WITHDRAWN

Donated to
SAINT PAUL PUBLIC LIBRARY

Letters to Gala

EUROPEAN SOURCES

Russell Epprecht and Sylvère Lotringer, Series Editors

American Journals
Albert Camus

Diary of an Unknown
Jean Cocteau

Letters to Gala
Paul Eluard

Letters to Merline
Rainer Maria Rilke

Letters to Gala

PAUL ELUARD

Translated by
JESSE BROWNER

PARAGON HOUSE
New York

First American edition, 1989

Published in the United States by

Paragon House
90 Fifth Avenue
New York, NY 10011

Copyright © 1989 by Paragon House

All rights reserved. No part of this book may be reproduced, in any form, without written permission from the publishers, unless by a reviewer who wishes to quote brief passages.

Originally published in French under the title *Lettres à Gala, 1924–1948.* Copyright © 1984 by Éditions Gallimard.

Library of Congress Cataloging-in-Publication Data

Eluard, Paul, 1895–1952.
[Lettres à Gala, 1924–1948. English]
Letters to Gala / Paul Eluard.—1st American ed.
p. cm.—(European sources)
Translation of: Lettres à Gala, 1924–1948.
Includes index.
Bibliography: p.
ISBN 1-55778-119-2
1. Eluard, Paul, 1895–1952—Correspondence. 2. Dalí, Gala—Correspondence. 3. Poets, French—20th century—Correspondence. I. Dalí, Gala. II. Title. III. Series.
PQ2609.L75Z48413 1989
841'.912—dc19   88-39025
                                                 CIP

Manufactured in the United States of America

Contents

INTRODUCTION *vii*

TRANSLATOR'S NOTE *xv*

CHRONOLOGY *xvii*

LETTERS TO GALA *1*

POEMS FOR GALA *269*

NOTES *293*

INDEX *339*

Introduction

Paul-Eugène Grindel, who would call himself Paul Eluard, and a young Russian girl, Elena Dmitrievna Diakonova—to whom he gave for posterity the name Gala—met in December 1912 at the Clavadel Sanatorium, near Davos, Switzerland, where they were both recovering from tuberculosis. They were both seventeen years old.

When they separated for the first time in 1914, before the onset of war, Gala returned to Russia. Eluard, mobilized at first as an auxiliary, then hospitalized, was drafted into the infantry. Gala returned from Russia in 1916 and, as life goes on in spite of war, they were married in February 1917, and had a daughter, Cécile, in 1918.

Some of Gala's letters from those early years have been found. Most, however, were destroyed by Eluard in an attempt to protect the sanctity of their private lives. Some of Eluard's letters were published in *Lettres de jeunesse* [*Letters From His Youth*] by Seghers. Those that are published here, all addressed to Gala, were discovered by their daughter Cécile on the occasion of her mother's death in 1982. They begin in 1924—twelve years after their first encounter, seven years after their marriage, near the birth of the surrealist movement—and end in 1948, four years before Eluard's death. All of these letters were preserved by Gala for over thirty years. We do not know if others were written, which were then either lost or destroyed.

Let us for a moment trace the relationship between these two people, as the letters encourage us to do. It was a relationship which, despite all its storms, all its separations, and all its disagreements, Eluard always considered an honor.

We know little about the first few years. Eluard and Gala are for the most part together, cheerfully participating in the same struggle. They write little to each other. Their reciprocal infidelities do not seem to cause any problems—at least, if one can believe the letters.

INTRODUCTION

They shy away from everyday sentimentality, and from any concept of mutual possession. As he often reiterates, Eluard has given himself over to a loftier, essential fidelity that venal affairs cannot endanger. Every great love flirts with utopia, and from letter to letter we are able to follow this pursuit of the impossible.

Through a paradox that he believes to be true, and which may well be, Eluard even maintains that it is his freedom that makes him faithful.

From 1929 on, the couple is physically disunited—without recrimination, without anger, all the more so as this separation will be marked by several happy, if brief, reunions. Eluard announces to Gala, not unkindly, that he has met a little Berliner and that he has a "good mind to go to Berlin for three days." He immediately adds: "But, of course, only if you have *no objection* to it. . . ."

Gala had no objection, and Eluard went to Berlin. It was a disappointing journey, during which he fell sick.

Behind this at least apparent simplicity of mores, which seeks something more than a bureaucratic fidelity, which shows their marital relationship clearly willing itself above bourgeois convention, these letters also betray a sense of menace, almost of despair. The feelings Gala was to have for Max Ernst, which first split the couple, even troubled Paul Eluard enough—along with arguments with his father and a certain general confusion—to provoke his departure on a long voyage around the world, in 1924, a "stupid voyage" during which his experience of his own solitude was so strong that he asked Gala and Max Ernst to join him in Asia. The effort was wasted: some time later, during a party given by André Breton, his friend Max punched him forcefully in the eye. "That pig Max Ernst. . . . A boxer's argument, on that superhuman level where I thought we were." Was Gala the source of the disagreement? We cannot know.

Their true separation came about in 1929, when Gala met Salvador Dali in Cadaqués. Luis Buñuel, who was present at the encounter, tells in *My Last Sigh* how Dali, overwhelmed, came running up, saying: "There has just arrived an extraordinary woman."

Dali himself has described and commented upon this decisive meeting at length, of which we find an occasional bitter echo in

INTRODUCTION

Eluard's letters—which, however, never lose that which was essential, a love stronger than separation and the desire for Gala's well-being.

This well-being is what matters above all. Eluard says so, over and over again, as if he first had to convince himself of it. And this well-being seemed, by all appearances, to be inextricably linked to Dali.

Dali has stated, and it is likely true, that Gala was the only woman with whom he had ever made love (Buñuel was sure of it). She stayed in Cadaqués, returned to Paris, and got back on the train to Cadaqués. At this point, Eluard's letters become very frequent. One always writes to an absence, and Gala was absent more and more. She was to remain in Cadaqués, by Dali's side, until her death many years later.

Eluard and Gala were divorced in 1932, but it is not the least peculiarity of their love story to find it prolonged for years afterwards, even after Eluard's 1934 marriage to the delicate and gentle Nusch, "Nusch the perfect," without his passion for Gala seeming to subside or his vocabulary to modulate. Despite the very keen tenderness he felt for his second wife, in his letters Gala remains his unique, irreplaceable muse, a kind of beacon without which all life drifts and founders on the shoals. The divorced couple saw each other often. It is fairly certain that they made love on several occasions, up to the war, their longest separation. It is only during the final years, after Nusch's sudden death, that the vigorous flame abates.

Meeting Dali again after the war, Eluard was disappointed to find him, and Gala with him, engaged in the pursuit of worldly gain. For his part, the "old useless and awkward fool," who had lately bemoaned the life he led as "of one defeated," is now the voice containing a million voices. Recognized and honored, Eluard receives homages and his many journeys are all triumphal—a penurious glory, if one believes his letters to Gala, in which his declarations of love have grown paler and more mechanical. Melancholy is his only faithful companion. In the last notes to his "eternal little girl," he confesses: "I don't know how to laugh too well anymore." Crushed by Nusch's death, he slips in this avowal: "Living is very difficult."

INTRODUCTION

♦

As in all correspondence, we find in these letters Eluard's daily concerns about health and money, as well as accounts of the sale and purchase of paintings and the various conflicts that rock the surrealist group. We see, despite Gala's having forsaken him, what importance Eluard places in the opinion of Dali, whom he calls the "thinking machine" and whose criticism he solicits, and how anxious he becomes when he sees Dali manifest a certain obsession with Hitler. It is absolutely necessary, he says, for Dali to find another subject of delirium.

We see him occasionally aware of the risks he himself is running, fearing to be—or to appear to be—an "abominable sentimental." We follow his relationship with André Breton, up to their parting (which receives this strange comment: "Leave the well-established life to others"), and all the many moments that give breath to a life—his "incommensurable rage" at the bombing of Guernica, right up to his conclusion, as World War II looms and, mobilized, he re-adopts the name Grindel, that "I'm becoming a funny sort of man."

And step by step, we follow his stubborn quest for "that which is no disgrace to poetry."

But above all, these are letters in which a man speaks of love.

♦

And, first of all, of physical love. Contrary to considerations of family reading, which are generally neutering, this publication gives an erotic coloring to the work and the life of a poet. And not for the first time. People are no longer astonished that poets should have a sexual existence, that they should speak of it and speak eloquently. It has long since been accepted that all public figures owe us their intimacy, their desires, their obsessions, their dreams—the detours of a heart of which they themselves are ignorant.

To burn these letters, or to bury them away in some prudish coffer for indiscretions yet to come, would be to pervert a life and censor a death. If some, who hold rigidly puritanical conceptions of our monuments, should balk and take offence in the name of their own virtue, others will jump for joy. Here is Paul Eluard in the raw, a surprising Eluard, an enriched Eluard, an Eluard grasping his life by the horns. The eroticism of these letters—daydreams, specific recollections, the narration of a fantasy or of glorious masturba-

INTRODUCTION

tion—becomes one of those magnified expressions of love, strings of simple words and powerful images in which, yet again, a great poet holds us captive.

He says as much himself. The beautiful description of sexual pleasure can be a medium of liberation, of self-perfection. It can even be the literal representation of this pleasure, since we find in these letters the ecstatic praise of "obscene cinema."

Let us keep to these heights. Let us not turn sex into prose.

And let us delve deeper. In all great love stories, each reader finds his own story. And so it is with these letters. Literary criticism, in its inevitable appropriation, will tell us all we need to know about the relationship they bear, either self-evident or concealed, to the rest of the *oeuvre*. As for us, their readers, we meet herein a man who tells us, insistently, that "without love, all has forever been lost."

Whether he loved Gala, or wanted to love her, even before knowing her and beyond their separation, whether he loved her in each distinct instance of his life or else—and one is not exclusive of the other, quite the opposite—loved her "for all eternity," these letters bring us closer to the struggle against time in which Paul Eluard always selected love as his weapon of choice. Love alone, he has often told us, has the power to unite past and future, to confound and defeat them. A strong love exists beyond the duration of things, and Gala is its pyramid. "I think of you as of the fatal light of my birth." He was born for her and through her. She is his point of departure and his destiny, she is his freedom, she is quite simply himself. He calls her "my child, my self." He goes so far as to say: "My being . . ."

We find in these letters the proof, betrayed here and there by momentary lapses, of this concrete identification. Eluard loves a certain manifestation of timelessness in Gala. She despises memories, she never speaks of the past. Free of all banal nostalgia for happy days gone by, she seems to him to be "the freest of all women." That is why he never made her acquaintance, never "met" her: he has *always* known her. It is a powerful emotion, before which time and space are obliterated. And should love persist after the object of love has receded, nothing could be more logical: One does not switch eternities *en route*.

Even before Gala's departure, this exalted optimism is occa-

INTRODUCTION

sionally waylaid by fits of melancholy that appear sporadically through the letters and deepen with the years. Thus does Eluard speak of a "great, resigned emptiness," of a "great, sad dream," as if the ambition has suddenly seemed to him too overreaching, an illusion perhaps, as if what he demanded of love has, on brief occasions, shown itself to be unattainable. In describing this lofty union, this fine defiance, he uses the appropriate word: "mystical." But he qualifies it with an unexpected adjective: "My concept of you, of our love, is becoming more and more mystical and despairing."

In identification with others, one runs the risk of losing oneself. The absence eventually engenders a doubt concerning the existence of the self. "I am in your eyes," he says, seeming to indicate that he exists only in her gaze. But if this woman is himself, and if the gaze is hers, on what shadow stage is the pageant of love played out? A doubt is born: "You are probably my imagination . . ."

Then he reassures himself: "I can speak seriously to no one but you, because I love you." If he can speak to her, she must exist, and from time to time respond. He even gives in to the common temptation of this experience, solitude for two, whose only comfort is well known: "I dream of being with you instead of being with the world."

The course of any love that is mapped out, as this one is, by letters the answers to which are unknown to us, is as incomplete as a forest path that is marked, from place to place, by rare milestones. Missing, too, is that which is said, or might be said, when the correspondents are together—as well as that which is never said. But—aside from the fact that letters reveal what nothing else can show us—that which they leave to the imagination, the cryptic allusions, the personal layout of the page (the overall use made of the paper, differences in scale in the handwriting), the abbreviations, the punctuation, the confidences, the lip service all bring us closer to the mystery of the human heart.

In the case of Gala, one of the women of the century, the mystery is enlivened. What we thought we knew of her is suddenly tinged with curiosity. The snapshot wavers. Who was she?

As with all human pictures, perpetually wavering, our picture of Gala is illuminated here by new glimmerings that can only help to

INTRODUCTION

push back the encircling darkness. And the dark-eyed figure will be asking us the same questions for a long time to come. This woman who was said to be grasping and cold—but how convenient it is to scorn enigmas—will be seen, during the war, sending money and even care packages to her ex-husband, now remarried. We infer her attentiveness to his work, and also to his life, and on occasion we even suspect her of amorous inclinations toward him. Her role as vigilant can be imagined. Suffice it to recall her words to Eluard, in one of her youthful letters: "Be above your pride."

And let us also remember that she tells him: "You don't love me the way I love you."

Gala survived Eluard by thirty years. For thirty years she preserved this correspondence, down to the telegrams and postcards—she who claimed to be the foe of all nostalgia. Did she reread these letters? We cannot know. Perhaps she had forgotten them. While life is present, one has a tendency to neglect its relics. It is death that gives weight to words. All that remains today are these remnants of an absence, fragments more durable than two bodies laid to rest.

Jean-Claude Carrière

Translator's Note

In most essentials, we have tried wherever possible to remain faithful to the Nouvelle Revue Française edition of *Lettres à Gala,* on which this translation is based. Jean-Claude Carrière's excellent introduction has been retained, for instance, and most footnotes have been translated directly from the French. However, certain minor editorial changes that have been deemed necessary are worth noting.

The NRF edition includes 15 letters written by Gala to Paul Eluard in November and December 1916. Though these may hold some anecdotal and historical interest for the reader, they were written eight years before the opening letter of this volume, and therefore bear but oblique reference to the relationship as it had evolved by 1924. For this reason, they have been omitted from the current edition.

The NRF footnotes are considerably more extensive than those provided here, compromising nearly 100 pages of the edition. These same notes have been edited and pared down to eliminate much of their bibliographical content and other information which the editors consider to be of mostly academic significance. The footnotes as they appear in this edition are designed to provide only the historical and anecdotal background essential to placing the love story of Eluard and Gala in its proper historical, cultural and art historical context.

Similarly, the poems appearing at the end of the volume were heavily annotated, the variants and final versions of every altered verse being provided. As this is an evolution that can only be usefully traced in the original language, a decision was made to omit those notes as well.

Finally, redundant notes and postal information were also eliminated.

Chronology

1895   Paul-Eugène Grindel—Paul Eluard—is born on 14 December in Saint-Denis.

1912   Eluard meets Elena Dmitrievna Diakonova—Gala—at the Clavadel Sanatorium in Davos, Switzerland.

1914   World War I; Eluard returns to France and is mobilized.

1916   *Le Devoir*, first work published under the name Paul Eluard.

1917   Eluard and Gala are married.

1918   Birth of Cécile Grindel.

1919   Eluard returns to Paris; early friendships with young writers, including André Breton, Louis Aragon, Philippe Soupault, and Tristan Tzara; *Répétitions*.

1923–   Eluard is a member of the Surrealist group; editor and
1938   contributor to *La Révolution Surréaliste*, *Le surréalisme au service de la révolution*, and *Minotaure*.

1924   Eluard's journey around the world; André Breton writes first Surrealist manifesto; *Mourir de ne pas mourir*.

1926   *Au défaut du silence; Capitale de la douleur*.

1928   Gala meets Salvador Dali; *Défense de savoir*.

1929   Eluard meets Maria Benz (Nusch); *L'Amour la poésie*.

CHRONOLOGY

1930   Eluard and Gala separate; *À toute épreuve; L'Immaculée conception* (with André Breton).

1932   Eluard and Gala are divorced; *La vie immédiate*.

1933   *Comme deux gouttes d'eau*.

1934   Eluard and Nusch are married; Gala and Dali are married.

1935   *Nuits partagées; La rose publique; Facile*.

1936   Eluard participates in the International Exhibition of Surrealism in London; "L'évidence poétique"; *Les yeux fertiles*.

1938   Eluard breaks with André Breton and the Surrealists; *Cours naturel*.

1939   World War II; Eluard is mobilized.

1940   Demobilized, Eluard returns to Paris; *Le livre ouvert*.

1942   Eluard reaffiliates with the Communist Party; joins underground.

1943   Eluard and Nusch in hiding from the Gestapo.

1944   *Au rendez-vous allemand*.

1946   Death of Nusch; *Poésie ininterrompue; Le dur désir de durer*.

1948   *Poémes politiques*.

1949   Eluard meets Dominique Lemor in Mexico.

1951   Eluard and Dominique are married.

1952   Death of Eluard on 18 November, in his home near the Bois de Vincennes.

1982   Death of Gala.

Letters to Gala

1

Postmark: Cristobal,[1] 12 May 1924—New York, 20 May 1924
Sender: M. Grindel—Papeete—Tahiti[2]
Addressee: Mme. Hélène Grindel,[3] 4, avenue Hennocque, Eaubonne (Seine & Oise),[4] France

My darling little girl, I hope you'll pass this way sometime soon. I'm bored. I have always written to you. You should have done the envelopes before you left. But you will be consoled by the way I'm going to love you. Wait till you get here to see the presents I have for you. You alone are precious. I love only you, I have never loved anyone but you. I can love nothing else.

Herewith 200 marks. If you find any objects, but especially any tikis, slates, or nazcas, charge them on account.

I'm sending this letter off quickly. I kiss you all over.

Paul

I have thought only of you every minute of your absence.

Could you ask Nierendorf[5] for Gurlitt's address (Postdamme Strasse no.?) or else look in the telephone directory, so you can pick up a tortoise-shell mask on Torrès-Strasse that Tual bought.[6] The latter has just instructed him to let you have it. If you foresee any hindrance whatsoever (customs, shipping, etc.), leave it. Otherwise, it would be much more convenient for Tual if you could pick it up.

Thank you, Gala, if you could do this. But please don't put yourself out.

Regards.
Roland Tual

LETTERS TO GALA

2

Telegram
From: Paris
Arrival Postmark: Arosa, 25 July 1925
Addressee: Grindel, Parksanatorium, Arosa Switzerland.

Sold several pieces rebought a magnificent Picasso we arrive Leysin Tuesday 10 A.M. mad with joy see you again.

Paul

3

[Paris, about 25 May 1927]

Thursday

Maya daragaya,[1]

you must be arriving or already arrived in Leningrad. I am on the rue Clauzel. It's six o'clock in the morning. I haven't slept. I am dazed and sad, sad. Last night at Breton's, I had a fight with that pig Max Ernst, or rather he punched me unexpectedly and pretty hard in the eye, I lost my vision and swung blindly.[2]

Marie-Berthe[3] had suddenly and for no reason become very abusive toward me. Max had told her (making a scene of it) that she couldn't hold a candle to me [*sic*].[4] He was scolding her for it.

First I blew up at the lady, then, feeling that the gentleman had misused me, I felt it appropriate to accuse him of lying and to get angry at him. In accusing him of lying, moreover, I demanded that he take back his filthy, boorish calumnies. And then came the well-aimed punch that would paralyze anybody. My best friend had hit me, disfigured me—my friend, that's putting it mildly, you know.

That's why Sir Pig practices boxing.

This will be well received amongst my enemies. He dared what

no one else has dared to do, hit me—and with *impunity*. I won't be able to go to the sales or do anything for eight days. My eye is disgusting. But it's not serious. But still, I feel quite calm about it all. I shall not see Max again.
EVER.
You can do as you like. Everything has conspired against me. I feel terribly sad and forsaken. It makes me think of that Pig Verlaine firing on Rimbaud, wounding him. What a miserable argument between Max and me: one punch in the eye, and everything's ruined. A boxer's argument, on that superhuman level where I thought we were.

I thought I understood the question. I was wrong. It is a question of strength.

Above all I don't want you to be concerned. Out of love for you, I will do nothing against him, for your serenity. But do not betray me. I couldn't go on living.

I kiss you all over. Paul
Write to rue Ordener.[5]

Nine o'clock

I'll wear dark glasses. Everything is fine here. Send me your address clearly written, don't omit anything: neither your name nor anything else.

I wanted to kill the Pig, but you are the one who would have suffered for it. I was denounced, robbed, punched. What misery. Be calm. I'm taking care of myself. Everything will work out, I swear it. But still, don't take this opportunity to stay away too long.

Your friend

Paul

4

[Eaubonne?] (toward the end of) 29 May [1927]

My beautiful, my adored one, I am pining to death without you. Everything is hollow, I have only your clothing to kiss. I miss your body, your eyes, your mouth, your entire presence. You are my only, I love you for all eternity. All the hardships I have endured are as nothing. My love, our love incinerates them. When you return I want to deck you out magnificently. Send me the measurements for your pajamas (!!!). For you, I want all that one can have, all that is most beautiful. Stay away the least amount of time possible. Come home soon. Without you, I am nothing at all. I fulfill all other desires in my dreams. I fulfill my desire for you in reality. It absolves reality.

Gala, my dorogoy, my all-beloved forever and always, come home as soon as possible. Nothing is worth depriving ourselves of each other in this way. Everything is fine here, despite my sadness.

Tual found some magnificent slates in Germany, notably a 3′ totem for Fr 1,800. If you find [any], have them write to me. In Russia, perhaps? Received the letter sent to my mother. Cécile is doing very well. Send a card to Mme. Vve. Salahum[1] to La Jouvence de l'Abbé-Soury. Rouen (Seine-Inférieure).

Nobody showed up yesterday to the Tanguy-America vernissage.[2] It was raining. The exhibition is magnificent. It's a shame that you won't be able to see it. That takes away all its charm for me.

We wrote, Breton and I, a manifesto that has come out: *Lautréamont envers et contre tout*—aimed against Soupault, who has just brought out an unworkable edition of the *Complete Works*.[3] I'll read it to you on your return.

I have two very lovely Pueblo (New Mexico) dolls. They are the prettiest things in the world. I'll put them in your room, where you'll also find all the presents I may happen to give you.

Don't write to Max. Marie-Berthe spoke badly of you. We fought. We are irrevocably estranged. But *be serene*. I have now completely calmed down. Nothing else will happen. *I swear to you.* You must forget his existence. From now on, everyone will despise him. I adore you, you know. You are my sweet and beautiful little girl, I kiss you all over.

Paul

I have your letter from Moscow in which you scold me for not writing. Poor thing. I don't have your address. Yes, come home as soon as you can. Your fidelity moves me. But otherwise, it would be so awful. Tell them to forward your letters from Moscow.

5

[Eaubonne, June 1927]

My little beloved,

I wrote to you, but I don't know if you got my letter, the address you had given me was very badly written and you had forgotten to put your name. I tried to write it, but I made a mistake, from very old habit I put Hélène Diakonova.

I've just had an idea. I'll ask Fraenkel.[1]

Your lovely letters make me happy. But I miss you. Eaubonne is sad without you, and rue Clauzel too.

To meet you in Berlin I hope to sell *La Gare Montparnasse*[2] and maybe Picasso's *Danseuse Nègre* (28,000) to Alphonse Kann.[3] Otherwise, I won't be able to. I don't know where to send the money in Berlin. Perhaps to Nierendorf. Give me his address and write him that I'll send a little money for you, which he can put toward your trip.

Tual found some marvelous things at Nierendorf's.

Breton and I found some dolls here from New Mexico (Pueblo). It's wonderful.

Everything is fine. Don't write to Max. I'll explain: we are estranged to death, forever.

My beloved, I adore you, I'd like to have you naked in my arms.

You are my source of life. When you get back it will be hot, you'll lie naked with me.

Naturally I'd like to join you in Berlin, not for the artwork but so as to be with you sooner, and to travel. And so as to be better able to tell you I love you, and to have you. All is going very well with my mother. You will be very [?][4] I kiss you awfully all over.

Paul

Give me your complete address again, carefully copied out.

6

[Eaubonne, June 1927]

My poor little girl, finally you give me your address. I've written you very often, but I'm afraid I put the address wrong.

Yes, return on the 5th if you can. I am fatally bored without you. I await you with mad impatience. I love you awfully. You must return quickly.

I hope to have some money to deck you out, on your return, in all that is finest.

Write to the Hotel Am Zoo that they should keep the letter that I'll send you there. Try to see Berger.[1] Tual made some marvelous finds in Berlin, especially some American stuff.

I have to go to Aubervilliers. Gabriel's[2] mother died and I don't have a car.

I love you, I love you, I love you, I love you. I love only you. Wait and see how I'll spoil you, I love you. I kiss you all over.

Paul

Don't write to Max—we are definitively estranged—I'll explain it to you.

7

[Arosa, March 1928]

My little girl, I wrote and wired to you in Berlin.[1] I hope all goes well. I don't know if you got my letter before your departure. I recommend two things: first, for the museum photos, choose the most beautiful pieces, and also the most strongly "imagined" surrealist ones, don't forget photos of North American and Eskimo objects, which I lack; second, buy without fail one or even *two* truly fantastic Klee watercolors *at Walden's* or at Flemming's if he's selling them at a *very reasonable* price. On further consideration, I find them marvelous (the Klees), *Les Bourgeons* for 1,000 RM. I'm buying it. Here is Max Flemming's address, Baderstrasse, I think: 42. Call him. I very much like *Le Grec et le gendarme*. Be very careful over there, he has some watercolors by an imitator of Klee (don't get them confused).

I adore Klee.

As in my Berlin letter, I tell you again to be cautious, not to tire yourself out too much, to remember that you are making this trip for your health. My Berlin letter was better. Let's hope you get it. I love you worthily of the light that you are, an absent light.

Yours alone.

Paul

There's an exhibition of Klee's recent stuff at Flechtheim, but it's probably too expensive and not as good.

Noll[2] tells me the photos have been sent; it seems the paintings are at rue Ordener.

8

[Arosa, March 1928]

My beautiful little girl,

you misunderstood. I thought that on Wednesday you would be not at Arosa,[1] but in Berlin, since you told me that you were leaving Sunday.

I am relatively pleased with the diagnosis. All in all, I am also *relatively* pleased with my illness, since otherwise, anywhere else than in a sanatorium, you would not have taken sufficient care of yourself. Here, you can have everything necessary: seven meals, rest, and in a marvelous climate. I myself am doing better, except for my ear and my teeth, which are being taken care of. *The weather is splendid.* All will be ready, as you can imagine, for your return, to receive you. Nelli[2] has sent the pieces to rue Ordener.[3] Received a *very* long letter from Bousquet,[4] very moving. Took some great photos. I'm sending you one. Stay as you please. I will bear the absence. There is already one long poem inspired by you. There will be another. And so much love and perfection that I place in you. I kiss you all over.

Your husband forever.

Paul

9

[Arosa, March 1928]

Thursday

My fair beloved, don't buy any books on primitive art for me, unless you find those that I have noted as being of particular interest. All this because I'm ordering two from Paris: Stephan, *Sudseekunst*, and Murray, *The Papuas*. It's going to cost Fr 200 but it's worth it, so don't spend anything on me (don't buy any ties). The only gift I need is you, next Wednesday, and to know what you have, how you can defeat it. It snows endlessly here. I don't go out. The doctor says that it's no good. I am tired and sad, yes, really sad, like an old, empty, dust-covered flask. Is everything going as you would wish? I should have advised you to write me. You can still send me a note. I'd get it on Sunday or Monday. A card. I kiss your nose, your mouth, your eyes, everything. I love you.

[unsigned]

10

[Eaubonne, March 1928]

Monday, 1 o'clock

My beautiful little girl, I arrived in good order this morning.[1] I went to bed to rest up for tomorrow. I'll pick up the money (250,000) tomorrow. I'm having lunch tomorrow with Oger, the clerk,[2] and I'm going with him afterward to pick it up.

I'm a little tired out by the trip. I'm having dinner with Nini[3] on Wednesday. They'll certainly come to spend the winter with us. Thursday night I'm going to the Folies–Bergère with my mother.

Don't move about too much unless "the pursuit of pleasure" dictates.

I adore you.

I'm going to sleep. Understood, as to the dresses. I'm happy that you like the woolens, very happy.

Take advantage of your freedom. One must always abuse one's freedom.

I adore you.

I kiss you *all over.*

Paul

11

[Eaubonne, March 1928]

Wednesday

My beautiful little girl it would be very difficult for me to list all the things I have been doing. Yesterday I had to pass by the Department.[1] I spent three-quarters of the day at it. And, of course, one piece is missing: the marriage certificate. I'll have it Friday. I hope I'll get it before I leave.

Saw Breton last night, very sad and weary of everything. Nothing new. I'm supposed to have lunch with him tomorrow. I bumped into Fraenkel at the automatic photos. Five francs a roll. It's funny if you make faces.

Spent last night in Paris. Tonight I'm dining with the Lavidières, who are going to stay at Eaubonne this winter. Your tiger jacket is going out tomorrow morning. I'm a bit dazed by all that I have to do: too much. Saw Crevel, who is well. Lunch with him on Friday, at his house, and on Saturday at Montlignon.[2]

Right now I'm on my way to the Company. Tomorrow morning to your dressmaker. Forgive me, this kind of life is impossible after that rest.

And all this despite a frightful sadness. Adventures but no strength. We won't be able to live here anymore. It's a hell. And after Marseille, people seem so ugly. It rains, it's cold. Work rules.

I love only you.

What a glimpse of the void in this life. Crevel wants to go on a long trip with us. It's the only solution, and living in the south. It's restful and merry.

Breton's been playing the phonograph nonstop, songs by Fortugé and Dranem.

"How miserable is our Earth on life."

La Bréchue[3] sends her love. The dogs are going to throw you a party one of these days.

I love only you.

Nothing exists but you.

Paul

12

[Eaubonne, March 1928]

Thursday

My very dearest, I still haven't managed to see your dressmaker. I was there this morning but she was busy. I have an appointment for tomorrow morning. Anyhow, you know, I "shopped around" a bit, and I hope you'll be pleased. And I'm still looking, because I want to find you some really viable stuff.

I'm going to the Folies-Bergère with my mother tonight. Tomorrow I'm going to the dressmaker's, having lunch with Crevel, and taking care of the Department with Oger. This delay is irritating. Falling as it does at the end of the month, I'm afraid of being unable to use the money well. You should tell me by express, in case I am either not paid on time or a good investment can't be found that quickly, whether it is really inconvenient that I prolong my absence by one or two days at the most. You know, I've been running around like a madman since Tuesday.

The Circus isn't showing any more. No fun anywhere. I see *very few* people and *very rarely.* And nothing bad—"neither hot nor cold." Everyone is very dull.

Apointment with Ratton[1] Saturday afternoon. I have to telephone Bouissounouse.[2] I'm bearing up fairly well under my exhaustion. I draw no pleasure from this city.

Friday

I've just come into the money from the Department. Also, spent the whole morning with your dressmaker. She's a bit alarmed at putting gray-brown lace on a blue background. Anyhow, I'm going back Tuesday to see how it looks. I've also ordered you a yellow afternoon dress. But none of this will be finished until next Friday. Still, if you want me to stay two extra days, I'll bring it with me. In any case, you know, the flounces on the blue dress will prevent its being finished before ten days or so. Consequently, that's no reason for me to stay. Anyway I'm bored. I'm leading a life that has nothing in common with *my* life. Obviously there's nothing funny about returning to Arosa. But it's more about what we'll find there than about what I'm leaving behind. Still, if you think that I can stay until Friday without putting you out, send me a telegram. It would be for purchasing deeds, but honestly!! I'm not at all in the mood. Anyway I don't have the time to go walking and even if I did it gives me no pleasure. In the telegram you can say if the dress should be made as you specified. In any case, no other solution could be found than using lace of the same color. Apparently, it's always done that way: one solid color. But perhaps gray-brown and blue will work together. Decide, or else I'll decide on Tuesday morning with my mother, who's coming with me. You forgot to tell me the total length from collar to knee, or else for the skirt. It's a bit troublesome, as I'm not too sure she'll be able to find the old measurements.

Don't get bored. Take advantage of your time as a "recluse."

Your letters are very nice, but not terribly long.

Love me, but if you have a mind to, take advantage of your freedom.

My all-beloved, I kiss you all over, *in reality*, I adore you, you alone and forever.

       Paul

Forgot to tell you that Nelli's pieces are glorious.

13

[Eaubonne, March 1928]

       Sunday night

My beautiful little girl,

I've been in bed all day with a magnificent cold. Out of caution I'll stay in bed tomorrow, too.

I don't have any fever. So it won't come to anything. I'm awaiting your answer for my Friday departure. I have to see Guénot[1] again Thursday morning, after the results. Anyhow, if you're too bored, don't hesitate to call me back. What miserable weather this is. At least it's drier in Switzerland.

Sold the Eskimo ivory to Ratton: 6,000. Not bad, eh? Got the painting from Van Leer,[2] magnificent. As for your dresses, I think it will work out very well. Made some investments on Sgard's advice, who told me to go ahead as if it were for him. Anyhow, everything would be fine without this cold. I had an appointment tomorrow with Bouiss[ounou]se. I won't go. Crevel came to lunch here yesterday. Cécile was pleased.

With this letter, my mother will send some photos of Jouk,[3] which should be good.

I love you, only you.

Paul

Your fur overcoat has been sent to Lugano.

14

[Eaubonne, April 1928]

Monday, 4 o'clock

My dear love, my sweet love, I'm still in bed today. I've just had a marvelous dream, one of those daydreams in which the physical emotions leave you with the entire weight of their desire upon waking—and the desire you drag around with you afterward, when you're awake, is so similar to the pleasure of the dream. I was stretched out on a bed, next to a man whose identity I cannot quite place, but a man submissive, who had always been and always would be a dreamer, and silent. I turn my back on him. And you come to lie down against me, in love, and you kiss my lips softly, very softly, and beneath your robe I caress your supple and so lively breasts. And very gently your hand passes over me, seeks the other person and wraps around his member. I see it in your eyes, which slowly cloud over, more and more. And your kiss grows hotter, moister, and your eyes open wider and wider. The life of the other passes into you and, soon, it's as if you were jerking off a corpse. I wake up, slightly tipsy, unable to renounce this pleasure.

I must admit that a return to Arosa doesn't seem sad to me, that in any case it is not a return to Arosa but a return to you, and therefore to my love. Consequently, I have but one desire: to see you, touch you, kiss you, speak to you, admire you, caress you, adore you, look at you, I love you, I love you, you alone, the fairest, and in all women I find only you: all Woman, all my love so great and so simple.

I'm doing better. Philippon came by this morning, says I should be careful but that there's nothing in my chest. For my nose, which was giving me great pain, he gave me a cocaine salve that instantly soothed me.

I have thought constantly of sending you books, but I only found some three days ago. And, out of caution, I'm reading them before I bring them away. You will get at least three, two of which will certainly please and enchant you.

I have said in all my letters that the dresses are coming along nicely, and that you should be prepared for myriad wonders. Don't count on it. On the contrary, I have the impression that they will just barely do. Still, so long as my beloved makes love entirely naked—and entirely dressed, too!

I received your telegram before the nap described above. "Kisses," it said. That's what disturbed me so. And also stirred up memories—in Arosa I will tell you how. But I am suffering awfully from your absence. My will to feel better is growing stronger and stronger. I was very flattered by a compliment from a very pretty little Berliner whom I met at Crevel's (whom we went to see in Berlin and who wanted to sell two little Rousseaus). Her husband was a [fairly] pretty homosexual boy, you found him "very handsome" even): that I was "big and good-looking, with a slim waist and wide shoulders." Let her keep her delusions! I'd consider it sacrilege to shatter them! Ha! Ha![1] I send you more photos of your Jouk, who has "*also*" been very "friendly" toward me, staying on my bed. I speak of you to him. He wags his tail, rubs his nose against my hand.

I will definitely be leaving Friday night. You yourself should leave Magadino early on Saturday morning to get to Arosa that night, unless you should prefer to spend Sunday in Magadino for certain reasons. Please be assured that I will not have a word to say on the matter. In that case, I will arrange everything at Arosa to receive you worthily. My desire for you will not thereby be diminished.

In any case, what is, is that your image does not leave me for an instant, that I love you in every way: in yourself, in all flesh as well, in all love. I am your husband forever,

Paul

I'm sending you a little drawing which I like very much. To be framed. And my photos. I am also going to be reimbursed for taxes that my father overpaid: Fr 4,000 or 5,000. I'm going back to sleep. To dream of GALA. I'll bring you a little poem.

I should sign Gala. The title *Décalques* has become *Comme une image*.²

15

[Arosa, late May 1928]

My beautiful little dorogaya

ya tebya lublu,¹ awfully.

I forgot to tell you to ask Mlle Bouissounouse to send me the following books:

Au Sans-Pareil (don't say it's for me or even talk about it)

Alexander Blok: *The Twelve* (1st edition).²

Paul Eluard: *Les animaux et leurs hommes,* one copy on Dutch or rice paper or Japanese vellum, and three standard copies.

— : *Exemples,* one copy on Dutch and three standards.

— : *Répétitions,* two of the Nouvelle Revue Française copies:

— : *Capitale de la douleur,* three copies.

Have her *wrap them very well* before sending. A pretty package. Naturally, she'll tell me how much they come to and I'll send her a money order.

A card from Max, addressed to Eaubonne, that says: Best wishes. Still, it's better than nothing.³ The German catalog bought by my mother has arrived. Very good.

I hope that you're traveling very comfortably right now. The Italian blushed with envy when she heard you were going all the way to Berlin, like her fiancé.

And now you're already drinking beer. You'll sleep well. I love you awfully. And then you'll be going to the movies, to the music hall, to the markets. You're going to find some marvels. You'd find them in the desert. And I kiss your lovely eyes very gently. Your [. . .]4 (anything you'd like)

[unsigned]

16

[Arosa, late May/early June 1928]

My sweet little darling, I would have written you sooner, but I didn't know where you were stopping, at which hotel. I'm sending you *Lord Jim*. It's the only one to have arrived. The others will come later, they say. I'm still very pleased to be sending you one.

I slept this afternoon, I'm bored. I'm reading the *Kalevala,* a wonder.[1] Yesterday, wrote a little poem.

A letter from Crevel. Indeed, someone, an American I think, asked him for my address, to ask me for a book. It's funny. I'm going to write to Bondy.[2] Write to Nierendorf. I'm returning the photos to him. A fortnight from now Crevel will meet up with us. Write to him, give him some information to tempt him a little: prices, conditions, etc. . . . It's René Crevel, 6, rue des Marroniers. Paris (6e).

My little one, I've found a little one that I'm sending you. I went for a solitary walk along our path, near the flooded areas.

You were quite right not to keep your promise. I wouldn't have been happy, you know. And be careful, will you. The little one should lose her headaches and be glowing. I want my letter to go out straight away.

I kiss you all over.

Paul

The poem in question that I could almost use as a preface.

I hide the dark treasures[3]
Of unknown retreats

PAUL ELUARD

> The woodland hearts the sleep
> Of a burning rocket
> The night's horizon
> That crowns me
> I go in head first
> Greeting with a newfound secret
> The birth of images.

I would rather leave the 14th than the 15th, and the 13th than the 14th.[4]
Louisa asks where you left the yellow wool.

17

[Arosa] 7 June [19]28

My darling little girl,

no letter yesterday, no letter today. And in your last letter, you said you were ill. I am constantly anxious. All today, I've even been a bit crazy, I'm having problems with my vision. I'd like to go away.

Our Chirico goes on sale 9 June. The silk is on its way, apparently.

Have you been to Seelisberg? If you decide on a place, give me the address immediately so that I can make all the changes.

My books, said to have been sent 31 May, have not yet arrived.

Do you like *Lord Jim*? Four years ago I found it somewhat entertaining.

I dream about the dresses you wear when it's very hot. I love you. Here, we are enshrouded in clouds and rain. We kiss you all over.

Paul

Guillaume[1] gave me an address for the remounter.
I'm writing and will send the painting directly.

18

[Arosa, June 1928]

Friday night, 9:30

My dear little girl,

I sent you the silk, which seemed very fine to me. Also sent *Chantiers*.[1] Bousquet and Nelli, it's good, really good. I don't know the exact price yet, but it's what Luisa told you. I haven't found any yellow wool. And the shopkeeper won't have any until Monday. It's annoying. Still, Luisa will get by. It'll be all over on the 15th. I'll leave on the morning of the 15th. Perhaps it would be better if you move in the day before. Or would you rather I spend the night at your hotel in Lucerne and we go for a walk the next morning? Decide for yourself. If Bürgenstock isn't better, Bellevue-Seelisberg seems very good to me. Don't hesitate to make that decision for yourself as well. And give me the address as soon as you've reserved the room under the name Eluard-Grindel. And write to Crevel. Give him all the information. And write a friendly little note to Nierendorf. I'm sending you Nierendorf's letter so that you can answer it. Tell him I'm going to return the photos. My books arrived. Very good. Your Hansie kisses your hands. The weather is filthy, rain and wind. I'm not writing any poetry. I don't have the energy to do anything.

Think how useful the little balcony will be to me, if we manage to get a sofa or a chaise longue. And Thorner says that Seelisberg is great. And if one falls sick, there's a very good lung specialist, Dr. Real, in Schwyz.

My ear, it seems, is doing very well. The other is intact.

After you left, the painter asked me to eat with him, and I'm eating with him.

A new era here: we are eating rather more badly than well. Right after you left, they made the dining room smaller. I take long walks, alone. I'm doing very well, except that I'm a bit crazy and get dizzy spells. Write a note to Bouissounouse. Give her our new address.

She wrote a frantic note, asking if the operation had been done, a 4-line note.
    As for me, I love you forever.
    And I dream about all of you.

              Paul

19

[Arosa, June 1928]

    My little darling,

    as agreed, I will leave on Friday 15 at 10 o'clock. I'll change at Thalwil. I am madly impatient to see you, to touch you, to kiss you. I've bought a cabin trunk (for this notorious journey).
    The weather is radiant. I'm dispatching the painting today.
    My letters are very boring.
    I adore you. Yours forever.

              Paul

    I'm going for a long walk. I'm in training. You know, in Lucerne we can buy a little, but very good, box-camera. We'll need it for the trip. So why not buy it now? I want to photograph you naked in all sorts of poses.

20

Arosa, 11 June [19]28

        The snow's rebellion[1]
        Soon put down under one sole shadow blow
        Just time enough to forget our dead
        To make the earth grow pale.

> By the rivers' flow
> Crystal girls with limpid brows
> Little ones flowering and weak ones smiling
> To play the water's role seduce the light.
>
> Setting suns and liquid dawns
>
> And when their kisses grow unseen
> They go to sleep in lions' jaws.

My beautiful little girl, Bellevue-Seelisberg seems very good to me. I'm leaving on the 15th at 10 o'clock, I won't go through Zurich. Seelisberg on the 16th. Try to find out what time I get in. I'll find out as well. Will you wear that lovely embroidered dress, if it's hot when you come to pick me up? Do you need some money? It snowed here this morning. It's cold. Luisa will have finished your jersey.

I love you, I kiss you all over.

Paul

I'm trying to make myself look healthy for my walk in Lucerne, so as to be appealing to you.

21

Postcard: View of Arosa
To: Mme Hélène Grindel, Terrasse Hotel, Lucerne
Postmark: Erased

Litzi-Rum, 13 June [19]28

My dear little Gala, this walk is very pretty I wish you were here with me.

Paul

Warum sind sie nicht hier, liebe Frau Gala. Shönstes wetter im schönster Ausflug.[1]

22

[Arosa, June 1928]

Wednesday 4:30

A letter for you. Send your address. We took that long walk. I'm tired restless. I had hoped to sleep, it would have calmed me. I'm horribly bored without you, I desire you awfully, I adore you. You are everything to me, all my thought, all flesh.

I adore you.

'Til Friday. Come pick me up.

Yours.
Paul

23

[Lucerne?, 25 August 1928?]

Saturday

My beautiful little girl, above all, tell me the truth. If it's serious I must come. If you're over 101° I'm coming.

As for my book, it will have no title. It will bear only my name on the cover. People will be forced to say: Paul Eluard's book.[1]

Today, 1st injection; the second on Tuesday. I've ordered a blue suit here, from Burberry's. It will be ready Friday night. I'll try it on Tuesday. That way I'll have it in Locarno, to do you proud. It's five o'clock in the afternoon, I was out with Cécile buying her presents. She was beaming with joy. She paid.

I'm tired. I'll stay in this evening. There's nothing to do. Last night, for 20 centimes, I went to look at the moon through a telescope. I came in at ten o'clock. Cécile and I have two adjoining rooms. I'm going to do a lot of work.

My poor little Galotchka, take good care of yourself. I adore you.

[unsigned]

24

Letterhead: Terrasse Hotel, Lucerne
[August 1928?]

My darling little girl,

I'm very pleased that you're doing a little better and that you can walk in the garden. Watch the drafts. They have been perfected here, in several directions.

There's also a celebrity here: a legless man. Unfortunately he doesn't walk on his hands. Monsters are forbidden to be funny.

Crevel had a minimum dose this morning and took to his bed with 102°. I don't think he'll ever be able to stand these treatments, which is a real shame.

I saw my tailor. If you're no worse, I'll leave Thursday at 11:30, because that way I'll be able to try on my suit. They'll send it to me. But I've already told you to tell me how things stand. If my presence is indispensable, don't forgo it for the sake of my elegance—quite hypothetical, for that matter. I'm going back up to Crevel, who's delirious. And I'm going for a stroll.

Day after day: STORMS.

I love you very deeply. No reason to doubt it. I'm not looking at anyone else. Nothing, nothing. I think of you. I look through the toy shops, what a good Swiss calls "trinkets."

Your Paul

I was counting on going out. But Crevel's got 104° even though he took three aspirins a quarter of an hour ago.

PAUL ELUARD

25

Letterhead: Café Haussmann [Paris. Hôtel Radio]
　　　　　　12, bd Haussmann, Paris
[March? 1929]

Thursday

My beautiful little girl, this is the only letter I'll write you from here. I've been prevaricating like no one's business, and I don't know when I'll get to Arosa. In any case I have to attend the board meeting[1] on Wednesday, because Hannesse, the ex-president and one of the three key figures to a resolution, has consented at my insistence to attend it. As I thought, this business did turn out to be a premeditated theft. Nothing to be had from the lawyer my mother had seen, an old piece of trash. Senile. I'm going to see another. I went to Raincy to see Hannesse this morning. At the meeting, I held back and announced that I wouldn't empower anyone. Saw Ratton. Nothing special. Going to the Fiduciary. I'm working like a dog. It is atrociously cold. Snow, rain, sleet. I fell sick from it yesterday. In general, failing strength, choking. I could never live here again. Pitiful women in Paris. Not one human face, not one temptation. But the cards didn't lie.[2] On the train, I made the acquaintance of a woman from Berlin with the face of an Indian, speaks English, gave me her address. If I don't see anything in Paris, I've a good mind to go to Berlin for three days. But, of course, only if you have *no objection* to it, if you are not too *bored* (!!!), if you don't feel as if you were being deserted, etc., etc. Answer me by return of mail to: Paul Eluard-Grindel, Hôtel Radio. Bd. de Clichy. Paris. By express mail. I've recovered a Masson (the forest) and two large and lovely Max Ernsts from the Gallery. Other than a pile of pottery that are at Naville's, that's all I had there. Bought some extraordinary records. Saw Bouissounouse. The movies last night: *White Shadows on the South Seas.*[3] Tonight, again with her, to the Concert Mayol. You see it gets no better!! I bought myself a fine pair of shoes. But I think that I won't buy you a dress, because, my pretty little one, I have found better, though *much* more expensive. It lends my room an enchanted quality. I hope you won't miss the dress. If you wanted a dress anyway, I could sell this present at a nice profit and buy the dress. You see I've done pretty well for myself. It will be my surprise, the most beautiful thing by far that you have ever seen. And enormous, my suitcase nearly full. The experts' opinion is that it is magnificent stuff. And I find it delightful. It goes with your lips, your breasts, your sex, your arms, and your curls. And decidedly, there are fewer attractive or easy women (except for whores, whoring, out of the question) in Paris than in Arosa. Ah! French women! Awful!!!! Long live Arosa! And what miserable cold.

I've already lost all my lovely color.

If I don't write another letter to you, it's on your recommendation and for your peace of mind.

I love you and think of you constantly. Tell Blum[4] that I've ordered his frames. They'll cost an average of Fr 50, very pretty. My portrait is in *Variétés*. Saw Sgard who said to sell nothing, that it will certainly go up. Tomorrow: Fiduciary. It never ends.

I adore you. I swear that I think of you endlessly, passionately. I kiss you all over. I adore you.

Paul

26

Letterhead: Paris, Hôtel Radio
[Montlignon, March 1929]

Monday, 1:30

My beautiful darling, your long letters "on your good stationery" really make me happy. I spent the day yesterday and this morning at Montlignon, in a dusty, mediocre atmosphere, but I slept soundly. Family was there, Albert, half dead, Clémence, René less badly off than the others. And my mother a bit upset, but with whom I behaved decorously! Cécile, very beautiful and very sweet, very sentimental with me. The preceding evenings had been troubled, but without you I do not have my tinted glasses, my emerald and fire glasses, my love glasses, and from all this I took away but an unbelievable disenchantment, a *suicidal* sorrow. Beauty has never, will never be enough for me. Without love, all is forever lost, lost, lost, wretched, ragged and steeped in base, ignoble poisons. There is no life, there is only love. I'll try to get to Berlin, I'll see that woman with whom I can barely speak. Perhaps she'll reanimate me, give me the energy to consider her other than a puppet, a statue. I'm trying this so as to get myself settled, so as never again to wander off, to find out if I can draw emotion only from you, from your love, even from your loves, your joys, your sufferings. My little Gala, I love you infinitely. I don't believe in life, I believe only in you. This universe that is mine, and that mingles with death, can penetrate life only when you are in it. It is between your arms that I exist. It is between your eyes, between your breasts, between your legs that I am called, where I will never be extinguished. The rest is just a great drudgery that only dreams of its own collapse, that has everything to fear from me. I am horribly sad and confused. I will not go to my appointment tonight with beauty, grace, youth, Sweden! Love is in Arosa. And it's not because you believe in love affairs that I will go to Berlin. I don't want to lie, within my love I have often found fancies for women very far removed from you, but it is becoming harder and harder. Am I still able to give life its due, howsoever small? That's the only reason I'm going to Berlin, to find out. All the signs seem favorable, but if it's like here!!! Only sadness and mystery tempt me. If I am disappointed, I'll have some important things to teach you, YOU, to demand of you. In any case, if you see any problem in my going to Berlin, you can tell me by express letter, or by *telegram* (better). I'll leave on Thursday, the noon train is best. Don't worry about being demanding. Anyway, I'm dreading this journey. I'm hopeful and fearful. And I'm especially afraid of believing myself mentally geriatric, of having lost all enthusiasm. I have abused life too much. And I love you too much (I say this with passion, with faith, from dream to dream; as concerns you I have switched universes, I have passed into yours. Look at yourself in the mirror, see your eyes that I love, your breasts that I love, your sex that I love, your beautiful hands, listen to yourself speak, please understand what you are saying, my only friend, why I only understand your language, why I'm giving you your freedom, what pleasure I draw from yours, why I want you to be daring and strong and submissive to your will alone, your will that is mine, that has been miraculously uplifted, like mine, by all our love).

I am waiting very melancholically for Bouissounouse, who is going shopping with me. I'll go to the company again on Wednesday. I have to make a decision: either to trust them or to resist. I'm supposed to see a lawyer again tomorrow. But even though the whole business is in a bad way, I'm pretty sure that it will all work out in time. The main thing is to lose as little as possible, and maybe to recover one's money. One needn't even think about making a profit. Anyhow, rest assured. I'll do what's best. I'll write to you on Wednesday night. I expect a lot from the presence of the old president, Hannesse. I will quash personal recriminations most energetically. And I have two honest allies in the future loan officers, whom I am supporting and have warned against the machinations of two or three very crude and energetic scoundrels. Don't worry about your present. It is engrossing and pretty, altogether made for you. You've probably figured it out, but even so I want to keep you guessing.

Life here is terribly exhausting. I am well rested today, anyhow. But long live Arosa! They are still skating on Enghien Lake. But it's just started raining. You see!

I'm going for my visa tomorrow. I won't buy my ticket until the last minute, and only if I don't receive a countermand from you. I'm very grateful to you for allowing me this freedom, for advising me so nicely to go to Berlin. But I don't know what to do myself. Will I be more tempted by Mystery (as well as by the risk of disappointment) or rather by spending a few days with you in Arosa? I still don't know. Will I, can I still have an affair that's worth the trouble? But here's Janine.

I adore you, I kiss you all over.

Paul

PAUL ELUARD

27

Letterhead: Hotel Am Zoo, Berlin
[mid-March 1929]

Tuesday morning

My beautiful little girl,

how miserable to be made this way. I am constantly ill. Last night was the most dreadful time I have ever spent in my life. It's partially the hotel's fault, where I have a room about thirty feet long by thirty feet wide by thirty feet high. All night long, a crowd of people knocked me about and frightened me. And the worst is that I dreamed that I wasn't dreaming. And I became rabid, like a cat, and I did a lot of shameful things. And I took three pills, and flushed hot and cold. And what a night. And yet, I went to bed at nine o'clock. I am dead. I sent you a package with two pairs of stockings and two cartons of cigarettes. But I don't know if they're any good. I had Kniga[1] send you 40 marks-worth of Russian books.

At Gurlitt's, I bought a long object from New Guinea like the one I sold to Ratton (5,000) for Salles,[2] and some bone from New Guinea (very beautiful). Both for 3,900 French francs, after bargaining her down by 1,000 French francs. Ratton will pay 3,000 for the bone, at least.

The weather is splendid. I saw Mops[3] and I am meeting her at 4:30. She's leaving for Lausanne in two days.

I am incapable of going out tonight. I'm too tired, and anyway nothing interesting is happening.

Misery of miseries. Write to me. If I don't get better I'll go straight home to Montlignon and take care of myself. I'm going to a doctor for my head. This can't go on any longer.

The Berliners are all attractive and friendly.

I love you, you know. Awfully. There is only you.

I kiss you all over.

Paul

28

[Berlin, 23 March, 1929]

Friday

My darling little girl, my lovely,

I'm much better. I think I must have been overwhelmed by the change in altitude.

I think I'm leaving Monday by car for Munich with Mops and two of her friends: a young man and a young brown-haired woman whom you went out with when you were here: Mme Apfel,[1] a lawyer's wife. We'll stay in the boy's house near Munich. It'll cost nothing and may not be unpleasant. We're going to see the castles of Louis II. This boy's car is enclosed and very comfortable.

This way, I'll go straight on to Paris. I'll be there on the 5th or 6th. Anyway, I'll write you from there.

At two o'clock I'm having lunch with Flechtheim and Grosz, whom I'll ask for a portrait (drawing).[2] Tonight to Berger's and to Nierendorf's, who's got some very lovely stuff from Bali, inexpensive, I'll have to see.

Tomorrow, Nell Walden.[3]

I'm having a good deal of trouble enjoying anything, I'm making an effort, and I miss you a lot, you the only beauty and the only intelligence. Still, I don't want to be too discouraged, but my greatest dream, my only dream, is that you love me, is to be with you, naked and tingling.

I adore you, my beloved little child.

Your Paul, forever.

PAUL ELUARD

29

Letterhead: Hotel am Zoo
Address: Bl. Bismarck 7000–7015
[Berlin, late March 1929]

My beautiful little girl,

a quick note to tell you I've just done a wonderful deal with a friend of Janine's: three silver Peruvian masks for 100 marks. There is a red and green one, very big, exceptionally beautiful, such as I've never seen before.

My mother is ill. She must have written to you. I leave Tuesday, unless Mops is still sick.

I love only you.

Paul

30

[Berlin, 26 March, 1929]

Monday

My beautiful little girl,

Yes, I have received the luggage checks.
I received your letter with the photos, which are great. I'm glad to have found all the books you wanted. Grosz did my portrait for nothing. Ugly enough for the French public. He also gave me a very strange banned book of his: *Ecce homo*.[1] I'm leaving tomorrow for the Bavarian countryside. It will be restful. Then I'll return directly to Paris with Mops and a friend of hers. Janine leaves tonight. She has been very busy all the while.

I'm beginning to grow distraught at the idea that you are existing without me. And, far from you, I am decidedly platonic in temperament. And it's quite demoralizing. And exhaustion on top of it all. Still, I'm much better than at the start. I've made some very advantageous purchases. Everyone has been very nice to me. I was shown some delightful things. And I'm very happy to go to Bavaria by car with Mops, her woman friend, a very simple boy (in love with her) and a little, "very little" 17-year-old homosexual (a licensed chef) who will cook very well for us. It's fun. Mops is unfortunately fairly (too) much in love with her friend Mme. Apfel, a charming person whom you know.

I have to go to the Austrian consulate for my visa, since I'm making arrangements for the luggage (very complicated what with all that I've bought). Come to think of it, I'll send you a Balinese statue by mail (declared value: 80 marks). I'll send it to you at the Parksanatorium. When you get it, send it by mail to my mother (declared value: 500 French francs). It's very fragile. Take every precaution. It's a very, very beautiful piece. Look at the markings in red on the face. I bought Fr 12,000-worth of artwork. But the silver mask alone (twenty centimeters wide) can be sold for at least 6,000 or 7,000. That Balinese piece is *very* beautiful. And I have the bone, a large fetish, a *very important* watercolor by Klee, a Klee drawing, some very beautiful books, two other silver heads, my portrait by Grosz. And my expenses, all travel from Arosa to Paris included, come to Fr 4,000. I think it's worked out nicely. Tell the Parksanatorium to be sure and forward your letters and packages to Locarno. I'm writing very small. Open your lovely twilight eyes wide. I adore you. The copies of my book on green paper will be as big as the reprints.[2] Thanks to Janine. Be healthy. Don't get bored. As soon as I arrive I'll wire you my address, in two or three days. Goodbye, my fair being, the only who disturbs me and whom I love with all my being.

I kiss you all over.

Paul

PAUL ELUARD

31

[Berlin, 26 March, 1929]

Monday night

My beautiful little darling, I have received another letter from you tonight. It makes me live again, for I have suffered the most awful pangs of self-doubt here. Exhaustion, you know! And all the people whom I understand. Used to you as I am, nothing can rouse any great desire in me. Except you! You are truly the sovereign of my body. And of my mind.

I'm very glad to be leaving for the Bavarian countryside bright and early tomorrow morning. If all goes well we'll be there Wednesday night. Write to me at the address I'm giving you. I'm leaving there directly for Paris on 5 April. With Mops and her friend.

No, I did not see the woman from the train again. Didn't have the courage.

Saw the Nell Walden collection today. They'll send me some prices in Paris. The Nell Walden woman was sick.

You know, I think that the mask that I thought was silver is gold. It is splendid. I'm going to bed immediately so as to get up early. I am fairly, very tired. Kidneys hurt. But for no reason, you know. Alas!!!!!!!!!!!!!!!!

I sent you the Balinese statue today. You'll send it on to my mother, just as carefully wrapped (declared value: 500 French francs). Exporting it from Germany would have cost me 26%.

Janine left tonight. She'll send you my book as soon as it's ready. So, until 5th April, write to me in Bavaria.

Oh! My portrait by Grosz! What a miniature! You'll see.

I love you, I'd like to have you on top of me just to know that I exist.

I'd like to have you, completely naked, your legs wrapped around me, kissing my nipples. Then, you'd jerk me off. (Now I exist. For the first time here.) I truly love none but you. Awfully.

Yours entirely.
Paul

LETTERS TO GALA

> Paul Eluard-Grindel, bie Herr
> Schlomann *Ohlstadt bei Murnau*
> (Bayern), Deutschland

32

Postcard: Munich panorama
Postmark: Munich, 27 March [19]29
To: Mme Gala Grindel

> Parksanatorium, Arosa, (Schweiz)

It is always the memory of the simplest moments, those most bereft of splendor, that proves the impossibility of destroying love.

> Paul

33

Munich [last days of March 1929]

> Thursday

My beautiful, adored little girl, we're leaving for Ohlstadt, where I certainly hope you'll write me. I'm thinking of you, don't worry. The mere thought of you is able to disturb me. I dream of you. You are always there, sweet and terrible queen of love's kingdom. I imagine you every which way.

But how lucky you are to be so easily excited by others. Each in turn. For me, You are all I need, naked to the waist, from the bottom up, from the top down.

Others, you see, others! —and yet, it is not opportunities that I lack. But they cannot break into our realm. They are not free enough, they want you to speak of love, and they can't, don't know how to speak of it.

I adore you!

> [unsigned]

PAUL ELUARD

34

[Ohlstadt, around 30 March 1929]

Saturday

I don't like, I can't get used to the idea of what you told me during those last days in Arosa: that you have no memories, that you don't like to have any. I've put my whole life in the love I have for you, I've put my whole life in *our* life. Otherwise I'd kill myself. Nothing has a beginning for us. Everything is present for us, everything *must* be present for us and at this moment I am with you as much in Clavadel, in Versailles, in Bray, in Eaubonne, and in Arosa[1] as I am here *with you absent,* with my great yearning for you. If I had to conceive of a past, a present, a future, I would kill myself. I want that no more than I want to enter the lives or amorous attentions of others.

My being, I can speak seriously to no one but you, because I love you, because I love only you. Please don't hold our temperamental moods against me. In reality, I want you so bedecked in sunshine and love, I want you so happy. I wanted to give you that freedom which no other would have given you. I offer you all possible pleasure, all enjoyment of yourself, but I'm so afraid of your losing sight of me, even for an instant. You should be very proud that no others can disturb me, despite my desire for them. In you alone my desires give birth to delirium, in you alone my love bathes in love. But my love must be filtered through your absolute love. If not, I'd kill myself. Forgive me for saying this, but it has grown by consequence of your indifference, however fleeting. We live very peacefully here, rising at noon, preparing our meals, playing the gramophone and flirting. Four boys and two girls: Mops and her friend Apfel. They are both coming to Paris with me. Flirting here is not much hindered by differences of sex. I myself am considerably put off by it. Mops and the Apple[2] are very nice, good buddies, but that's all. The Apple is charming but a bit too easy. And without restraint. All these people are extremely sweet to me, in love with me. In any case, nothing, my beloved child, my sole being, for you to worry about. I couldn't care less about the others. I dream that you are here. It's the real countryside, you could live here practically naked and very serene and love me. Will I never have you as others have you!?! I am unhappy, unhappy. My love is too great for me.

My little one, I have your letter of the 28th. I am sending you this one express, since you tell me you're leaving Tuesday and with the holidays I'm afraid you won't get it before you leave.

Your letter does me a lot of good. I am comforted, the day is sunnier. Send the Bali to rue Ordener. I told Janine to send you *L'amour la poésie*.

My cold is cured. It's like Imst[3] here, and the weather is radiant. I adore you.

Paul

Ah! How I wish I could be with you—here—and also in Locarno and in Paris, at the Hôtel Radio. How I would make love to you. I only want to make love with you. The others are distraction, pure dilettantism.

35

[Ohlstadt, around 1 April 1929]

Monday

My beautiful little darling, I received your long registered letter, with your proxy, very ingenuous indeed, for the Company (but I will be in Paris on 10 April, and determined to defend myself—and I have some very clear-cut ideas about my defense. I have confirmed my arrival to them). Your letter gave me extraordinary joy. I, too, am only with you. Everything else is just a hobby. You alone in the world are not a hobby for me. You are my great Reality, my Eternity. When I think of you with any concentration, I am horribly disturbed.

Bouissounouse sends me the wrapper and the ad for my book. I'll lose no time in sending it to you. It is for you, for you alone, that I wrote this book. Not one thought, not one line that isn't about you.

PAUL ELUARD

You are all the imagery, all my joys, all my sorrows. The book has been sent. You'll have it in the next few days. It was sent to Arosa. It is already on sale in the bookshops.

Crevel is going to take a cure at Manoukine's (the doctor whom Demikeli spoke about, in Saint-Cloud).

There has been a terrible *foehn* blowing yesterday and today, throwing everyone to the ground. We get up at noon, we eat all the time, we are really getting a rest. I'm doing very well. The cold is well and truly gone. I leave here on Saturday with Mops and Mme. Apfel. We'll spend the night in Munich, and leave Sunday morning in third class so as to arrive in Paris that night. In third, because it only costs 40 marks, and with two meals and three people, the time passes quickly. I'll probably stay at the Hôtel Terrasse, but in any case, I'll wire you my address as soon as I arrive. I'm sending this letter to Locarno. I am cheered by the thought that you'll surely find a serene climate and some warmth there. Our departure from Arosa would make it seem empty there. Here I am adored, almost embarrassingly so. Mops is really very nice, very good, very simple, and all her friends, too. Send her a card, quickly (same address as me).

I adore you, truly, completely, and I'll never have anything real for the others.

You have a handsome little boy and you paid nothing. I kiss you all over, at length, all over, I penetrate you.

I love you.

Paul

36

Postcard: Strasbourg panorama
Postmark: Strasbourg, 3 April 1929
Addressee: Mme Gala Grindel. Hôtel du Parc, Locarno
   (Switzerland)

4 o'clock

No problems passing through Strasbourg. The mask is very beautiful.

Be in Paris tonight at eleven.
I do not forget you for one instant.

> Paul

37

Telegram
Postmark: Locarno, 5 April [19]29
Sender: Paul, Hôtel Radio, Bd de Clichy
To: Gala Grindel, Hôtel du Parc, Locarno (Switzerland)

I am nothing except when I'm with you. Paul

38

Postcard: Advertisement for the Le Radio brasserie
[Paris, about 10 April 1929]

My little girl, I'm going to Max's. I'm very happy to get your letters. I'll write you at length, tonight. I'm tired. Go to Arosa, but I'd really like you to meet me in Marseille as soon as possible. I am dying for want of seeing you. Literally. I'll leave here around the 18th. You should consider seeing me again, instead of moping. Otherwise, I'll kill myself.
I'm fed up to the gills with the others.
I adore you.

> Yours.
> Paul

PAUL ELUARD

39

Envelope: Express
Postmark: 10 April 1929
Addressee: Mme Gala Eluard Grindel, Hôtel du Parc, Locarno (Switzerland)
Sender: [Paul Eluard], Hôtel Radio, 64 Boulevard de Clichy, Paris

Tuesday night

I was in Meudon with Max today. It's really a perfect spot, no matter how you look at it. He's very well set up. I bought a very beautiful painting from him (Fr 2,000) for Bousquet. Also, a very beautiful human head from New Guinea that Flechtheim had given him, and a lovely little canvas.

I am now *very* tired. I can't wait to leave Paris, but I'd like to be able to meet up with you. At the end of the week, I'll probably go to Brussels for two days with Aragon and Breton. Tomorrow I'm going to the company. The day after, I'm on publicity duty all day. I am weary, drained. I'm coughing. I can't wait to leave.

Wednesday morning. I have received your express letter announcing your departure for Arosa on Saturday. It's a shame, because the climate in Locarno is surely better for you. Still, you obviously can't stay there alone. As for Arosa, I explained to my mother that it's for your health. Will you stay for long? I don't much enjoy explaining by letter my needs and reasons for seeing you again. It's too complicated. Given my exhaustion, the expense, and the complications that it entails, it would clearly be a mistake for me to remain in Paris too much longer.

1st, I still have things to do here, but I'm afraid of falling sick again (I'm coughing, I'm spitting, I'm very thin).

2nd, The Apple[1] is very pretty and very nice, but too abnormal. Mops is leaving here today, because she's very jealous of her. She was deeply in love with her, and has vaguely come to realize that the Apple loves me (she thinks I don't like her at all).

Only, the complication is that the Apple loves me, dreams of divorcing, of staying in France, of walking the streets to stay if need be, won't do anything about it, but will be very unhappy if this goes on much longer. She can't make love without crying at the thought that she has to leave soon, she's losing weight, she cries, etc. . . . <u>I hate that.</u>

And only my leaving can stop all that.

3rd, the real reason: it's that I love you and dream of being with you. The first night, I'll make love to you three times. And I want you naked all night. I'm going to jerk off thinking about you.

And I'm fed up with the rest, I want only you. If I love you it's lovemaking that I want, awfully. And to hold you in my arms, to lick you all over, to crush you, to make you lighter than ever, wetter, hotter, softer and harder than ever. My whole tongue is in your mouth, in your sex, my sex drenching you with come. It's all over your hands, your belly, your breasts, your face madly alive, and we start caressing each other again, kissing each other, drilling into each other. I want to love you more than ever.

My Gala, I make love very often here, too often. But what wouldn't I give to spend one night with you. Everything.
only

I'm worried that you'll want to stay a long time in Arosa. What then!!!!!!!!!!!!!!!!

I'll be in Marseille on the 18th at the latest. And you can't get there by then. I'll wait for you there as long as I have to. You know, I wanted to go to Carcassonne with you. I wish that you had some desire to see me again. You scold me for telling you to stay in Switzerland as long as you like. But you wrote me that you wanted to stay there much longer than originally planned, and asked me if I would be angry.

Of course not, not angry at all, but sad, *mortally* sad. Well, enough!!!

You surely believe that I love you. Don't have your flows[2] when you come to meet me. Be always, endlessly, beautiful and disturbed. Take care of yourself, don't wear yourself out (I mean no long walks, and *no drinking*). Tell me if the husband of the red woman[3] is still there. If not, I'll send her a line, out of courtesy.

Answer me nice and long.

I am yours, Paul.

PAUL ELUARD

Êtes-vous fous has come out.[4]

> Here is the dedication:
> to Paul and Gala Eluard
> How miserable is our Earth on life
> (song by Fortugé)

Very nice, isn't it. You'll get it in Arosa.

40

Letterhead: Hôtel Radio, 64, boulevard de Clichy, Paris
[Paris, mid-April 1929]

My beautiful little girl,

I did my publicity duty today with Crevel. I am exhausted beyond all measure. I love your letters. They comfort me. I am drained, literally. To the last drop. Tonight I am going with Max and Breton and the ladies to see *La Belle Hélène*.
Publicity is deadly, deadly, deadly. I've had it.
Nothing definite yet with the Company, but some progress: decision to put everything up for sale in a month if it's not worked out. We'll work it out. I said I wouldn't put up another penny. But then I could sell my share and lose very little.
I don't know when I'll be leaving for Marseille. If I'm still just as tired, I'll leave in 5 or 6 days. Otherwise, around the 22d. Consequently, reserve your ticket. But I'll be madly ecstatic if you're there before 1 May, madly ecstatic. I, too, dream of having you with me. Alone and amorous, very amorous. You are my only and the only beauty, the only intelligence.
I kiss you all over.

Paul

41

Postcard: Hôtel Radio
[Paris, April 1929]

My little one, I don't quite understand that "please let me return to Arosa." I didn't receive the letter in which you speak of it. Do as you like, but think about the fact that I may be obliged one day to go to the Parksanatorium. Stay in Switzerland as long as you please. I am very pessimistic, but am bearing up very well under the idiotic love affairs that I lead. But very, very pessimistic, very, almost too much so. Love with others than you exhausts me, disgusts me.
Gala, Gala, Gala, Gala, Gala, Gala.

Paul

42

[Paris, mid-April 1929]

Saturday

My dear little child, all is well here. I'm sending you today the standard copies (3), your copy on green paper, and Blum's copy. I did what was necessary at the bank. I was at Montlignon, I'm returning there tomorrow, Sunday. Then, the company and my publicity duty with Crevel. The book is in all the bookshops. I ordered myself a lovely gray suit.

Everything is going very simply with Mme. Apfel, calmly, no exhaustion, onanism for two, etc. . . . Saw Crevel, Breton, Janine, will see Max tonight. I love you and think of you continuously. I have a deep yearning for you. I love only you.

I kiss you awfully, all over.

Paul

43

My address: Terrass Hôtel, rue de Maistre (corner of rue
 Coulaincourt) Paris (18e)
Paris, Monday, 15 [April] 192[9]

My beautiful little girl, my sacred little girl, the 30th does indeed seem a long way off, and your flows very poorly timed. I still have a lot to do, but I hope to have finished as I had planned, around the 20th. Paris bothers me, I am generally more than tired, and I have an uncontrollable desire to see, to have you again. We shouldn't be apart for so long. I am happy to have affairs, but not to be deprived of you, the perfection of love, of womanhood, to that extent. The Apple is very nice, she adores me, she is very pretty and full of sexual imagination, but deprived of you I could grow to despise her. I am like you, most exactly, and anything I could do in that area could only be to your advantage, could only make me want to have you. I miss you constantly. You haunt my every move. Your presence is sovereign within me.

I'm going to Eaubonne with Ratton in a while. He wants to see the large pieces again. I'm having dinner at his place tonight. If he doesn't buy anything I'll sell some stock and send you the money straight away. You'll have it for the invoice on the 20th.

Yesterday I went for a drive with Max and Marie-Berthe, she's very sweet, much better than before. They'd like to come to Martinique with us. They're spending the summer near Arcachon and would like us to rent a house with them. Max recently had an intrigue (abducted a woman) that made a lot of noise. It was bound to happen.

I've had his paintings sent to Bousquet. We're preparing a 132-page number of *Variétés*[1] that will be very handsome. It will supplement the *deluxe* editions of Péret's (magnificent) erotic poems. I am very elegant here, very handsome. Everyone adores me. Mops did my portrait and that of Crevel for a Berlin paper (with an article by Klaus Mann, Thomas's son). The publicity hasn't been sent out yet, but I've already received some letters. All of this to give you a high opinion of he who really loves and desires only you, who finds you so much to his taste, so velvety and hot and soft, he who thinks with you, who cannot leave your head without the world coming to an end.

In the next few days I'm going to a very good specialist in general diseases. Today I'm very well. Write to me if there's any chance of your meeting me in Marseille before the 30th to make love. Otherwise, come the 30th. But what fortitude I'll need.

My beloved, my only beloved.

I kiss you all over and let myself be kissed all over by you.

I am in your eyes.

Paul

44

Letterhead: Hotel Belgravia (London), Grosvenor Gardens, Victoria, London S.W.1.
[mid-April 1929]

Wednesday morning

In haste, my beautiful little girl. After many difficulties, I have an appointment in a little while with Oldman,[1] who was in the country. I hope to find some very lovely things at his place that I can sell back to Pierre at a very good profit.[2]

I'll leave Paris Sunday morning so as to arrive in Marseille that night. As you will already have left, go directly to the Hôtel Beauvau, 4, rue Beauvau. If I can't have got a room there, I'll leave my address at the reception desk. And perhaps you could also ask for Gaillard,[3] who should still be there.

I got here last night. I'm leaving again tomorrow. I won't forget your turquoise. Nor your gifts in general.

I adore you. I dream only of Monday when you will be arriving. If you can, wire me your arrival time from Geneva. But if I'm not at the station, go to the Hôtel Beauvau where you will find either me or Gaillard, or my address at the reception desk.

I kiss you all over. I adore you with my whole life, *forever the same*.

[unsigned]

45

Telegram
Postmark: Arosa, 26 April 1929
From: Paris
To: Grindel, Parksanatorium, Arosa, Switzerland

Will be Sunday Hôtel Beauvau probably otherwise ask address reception desk.
Madly impatient Paul

46

[Marseille, late April/early May 1929]

Thursday

Last night, in Geneva, I didn't sleep a single minute. A crazy restiveness, like never before. I got up at 5 o'clock to catch the 6:15 train. The trip very tiring. Stormy weather, packed train. The customs went like clockwork. Slept about two hours on the train. Aside from that, I am forgetting that that entire night of insomnia produced a poem for you, which I like very much because it is a good proof of my love. It makes you "absolute queen." Found Gaillard, who went out to let me wash up. Very nice, but very sluggish, very melancholy. Tonight we're going to the special cinema. It costs Fr 20 and is apparently very good. I am not too tired, just a little too nervous. I hope you received your package this morning and that you weren't too unhappy with it. In your store, there were only some beautiful ties. I bought two blue ones. And in the House of Knitwear, a little sleeveless sweater, in a very lovely solid blue, and very cheap: 24 Swiss francs. It goes very well with my suit and ties. Also found a blue hat. I ran like a madman. Didn't buy any books. In the Zurich station, I ran across the Hindu woman from Arosa, with a really repulsive guy. She didn't see me. In Geneva, saw Dr. Serner, who also didn't see me. Marseille, what noise, what smells, how many breasts bouncing under dresses, how many pimps. The opposite of Switzerland. Life, a living city. And I'm not forgetting those Swiss pigs. I'm bringing you an all-round wonderful dentifrice: Bi-Oxyne *paste*. If you find any, buy it. It gives you teeth like snow.

Friday morning

I won't have any letters from you until Montlignon. But I expect them there at my arrival, Monday morning.

Obscene cinema, what a marvel! It's exalting. A discovery. The incredible life of enormous and magnificent organs up on screen, the erupting sperm. And the life of amorous flesh, every contortion. It's glorious. And very well made, madly erotic. How I'd love for you to see it. If you come to Marseille you'll go with Gaillard, who is the veritable incarnation of respectability and has already accompanied several very "bourgeois *ladies*." Well, I'll tell you all about my feelings. I was very well-behaved, didn't see anyone. And that's enough. The film gave me an exasperating hard-on for an hour. I almost came just from watching. If you had been there, I couldn't have held back. And it's a very pure show, no theatricality. The actors don't move their lips, at least not to speak; it is a "silent art," a "primitive art," passion versus death and ignorance. They should show it in all the movie halls and in the schools. It would result in workable marriages, the first, by sacred, many faceted unions. Poetry has not been born, alas!

My darling little girl, after all that, and some soporific, I slept well, from 11 to 8. I'm not tired. It's hot, but thundery.

Life in Marseille is much more expensive than before. The room: Fr 30, in a little hotel. But I'm still managing to economize, and you can dream about your gifts. Be serene. Think of all I've promised you. I hope you have a good room, no noise. My handsome little girl.

I believe you have no doubts about my love for you. There are no doubts to have. You can rest assured. AND FOR YOU ALONE! I kiss you all over.

Paul

47

[Marseille, May 1929]

My beautiful little girl, I was very happy to get a letter from you. I wasn't expecting it. I hope you got my first, very long letter. They have to be forwarded to you in any case.

There's nothing new here. I am well. I'm sort of in training for city life. I brought my poems to a typist. I'm going to buy myself an overcoat. There's an enormous crowd in Marseille.

A flattering (though unwitting) word from Baron[1] to Gaillard: "Eluard? Yes, sure! But still, you can't forget Apollinaire." Holy Innocence! Max Ernst was very restrained.

Finally, I've had a decent haircut. I wish you were with me. It would be so much better. I adore you. My dove, I kiss you all over.

You did well to change hotels. I think that the beach, especially, is better. And the people won't be the same. Here, the weather is fine.

[unsigned]

48

Hôtel Alexandra, Nice [June 1929]

Monday morning

It's funny—all these departures, all these stopovers in Nice. The Hôtel Alexandra is across from the Hôtels Beaulieu and de Hollande, where I stayed before my voyage, 5 years ago, I cried there—how I cried—5 years ago.

Radiant weather, the palm trees, the window open, a very lovely room. (I'm awaiting the doctor for my knee, which is still killing me.) This morning, the same feeling as five years ago—but the feeling of departure attenuated by my return.

This Hôtel Alexandra is pretty good, and inexpensive: room and board Fr 50 for a large double room over the gardens. Very beautiful wallpaper and lovely moldings on the ceiling.

Last night I went to bed on arrival, very tired by the trip and the heat on the train. I'm going to rest long and well, I think. I never expected this kind of weather. Marvelous. I think of you—as of the fatal light of my birth.

I love you. I kiss you all over,

Paul

All my regards to Gaillard.

The doctor says that my knee is not serious, but that I should wear a bandage for walking, and tomorrow he's giving me ignipuncture.[1]

49

[Hôtel Alexandra, Nice, June 1929]

Tuesday morning

My dear, dearest, last night, life was too unbearable, so I got drunk. It was immediately much worse. Monstrously worse.

I feel better this morning. Not sick at all. I dreamed a lot. Obscene nightmares, dirty and sad. But the weather is really fine.

After lunch, I'm going to get my ignipuncture done. Afterward, in a while, my knee will have to be x-rayed. Out of caution, because there's a small fracture.

But the main thing is, with my knee bandaged, I can walk.

Nice is beautiful, as far as climate, sea, greenery. But provincial. The hotel is perfect. And such good wines!!!

Thanks for Keller's[1] letter. He wants to go around the world, etc... 9 pages.

That's it. No chance of any intrigue here. And I prefer my room, which is very pleasant.

My regards to Gaillard.

I give you a big kiss.

Paul

50

[Nice, June 1929]

Saturday

It's better after all that you didn't receive that letter. It was very unhappy in every sense of the word.

But tonight, when I have the sensation of living, I am happy, very happy, my Gala, my ONLY, that you were spared any pain. And I'm breathing easy. It's when I'm very unhappy, and Tuesday night I was very, very unhappy, that I don't want to see you.

But when, like today, I have three appointments, every success, new books, and life resumes itself—then *I hate to be unfair* to you, and the thought of you, your existence within me, takes the place of that life, and I dream of being with you instead of being in the WORLD. The poem, which I'm not sending because it would ruin this letter for you, the long poem will show you how unhappy I was.

And everything was involved. I don't want to tell you about it because *it's over, totally avoided* now, but I was threatened by horrible things, worse than death. Love was *no longer present*.

And it seemed to be a punishment. It's a frightful Christian idea, demoralizing and truly impossible to bear. And you had written me a little clumsily (I had lost my freedom of spirit).

My darling, all of that is over, over, over. I love you, I love you, you are real and beautiful. LOVE IS ABOVE EVERYTHING. WITH GALA, MY GALA, all mine in a world that is all mine.

Send Gaillard all my love. Did you receive the letter with the keys?

Sunday

My well-beloved,

I'm happy that you want to come. That's what was needed to be written. VERY HAPPY. (Jerked off twice today at the thought of you being here.)

This way, with this temperature, I'll be able to adore you NAKED for hours on end. We'll go out only to see the marvelous *kino spezial* [sic]. But come well before your flows. Come Tuesday, for instance, by the same train as me. Wire me.

We will live on love, love alone. Tomorrow morning I'll wire you and send you Fr 1,000 by wire, if possible (it's a holiday).

Herewith the poem in question and a drawing[1] for your entertainment. You can show them to Gaillard if he's interested. I am dazed with excitement, with dreaming about you:

NAKED
eyes, mouth,
and sex agape.

Received Gaillard's telegram. Have him give you the drawings, photos, and manuscript—for me. Understand, and make him understand, that I wish we could sometimes possess you together, as we had arranged.

I've suddenly thought of something quite worrying. Providing that I didn't address my letter to Montlignon, that I didn't do the opposite of what was necessary, write your address on the letter that was inserted. It would be rather bothersome, because that letter was *incredibly* intimate. That's exactly why I sent it express. Sometimes my mind is so empty and stupid.

While I'm thinking of it, I can tell you now, since it surely isn't so, that the doctor strongly feared a bacillary (tubercular) arthritis of the knee, and that without knowing that I had had a lung complaint.

The ignipuncture did me a lot of good, because, with my knee still bandaged, I can walk almost as before.

[unsigned]

A prison uncrowned[2]
In the open air

PAUL ELUARD

A window in flames
Where the lightning bares its breasts
A night all green
No one smiles in this solitude
Here the fire sleeps on its feet
Through me.

But this gloom is pointless
I can smile
Doltish face
Whose desires death cares not to wither
Perfectly free face
That will forever keep its look and its smile.

If I live today
If I am not alone
If someone comes to the window
And if I am that window
If someone comes
His new eyes do not see me
Do not know my thoughts
Refuse to be my cohorts

And divide so as to love.

51

Telegram
From: Paris
To: [Mme.] Grindel. Med. Hôtel. Cannes
Postmark: 17 June [1929]

All well except my missing you. Kisses: Paul.

52

Letterhead: Terrass Hôtel, 12 and 14, rue de Maistre, Paris

[June 1929]

My Gala, Gala, Gala, you must forgive me. Without at all wanting to, I have behaved badly toward you by not writing. All of this comes from your telling me to write you at Régina,[1] when you weren't even there, and my obstinacy, because of the express letter, at not wanting to write to Régina, thinking that my letters would be stolen.

But I have been punished for it, very sad and distraught. I knew I wasn't wrong about G.[2] I only regret what I had to endure because of it.

Try to get a letter that I sent to him from Holland to you. Tell him to write me. It will be difficult for us to be together for now. The A. still has another month coming. I can't leave her. We're going to Brittany. You to Switzerland, to see B.[3] But you know, my lovely, it seems ridiculous to me, sweetly ridiculous, these two separate departures, when I love you so, when I am so proud, so close, so fraternal to you and you alone, you, Gala. And yet, what's the point of us meeting too soon. Cannes was marvelous, but Marseille, Carcassonne were awful for me. I couldn't make you go through that. *For me,* G.'s attitude was abominable. Well! But still, those trips to Belgium and Holland with the A. were not unpleasant, but your ghost followed us, because you are Truth. I could have made that trip with my Gala, the eternal one, the one I love awfully and with whom I fight just as awfully. But life, awful life. . . I played baccarat in Belgium and won 12,000 Belgian francs (8,000 French). In Holland, I bought a fetish, one of a kind, New Guinea (3 feet), Fr 20,000. A glory. I'll sell it one day for 200,000. Certainly. And a very flat uli,[4] ancient and very beautiful, like a Modigliani, and various other things here. My mother bought an old, very lovely Chirico (15,000) as an investment. But it's in a safe place. Then, some books on Blake. And perhaps a Goethe: Fr 1,200, unique copy. Then I saw

Keller. He had a very beautiful little Rousseau, reproduced in color on the cover of Basler's book on Rousseau (Librairie de France[5]) (perhaps you can see it, ask around the bookshops for the book). He was asking 6,000 for it. He didn't want money, but told me to give him a Negro piece later on. I'm very pleased. But I adore you and the only pleasure I can take in all this is to believe that you'll see it, that it will please you. I'm looking for a nice apartment. We can have all our things there and use it as a base for our travels. But also we'll meet there, make deep love there, the two most united beings in the world will go there to cancel out all the others.

I need to sell some stock to get money. I'll send it to you Wednesday without fail. By wire if you're in a hurry. That way you can go to Arosa. How stupid this all is. Stupid because there doesn't seem to be an end to it. Wire me often and intelligibly. Herewith a telegram[6] that I couldn't quite understand.

I kiss you all over, awfully, at length.

Yours alone forever.

Paul

53

[Paris, July 1929]

Tuesday

My beloved little girl, first of all I have only this to say to you: how I long to see you naked, to hold you, to kiss you, to make love to you. And we are apart and I no longer have much hope of keeping you. You see, for the moment, I have the unmitigated company of the Apple. If I let her go to meet you, how long will I keep you? And I'd find myself alone again with even more time to waste on my hands, feeling horribly lost. Since you have B. or others who'll come along, I can't eat my heart out in solitude. The Apple, pretty, pleasant, and submissive, is a lifeline for me.

But she still doesn't wipe out the horrible sadness of not having you anymore. That which *is* does not frighten me, but that which *might be* will be the end of me. I won't be able to go on feeling forsaken. I know now that nothing can stop you, you are pitiless—and I wouldn't want your pity anyway. And I myself am so changeable. But I can't be there anymore, as a "spectator," I can't for a moment think that I am not everything to you, that the rest just exists as a function of me.

You, you are the only being that I have ever loved. I love, I believe only in your image.

Go to Arosa if you want. But if you sincerely *must* be with me, I'll send the Apple away, but afterward, you'll have to be entirely at my disposal, you can't leave me any more than I could call her back, you can't leave me alone. The Apple won't understand my sending her away so soon. She still has some time. And later on, I may not be able to have her as easily as I'd like.

Please understand what I'm telling you. I have to stay here two or three days in any case. I was planning to go off somewhere afterward. I'd go with you. Maybe it would be better for you to go to Arosa now? But for how long!! For the moment I'm not alone. Maybe you had better take advantage of it.

I'll send you Fr 3,000 on Wednesday, tomorrow night. I am at your service. Think about it, send me a long, clear telegram.

I adore you, I kiss you all over. I love only you.

Paul

Tuesday midnight

I reopen my letter. I went to the circus this evening (a big German circus) with Cécile and my mother. I just got back to the hotel. All evening I thought of nothing but you, I saw nothing but your ghost.

You can go to Arosa now. It will be better than later. I'll have an apartment at the end of the month.[1] And we can meet there. My Gala, Gala, my well-beloved, my only. But I assure you that never has my fate seemed more tragic, never has my thought been so far from all rest, from all hope. The form of love—You—has veiled all other forms of life. Go to Arosa. It will be simpler, more practical. Life without you can't last too long.

Or else command. Under any circumstances, I'll accept your will—but without hope. I love you—under any circumstances—I love only you. You can be sure of that. And whatever you decide, I will have neither thought nor word of reproach. We have willed what you will do—under any circumstances.

I adore you. You are my little, my beautiful, my fine and voluptuous and inspired GALA.

54

[Paris, July 1929]

My beautiful, my Gala forever,

I am waiting for an answer on a cheap and very pretty apartment, on the Butte Montmartre, very bright with a good view of Paris, and big. If I get it (it's not easy) I'll wire you immediately. In that case, I'll put all our things in one room, and I'll come to meet you wherever you like. You'll have a lovely room. Where shall we go? To some place fairly warm? But not too.

It's cold here as well. And exhausting. Give your address only to me. As far as my mother knows you're still in the south.

For the moment I'm strapped for money. I've bought a lot and the apartment will cost quite a bit (rent and moving in). I'll have to keep expenses down at first.

If it works out, we'll be in the sunshine in a quiet, dustless street, in a new building.

Herewith a letter that I left in my pocket a long time ago.

I love you terribly. I hope that by the 20th, at the latest, we'll be together. Or earlier if you like, but I have to prepare the apartment and it's not very comfortable. If you don't think the 20th is possible, let me know. I won't be angry, but I'll have to go to the country and to keep the A. with me so as not to be alone.

Think about where we'll go with Cécile. Breton is in Brittany. Goemans[1] is going to Cadaqués, in Spain, with some Spaniards who made a wonderful film.[2] We'll have to find somewhere very cheap. Crevel's going to Switzerland: Leysins or Arosa. He had his operation. He's feeling better, but not strong. I adore you. I am miserable without you.

I'll write to you often. I wasn't sure of your address before.

I'm sending two books and two copies of a very funny record album: the spare copy for whomever you like.

[unsigned]

My beautiful little girl, I'm really happy that you're doing better. I want you strong and calm and amorous when we meet. Your letter seems to suggest that I won't see you before 1 August. I'm not quite sure what I'm going to do, myself. I'm still waiting for the manager's answer on the apartment. Paris is becoming unbearable. It's very hot here right now. In any case I'll leave for the holiday weekend of 14 July. But you can always write to the Terrass Hôtel. I hope B. is getting better. Be very careful. I'm always afraid of you falling sick.

I'll write you little, but every day. I'll be sure always to give you my address.

Perhaps we could go to Évian first. It's very good for the stomach. And then by the shores of Lake Geneva. What do you think? Then afterwards, maybe to Spain. Or by the sea.

I'm counting the days. If you want to come with me beforehand, write, or wire.

I adore you alone.

Paul

55

[Paris, July 1929]

My beautiful, my only, my all-beloved, I am impatiently awaiting your answer to yesterday's letter. Also whether or not my books amuse you. I'd like to know when you can meet me. The A. can stay with me until about 10 August. But if you like she'll leave earlier. I myself live only by the idea that every day, that light and love, in any case, bring me closer to you.

I'll meet you whenever you like, wherever you like. These past days, I've made some quite brilliant deals that will greatly help toward the rent and moving expenses of our apartment, which are fairly costly. I am impatiently awaiting the manager's answer.

At the company, a settlement has finally been reached, and concluded. I remain, with the four richest and most serious [shareholders?]. And I hope that, henceforth, there's nothing more to be lost. I was very busy with it all. I'm going there again this afternoon. If I can wait a while, there may be something to gain. With interest, I have Fr 246,000 in it.

Little by little, I've been persuading my mother to buy important paintings, which will go up. She's already started.

Keller, as I told you, has been very nice. I see him fairly often. See you soon, my lovely little creature.

I kiss you awfully all over.

Yours forever.
Paul

56

[Paris, then on the train to Brussels, around mid-July 1929]

Saturday

I think I'll have the apartment Wednesday morning. I'll wire you immediately. There are five large rooms: living and dining rooms connected by a large opening without doors, one lovely round room for you, a lovely room for Cécile, and a very large maid's room where we can put cupboards and junk, a large entrance hall, a bathroom, a kitchen, a stairway and a service entrance, large windows everywhere. The first floor is sunny, you can see all of Paris, on a very, very quiet street. There's a school yard opposite. It will be really nice.

Nine P.M. I'm on the train to Brussels. Paris was too awful for the holidays. I'll be back at the Terrass Hôtel Tuesday. I hope your letters will be waiting there for me.

I think of you endlessly. This trip would be so good with you. And love. I really, truly love only you.

Paul

57

Terrass Hôtel, Paris

Thursday [July 1929]

My beautiful little girl,

Herewith some letters for you. But avoid having people write to you at Eaubonne. I'm just back from Belgium, pretty tired. And I lost Fr 6,000. I won't gamble anymore. It's nothing, I'm still up 10,000 in all, but I think my luck's turning. Other than that, I made some great sales on some pieces, and I hope to sell a Crevel manuscript for Fr 4,000. Not bad.

And I've got the apartment, I think. I have to sign the lease tomorrow morning. As soon as it's signed I'll wire you with some money, because I'm still not sure exactly what it'll cost and I'm keeping what I have for that. In any case, you'll have the money in 5 or 6 days at the latest (Fr 3,000). I'm owed money. Everyone says I'm looking well. Crevel left last night for Leysin. He'll write you. If I meet you in Évian, we'll work it out to go see him.

As for the apartment, as soon as it's definite, I'll order everything that has to be done on it, so it will be done over the vacation and we can move in late September. It will be great.

The heat here is miserable. And I still have a lot to do.

I'll have a lot of new things to show you. We're far from being ruined. In any case, we can't lose anything at the Company.

I only wish I could have sold the house.[1] And it's harder than I thought.

Received a letter from Gaillard, who complains that this whole business has done him a good deal of harm.

I have a magnificent complete edition of Goethe. I'm having you sent the *Variétés* issue with my article on Péret. And rest well assured. I love you awfully. I'm waiting to see you. Only that.

Paul

58

[Terrass Hôtel, Paris, July 1929]

Monday, 6 A.M.

How are you, my beautiful little girl? You're still asleep. Your body is curled up in sleep. I'd like to caress you, hold you, make love to you. Would you like us to meet in Évian next Monday or Tuesday? Cécile's awards ceremony is next Sunday. We'll leave straight afterward. Perhaps you can go on ahead and wire me your address here (Terrass Hôtel). Choose a good hotel, but not too expensive. It shouldn't be more than Fr 150 for the three of us. I think that's possible. Or else, which would be simpler, take any old hotel and we won't stay there. Perhaps we'll go to Thonon-les-Bains (1,000m), certainly to Leysin, we'll see. Anyhow, do just as you like. I only ask you to love me terribly. To begin thinking of me only.

My mother wrote you a letter in Cannes, it was returned to her. I told her you were in the Marseille area, that you're moving around and that I don't have your address.

As soon as you're in Évian, write to her.

Business is very good. This morning, I'm busy arranging the apartment. And I'm hoping to sell a bunch of Negro and pre-Columbian *junk* next Thursday. Goodbye, my Gala. I adore you, you alone. I kiss you deeply all over.

Paul

59

[Paris, July 1929]

Wednesday, 8 A.M.

Gala, my well-beloved,

this is my last letter to Arosa. I will very probably be in Évian with Cécile on Monday or Tuesday. The best thing now would be for you to leave immediately and to wire me the name of the hotel where you will be. I have to have the telegram *at the very latest,* at the Terrass Hôtel, 12, rue de Maistre, early on Monday morning.

Sooner would be better.

I am in a mad rush to see you. You are, of all flesh, the most desirable, of all eyes the deepest, of all sexes the hottest, of all passions the wildest, of all women the most beautiful, the most daring, the most free.

Yesterday I went to see the apartment with Moreux,[1] the decorator. It really is a pleasant apartment. Your room is lightly rounded and you can see all Paris from your window. The shame is having to put a large wardrobe in there. It would be prettier without one.

And we are horribly furnitureless. We can't use the things from Eaubonne.

Anyhow, well and truly moved in will cost us a few fetishes and a large Chirico. It's worth the trouble. We'll get more pleasure out of it. And I've bought so much! And good stuff. And there'll be some deals to attend to. And tomorrow, I hope to stick an old American woman who knows nothing with a pile of junk that I'll bring over from Eaubonne and Montlignon to put in the safe. It'll be great.

You'll have to take care of the fetish. Is it pretty? Have you seen it? Try to get the photo. Give your address in Évian. Thanks very much for the book of Children. Very beautiful pictures. There are a lot of books I'd like at the moment.

Do you need anything? Yes, there is central heating, fully equipped bathroom, w.c. for the maid or friends, etc. . . Very large windows, a school yard opposite, the Sacré-Coeur clock tower, not a car on the street. It's a brand new building. And I'm having everything arranged marvelously. You'll see. And we'll have a telephone. And a lovely phonograph.

Maybe it would be simpler if we went to Leysin first. Easier to find one another. I think that's better. Anyway, decide as soon as possible and wire me your address very quickly. Really, you can decide. I don't care either way, myself. And as we're going there in any case, it would perhaps be best. You'll find a place: a *pension,* not too dear, not too bad. Very clean: for Cécile. They'll tell you that in Arosa. You could call ahead for the rooms and leave. Or ask Crevel by telephone; he's at the Grand-Hôtel. Anyway, do as you like, really.

I adore you, you know. I'm sick at the thought of seeing you again, of taking you back. I kiss you all over, all over.

[unsigned]

60

[Paris, early September 1929]

Well, my little girl, I have a lot to do and it's as hot as the Sahara. I've bought some lovely furniture, almost everything for Fr 11,000. All I've ordered from Moreux are the sideboard, the bookcase, and your dressing table.[1] Believe me, it won't be bad. But I only want you to see it fully installed. In the early part of October. We'll have a very good bed, the best there is, a splendid American hospital mattress.

I'm fine, I love you.

I'm going to see the doctor next Wednesday.

Write me often. I adore you.

Goodbye, my little girl.

Paul

61

Paris [early September 1929]

Tuesday

My beautiful little girl, yesterday morning I went to pick up the Goemans at the station, and they passed on your letter and Cécile's. I don't quite know what to send Cécile. She must have received the large package I sent her from Toulouse. Anyway I'll send her two books tomorrow. I hope she's on her way to recovery. I'm seeing a painter for the apartment at two o'clock. I hope everything will be done by early October. I'm seeing a doctor Thursday. I'll write you right away. I'll also stop by the cosmetics shop this afternoon. It is still very, very hot here.

Be serene. I love you awfully.
I kiss you all over.

Yours forever.
Paul

62

[Paris, September 1929]

Thursday

My little girl, the heat here is still miserable, and it's hard to say how people are surviving.

Despite that and despite some pretty unbearable heart palpitations, I'm doing fairly well. There's nothing new. But I feel as if I can only live in the most absolute inertia. Unable to think, unable to act.

I am only very happy, *very*, to know that you have pleasant memories of my presence alongside you in Cadaqués.[1]

Rest well assured that I love you and that I'll always love you.

I received your letter. Very glad that Cécile got her Papers. I'm leading a pretty despairing life here.

I love you.

Write my mother, at Montlignon, that Cécile is feeling better.

Paul

63

[Paris, September 1929]

My adored little girl,

I sent you 1,000 pesetas yesterday. That's the limit. Come back when you like. The heat has finally passed today and I think it's going to rain.

Come back around the 22d or 23d, if you like. I would really have liked for us not to have to live at the hotel, we'll have to anyway.

Last night, I jerked off magnificently thinking of you, imagining you lascivious and unleashed, as you taught me to see you. I adore you and desire you terribly.

I drew some overpaid funds (30,000), a registration refund, and I bought a very beautiful fetish from Cameroon. Also bought back from Ratton a very beautiful Dali canvas (tell him) that I made him buy (a 12 or a 15).[1]

The apartment will be ready around 5 October. How is little Cécile? Give her a big kiss. I wasn't able to send you the lipstick or the lotion. It's complicated. Perhaps you'll be able to do without.

I dream of you. I want you to be supremely elegant in Paris. I'll take care of it. I am most incapable of writing to you right now. But I'm very well and not exhausting myself. Don't worry about anything.

Saw Keller, with whom we'll be able to do some business. He presented me with the barometer.

Be very nice and send a card to the Goemans.

I kiss you awfully all over.

Ys. forever.
Paul

Keller is here and sends you his very best. Gala. Gala. Gala.
My very best and most sincere wishes to Dali and Buñuel. Gala.

64

[Paris, September 1929]

Gala, my sister, my friend, my lover, your letters give me great pleasure. And also I love you and you are my only and the greatest mystery to me. The mystery of your body, so beautiful, so young against me, voluptuous and forever offered me in your marvelous eyes. I love you, I love only you. You can be sure of that, absolutely sure.

I'd really like you to come home. But I'd also prefer you not to stay too long at the hotel, which might make you sick of Paris. The apartment won't be ready before 4 or 5 October. Why should you go to Barcelona? You'll wear yourself out. What kind of people will you run into there? Anyway, my lovely darling, you'll do as you like. I only want you to have fun, I only want you to be free.

But I don't know what to say. Above all, I'd like to see you and have you. Yes, come home. Come, come, I love only you, I desire only you, I understand only you. It's you I want. Come, come, come, my most beautiful, *my only being,* Gala, Galotchka.

I'll send you a bit more money. And warn me of your arrival. And I'll make you elegant and happy.

Give Cécile a big kiss for me.

I love you, I kiss you awfully all over.

Paul

Do the impossible to bring back some Dali paintings: *Le jeu lugubre,* my portrait, and the two others. It would be *very* useful. Breton is here, at the Terrass. Write to me at the Terrass Hôtel, 12–14 rue de Maistre, 18e.

PAUL ELUARD

65

Postmark: Paris, 90, rue Duperre, 11 January 1930
Addressee: Mme. Grindel, Hôtel du Château, Carry-le-Rouet (Bouches-du-Rhône)
Arrival Postmark: Carry-le-Rouet, Bouches-du-Rhône, 13 January 1930

Saturday

My darling little Gala,

received your cards, some of which are very good. Very well chosen in any case. (Don't send me any Marseilles jokes.) It's raining, it's cold, there's a taxi strike and I am ever so sweetly missing you (a great melancholy, a great determined void). Keller came with a guy who chose Fr 30,000-worth of pieces (the Carolina, bought for 3,000—10,000; the slate totem, bought for 400—10,000; and three little pieces) but they're going away until Thursday and won't come to pick them up and pay for them until they get back. If it's confirmed, as I think it will be, I'll come to meet you on Friday and expect to find you in Marseilles. I'll give Keller a fairly handsome piece as a commission.

Between now and then, I'm going to try to get my mother's car to go east tomorrow morning to look for postcards with Breton, who sold two pieces.[1] We'll try to be back Wednesday. It will distract me, for I'm missing you and missing everything. I love you, only you. I have made you the subject of all my dreams, the simplest as well as the most bizarre. Char had you sent a blouse. I'll bring it to you. He's in Marseilles, "c/o M. Jules Armani, 378, rue Paradis." Send him a card.

I love you, I kiss you all over, with my eyes, my hands, my mouth and my sex. Ys. forev.

Paul

66

Postmark: Paris, 16 January 1930
Addressee: Mme. Grindel, Hôtel du Château, Carry-le-Rouet (Bouches-du-Rhône)
Arrival Postmark: Carry-le-Rouet, 17 January 1930

Thursday, 1 o'clock

My sparkling Gala,

I'm back. I'm expecting Keller at 2:30. I hope it'll work out and that I'll be able to meet you. I am awfully restless. I yearn for you so much. It's driving me crazy. The idea of meeting you, seeing you, kissing you, is killing me. I never want your hand, your mouth, your sex to stray from my member. We'll jerk off on the street, in the cinemas, the window open. This morning I jerked off magnificently while thinking of you. And my imagination isn't weary. I see you everywhere, in everything, above everything. I love you to death. Your sex swallows mine, covers my face, it covers me with your beauty, it covers everything with your beauty, your genius. Everything about you is beautiful: your eyes, your mouth, your hair, your breasts, your pubes, your ass, your sex, your legs, your sex, your hands that can't let go of what they're jerking off, that space between your thighs, near your sex, your shoulders. The thought of each part of your body makes me drunk. And everything you do souses me, terrifies me, tortures me, elates me, everything you do is perfect. If this deal is clinched, I'll leave tomorrow night to be in Marseilles Sunday morning. I'll go to the Hôtel Bristol and I hope you'll join me there right away. Char is in Marseilles. I hope to see him.

I'm waiting for Keller.
It's come off: 29,800.
Great. I'll leave tomorrow night.
Best to Dali.
I adore you.

Paul

PAUL ELUARD

67

[Hyères, around 20 January 1930]

Wednesday night

Your letter did me some good tonight. If you don't mind, write me a lot and often—and well. Since you left, I've been going through a ridiculous crisis of melancholy. I'm full of you. I don't talk, I think endlessly of our whole life, of our love, of our greatness. I'm not sleeping too well: so many dreams about you, and you're also there every time I wake up, greater, more fine, more alive than ever—but desperately unattainable.

You must forgive me, you know. My head is rather unwell.

I recently read *Jude the Obscure*. It didn't help at all.

I imagine your coat around your slim figure, so pure, so lovely.

For three hours today I tried to phone you. Not succeeding, I looked for a taxi to take me to Carry. None of them wanted to, it's too far. Or else they asked crazy fares. And I only have Fr 4,000 left, which I'm nibbling away at. The hotel here costs Fr 40, all included. As for Noailles,[1] I ran into him. I was with the Apple and he invited her over tomorrow. I'm very upset about it. But you know, Hyères is so far from Carry and you'll really have a much nicer trip to Spain.

I want you to be happy, but one of these days, when I'm merry and healthy, I'll try to have you be so with me.

Savinio[2] is in issue No. 5 of *Bifur*.

The weather is very good here, but it's very sad and I'm leaving for Nice in two days or on Saturday.

Write to Char's guy to forward me your address. In any case, *use telegrams*. If I'm in Nice on Wednesday night or Saturday morning, I'll wire you my address.

No news from Char, who should have been here yesterday. I'm afraid of leaving before he comes. Where can he be? I love you infinitely. You're in my head every minute of my life, day and night. I kiss you awfully all over.

Paul

68

Postmark: Paris XVIIIe, 30 January 1930
Addressee: Mme. Grindel, Hôtel du Château, Carry-le-
  Rouet (Bouches-du-Rhône)

Thursday

My sweet darling,

I stay in this apartment arranging my cards, lounging around. The weather is lovely, but I don't have any desire to go out. A splendid silence. In the postcard style, I am "crowned with melancholy, decline, and neglect."

How can this go on? Never again will anything open itself to me. My health is excellent. The cards have had a great effect.

I was hoping for a letter from you. If you're comfortable in the south, stay there, I want you to be happy and free. I am very calm, very faithful, very calm. If it bothers you to write, wire.

Some metal has been put on the sideboard. I hope that you found some cards today. And that you've been gluing your chromos. I'll go for your knitwear tomorrow.

My only, my most lovely,

Paul

69

Postmark: Paris Xe, 3 February 1930
Addressee: Mme. Grindel, Hôtel du Château, Carry-le-
  Rouet (Bouches-du-Rhône)
Arrival Postmark: Carry-le-Rouet, 4 Feb., 1930

Saturday

My little darling, finally a letter. And straightaway I come out of my neurasthenia, my profound solitude. I'm in bed today, despondant and still "needing to vomit." Well then! I'm going to get up, I'm going to go out. You know, I believe you! I believe you! I BELIEVE YOU! Nothing's lost. Your letter cured me. Please don't hold it against me for having been engulfed these past two days in the pit that is your absence. If it takes on such proportions, it's because I love you. And how!

And also, ridiculous and ferocious migraines!

But your letter, your letter, your letter—Gala.

Gala, when the thought occurs to me that all is over between us, I am truly *like a man condemned to death,* and to what a death.

My little girl, when are you coming home? I'm fine now. But write to me. I kiss you all over.

Paul

A little entertainment for you: Yvonne[1] is with Rott[2] and Goemans has gone on a trip! I'm waiting for Char and his cards.

Char will explain to me what you found for your chromo collection.

70

[Paris, early February 1930]

Monday. It's 7:30. Odette hasn't come down yet, and so I was awoken by the doorbell's fierce ringing. Your express letter. And I am bright and joyous. This time I'm going to get up early. Since I came home, I've been getting up at 4 in the afternoon. It did me good. I'd arrange the cards, my mind a blank. I wish you were in my bed this morning—and always.

Breton (and I too) received letters from some young unknowns offended by *Cadavre*.[1] He's finished the *Second Manifesto* and is giving it to the publisher today. It's absolutely magnificent, irrefutable. We found the proof for Poe.[2] Bataille is executed with a magnificent sentence by Marx on "toe-philosophers and excrement-philosophers." And as a preface: the report of a meeting of the most famous French psychiatrists (published in the *Annales medico-psycho-*

logiques) in which they call for a lawsuit against the author of *Nadja*. Professor Janet announces that some *madmen* triumphantly pointed out to him the passage in which Breton says that, locked up, he'd exploit the light of reason to kill the doctor. Etc. . . . It's perfect. Sadoul (and Caupenne) is deeper and deeper in the shit because of his letter. Goureaud is demanding a public apology to France, under the flag, on the Place Saint-Cyr. Obviously, there's no question of one. And so, the military authorities will prosecute for death threats (it could mean up to 5 years in prison).[3]

Thirion is abroad because he's being threatened with arrest for the unrest in the East.[4] The Goemans Gallery is going to close temporarily, because Goemans has gone off in despair, who knows where. And I'm afraid that Rott will give Yvonne the brush-off.

As you see, things are going fairly well. The whole world is agitating against us. And yet our position has never been more clear, firm, and lofty. The young people in the schools, in the army, in the factories are with us. Every day we see evidence of it.

Breton is exhausted, disheartened (Suzanne[5] is ill and nervous). Yesterday I managed to drag him to Luna Park. It was two years since he had gone out like that. We spent an hour on the bumper cars. He was elated, relaxed. Forgive my writing and my style: I only have a tiny little pencil. I was told about a spot where I could find some lovely chromos for you. I am, we are impatiently awaiting Dali's cards. Tell him and give him our heartfelt thanks. In *Documents,* there is a psychonalysis of *Jeu lugubre* and its author, with a tracing (!!) of the painting. Anyway, I'm sending it to you. Dali really must write a clear and energetic article.

I am tirelessly preparing for your arrival. Before you have your flows. I'll have a lot of things to show you and read to you. And some little gifts! Take advantage of the good weather. Here it's perpetual night. But come home as quickly as you like.

I'll go to see Touraine[6] some day soon, for sure. Char is arriving tomorrow morning "covered in cards."

I love you—and only you. Out of everyone, I trust only you. I kiss you all over with my eyes, my mouth, my hands, and my sex,

Paul

PAUL ELUARD

TO HEAR TO LISTEN TO UNDERSTAND[7]

> Prow-shadowed love
> Sea masked with kisses
> That the mouth meets anew
> Backlit glances
> Forsaken by the eyes

That's all for now.

71

[Nice, March 1930]

Friday

My beloved Gala, finally your address. I was incredibly anxious. I cried from anxiety, from misery. It turned my hair white. But this letter comforts me a little. How could you have been waiting to hear from me, not having given me your address[?] Never mind! The first thing is to cure that exudate.[1] You know how it turned out for me.[2] Be very careful.

I felt like coming to get you in Barcelona! Rest assured that I love you, that I want all that you want. I think of you ceaselessly, every minute. I wrote some poems, two of which are for you, which I'll send you.

I'm going to Avignon, Hôtel Regina. All three of us[3] are leaving tomorrow morning to join Breton, who has been most unexpectedly betrayed by Suzanne.

I want to mail this letter at once and wire you.

I'm fairly well. Char is very sweet. Write to him at the same address. He's very fond of you.

Friendliest greetings to Dali. I adore you. *Always* be serene.

Paul

Buy some color glossy cards of the exhibition.

72

Letterhead: Hôtel Regina
Avignon [April 1930]

Wednesday

I'm writing you one more note in Barcelona in the hope that you're not yet in Málaga, because I'm very worried about that quasi-tropical climate for you—and also about the well-known lack of amenities—and about the inadequate food they have there.

Don't be shocked or angered by my telegraphic suggestion of this morning to go to the Riviera, to Switzerland, or to the Black Forest, but I think that otherwise you risk aggravating your condition, or at least prolonging it a good while. Anywhere you go, I am happy to go with you, if you like. But Málaga is so far away and so isolated.

Anyway, if you insist on going to Málaga, I'll come see you soon, as soon as I have some money—and I will have!!—because I need to see you, because I love you terribly, truly. I dream about you all night—and all day, about your eyes, your body, your mind, your sex. I have always loved you, passionately, and always will. Think carefully about this cure you must take. I am very anxious. Out of love for me, think.

I kiss you and make love to you.

Paul

N.B. I have submitted my resignation to the Company, and I think it'll be fairly easy to sell my stock.

Keller has two clients at the house.[1] I'm waiting for news.

Dali's drawing for Breton's book won't work. Why such an obscene drawing?[2] It doesn't make any sense, really. Tell him. Breton feels very awkward. He doesn't dare ask him for another.

Don't hesitate to wire me or write me a little note every day.

I'm doing well, but going gray.

PAUL ELUARD

73

[Avignon, around 10 April, 1930]

> Friday morning

My beautiful Gala,

I have received your telegram, which makes me happy. It's very good for me for you to write quite often, to give me an idea of your love. If you could only recover completely!!!

I'm returning to Paris on Tuesday with Char, Breton, and the woman from the Moulin Rouge who's with him.

I don't know if the Apple will stay, because she's beginning to wear on me a bit. I'd like to be alone (with the thought of you, of being faithful to your eyes, to your body). I'm compelled to return because of money, for I have a lot of things to take care of. I'll try to sell some things, the 15th is rent day—the carpenter, etc. . . . 1 May is Pierre.[1] Anyway you can be sure that if all runs smoothly at this end, I'll come to see you in Málaga. In any case, I'll do all I can to send you a little money.

Breton, Char, and I did a fairly long book of thirty very beautiful poems, of which Char's printer is going to run off 200 copies free of charge.[2] We'll have the proofs Monday. It'll bring us each Fr 1,500 (Fr 1,500 for you!!!). I'm sending you Aragon's book on collage— quite extraordinary.[3] Read it well—it's worth the trouble.

I don't understand the sense of Dali's drawing for a book by or about Breton. Make him understand *very nicely* that it's unusable. Erotic is one thing! But the onanism is too poorly interpreted.[4] To be fair, this happens very often, for that matter.

Char will send you his magnificent book of photos on Monday or Tuesday.[5] I love you as ever, desperately, fervently. You are everything to me, everything, everything. I kiss you awfully all over.

> Paul

For your entertainment I'm sending you the sequel to Vasco's idiocies.[6]

74

Letterhead: Regina Hôtel
Avignon [April 1930]

My little loved one,

write to me in Paris, where I'm returning soon.
I'll wire you to find out whether you got back safely. I'm a bit concerned.
I love you as you know I do.

Ys. frvr.
Paul

Best to Dali.

75

[Paris, April 1930]

My beautiful Gala, my marvelous treasure of flesh and spirit, I'm leading quite a sad life without you. My only delights are in endlessly perusing your naked photos, where your breasts are soft enough to eat, where your belly rises and falls and I lick and devour it, your sex is open wide over my entire face, then my sex plunges in to the hilt and I grab the cheeks of your ass which move marvelously, like the springtime. You have the most beautiful eyes in the world, I love you, you take my sex in your hand, your legs are spread, your body gently arches, you jerk me off furiously, I crush your breasts, your hair, and suddenly your hand is covered in sperm and you're strong and sure of my power over you, of your power over me, of Everything. You are still the troubled child of Clavadel. I'm going to struggle to find some money, to send you some and to come see you, to bring you gifts. For the moment I'm going through a very dry patch, but I'll use all my resources to get through it. You'll see. The Apple left for Berlin a few days ago. I haven't seen my mother yet, but I'll tell her you were sick and that you were advised to rest and that you've been in Málaga the past few days, invited by some acquaintances of ours. You can write, with that in mind. And be sure that I want you to be happy, at all costs, I want you to feel as if you were beaming, and taking joy in everything. I adore you. I kiss you all over,

                                    Paul

I'm sending you *Variétés* and a book by Freud.

76

[Paris, April 1930]

> A porcelain song claps its hands[1]
> Then begs and dies in pieces
> You will recall it poor and bare
> Morning of wolves and their bite is a tunnel
> That you leave all clad in blood
> To blush for the night
> How many living to be found
> How many lights to be put out
> I will call you Visual
> And multiply your image.

                                    Saturday midnight

My one and only, I'm grateful to you for writing me often. But I'm writing you in Málaga. I'm afraid that my letters will be lost. They're addressed to Dali. We should have arranged for you to wire me the date of your departure. I am reassured by the details you send me. But will I get to Málaga? For that I'd have to settle Fr 40,000 of debts. And even if I sold the house it wouldn't go fast. And the worst is that I'd probably need your signature. Maybe the power you vested in me will be enough. Anyway, we'll see. At the moment I have hardly any money left, Fr 1,200 to be precise. I am desperately clinging to the idea of seeing you again. As I see it, you're planning a long stay in Spain. It's already been a month since I've been without you. This sickness is overwhelming me. What good is our apartment, with so many worries! What madness on our part! Don't be upset by such talk. But at times, and only at times, everything gets away from me, everything is lost in the precious time in which I might have had you.

If your love for me has grown weak, you should tell me. Under any circumstances, I want and would do anything for you to be happy. My darling child, don't read anything in all of this but my love for you. In any case I'll have the strength to guarantee our lives. Things are coming along but lazily, slowly.

Thanks for the sumptuous cards, a bit embarrassing for the album!!!!!

I kiss you awfully all over.

Ys. frvr.
Paul

77

[Paris, April? 1930]

My beautiful little Gala,

I'd prefer you to come home after your flows have ended—but as soon as possible anyway. I am torn between the desire to see you, to hear you, to read to you, to show you things, and the feeling that the only way I can really say hello to you is by making love to you. And I think it would be best not to weaken that feeling. I adore you. My life here is very monotonous and very calm. I spend the night here with Char (very sweet). Breton comes fairly often, because he's very disheartened. After some scenes, Suzanne went to live with Yvonne two days ago. I think she'll go back to rue Fontaine soon, but even so things aren't so good over there.

I wrote you a long letter a week ago, then sent you that package. Then I wanted to write to you again—and here we are. I think of you constantly, look at your photos. I've been very faithful to you.

But I miss you terribly.

This afternoon and tomorrow is the Tual sale. I won't buy much, nor spend a lot. We have three months to pay.

For your return I'll prepare you a little batch of presents.

I'm receiving a lot of clippings at the moment. I'm working just a little bit on two poems.

I'm making endless preparations for your return. I want to be very precious and very pure when you see me again.

I'm very glad that you like the white and black suit. Those three pieces are pretty voluptuous. I imagine you dressed in the blouse and the dress, but with nothing on underneath. Or else in the skirt and sweater. Your nakedness at the ready beneath this shameless apparel. And my sex stiff and hard, seeking yours or your hands.

I love you, my soft and hard, voluptuous and very intelligent and most daring queen.

I kiss you awfully.

Paul

Best to Dali.

Aragon and I are preparing a homage to Breton, to be published by Kra. Ask Dali to contribute something, on a specific subject, such as Breton's theory of art appreciation, for example.

78

[Paris, April 1930]

My little one, my most intimately beloved, forever to me, I hope you are well over there, that it's warm. Here it's cold and sad. I can hardly hope to come see you, because money . . . yes, there's a lack of it. And my struggles to find any are in vain. *The minute* I have any I'll send you some, but in truth I couldn't be living any worse, hand to mouth, crisis to crisis. But if you are really in need, wire, I'll sell anything at any price. But unless it's absolutely necessary, I'd prefer no one to know that I'm so broke. I've just paid 7,000 in rent (heating, etc.).

Everything's gloomy. Desnos and the others continue to go all out against Breton, against me and against Char.[1] We don't respond. It's impossible, too low. But it'll end in a brawl. Breton's at the end of his rope. Since Suzanne left, he's been going with a dancer from the Moulin Rouge, who left him yesterday. They're all pricks and bastards, all of them.

My mother was very sick two days ago: hepatic colic. Write to her. Cécile is tall, thin, and melancholy.

I wrote to Noailles about the Picasso. I'm going to the Company about the sale of stock. Did I tell you that I quit?

Etc. . . . etc. . . .

But all of this is *nothing*, since I still have my love for you, complete, devouring. I allow myself long moments at night with you, I go to sleep with you alone. I don't want you to have any worries, you shan't have any, *ever*.

Mayakovski committed suicide—sorrows of love.[2] It complicates the lives of Ella[3] and Aragon.

After the holidays I'll send you some books. Char's, ours, which will have come out, I hope you'll like them very much. It's only done for you. Char's book is dedicated to Gala and Paul Eluard.

Thank Dali for his wonderful drawings—everyone thinks they're magnificent.

I adore you.

I kiss you all over, I penetrate you.

Ys. frvr.
Paul

PAUL ELUARD

79

[Paris] 27 [April 1930]

Sunday

My Gala, because I couldn't live if you weren't mine. I think *endlessly* of you, but I miss you so much that if I had any money I'd go live in a hotel. You don't know, you can hardly imagine the atmosphere of this apartment which I really wanted for you and that you lived in so little[1] and the winter. And the neighborhood, the street corner we used to pass together, everything I had dreamed about: where to take you, your dresses, your entertainment, your sleep, your dreams, all the awkward things I've done, everything I wanted to redeem.

Everything is sinister, everything is dismal. The idea of death is becoming more and more confused for me with the idea of love. I believe I have lost you. Why are you so far away? I've been loving you for seventeen years and I'm still seventeen years old.[2] I have yet to do anything and I can no more see the future than when I was seventeen. The idea of evil was born today with my love for you, without redemption. I know no more than I ever did how to figure out how to keep you, to have you, how to make you love me wholly. Why are you so far away? I was horribly upset not to receive the telegram I asked from you for five days. And when I received the telegram last night, it stunned me silly, brought me nothing. It left me all my misery, all my idiotic torment.

If you knew how I want to see you, how I want to have you with me as I did last year in Cannes. I know very well that I can't keep you, that the abomination of a shared life is beyond our reach, but I feel as if I haven't had you for years. And I've lost my taste for life, for walks, for sunshine, for women. I've only retained the bitter and terrible taste of love.

But don't be unhappy. I had to tell you all this, don't you see? I've already written you two pessimistic letters, without sending them. But I can't be silent any longer, or I am irretrievably lost.

Cécile has scoliosis (curvature of the spine). It's not serious so long as it's carefully tended to. The other day I went to the movies with her, and I was struck by her melancholy, her listlessness. So I insisted that she see a doctor at once. I'm obviously going to have to sell the house at any price, or else mortgage it. Because she's got to go to Switzerland to lie on her back for a few months. I was hoping to sell Pierre's[3] Picasso to Noailles, but I'll no longer have anything to do with that person. The Goemans Gallery is closed. Keller, Ratton, etc. . . . nothing doing. The pieces and paintings are unsellable, even at a discount.

And the worst is that I can't come to see you. It costs too much. I paid the carpenter. Pierre wants to be paid his Fr 23,000, but he won't get a penny out of me. He'll take it in kind or I'll give him back the Picasso. I'm selling books. For the moment it's the most profitable. Our books especially. For instance, your copy of *Au défaut du silence* is worth a lot.[4] Breton's been offered Fr 10,000 for his copy on rice paper no. 1, bound by Legrain along with documents, the *Champs magnétiques,* etc. . . . I can sell my collection of *Littérature* for 5 or 6,000.[5] *Please understand me,* my beautiful little girl, my darling child whose eyes and sex are forever new, in all these money problems the only thing that kills me is *not being able to go to Málaga.* To be stopped by that, when my love is tormenting me so. And we have so much: company, house, objects, paintings, etc. . . .

If I could hold you in my arms, I would become once again the man I was for you at certain moments. I adore you, there is only you for all eternity. Mayakovski killed himself out of sorrow in love, for a woman who married a Polish diplomat. But in the letter which he left, he says not a word about that woman, but to his wife, Ella's sister, he says, "Lili, love me." I cried when I read that. You know it.

Crevel, our poor friend, is in Paris, more tragic than ever. His side is hideously shrunken.[6] Write to him here, rue Becquerel. I'm not sure of his address. Yvonne Georges[7] is dead. Cohen, the architect who was in charge of my house, is dead. Noll's been chucked out. We won't be seeing him anymore, I believe. The woman who was living with Breton left under the pretext that she is a woman and not a child.

Ella is worse than ever, disheartened by Mayakovski's suicide. She gave her tuxedo to Char, who is exactly the same size. Did you receive Char's books[?] If you did, thank him, and say you got them very late. He's still living with me, very sweet but terribly gloomy. I keep going to the movies, alone, because of the darkness. I hope to send you *Ralentir travaux* any day now. It's a very good book, but quite sad. My beautiful little Gala, my darling, maya dorogaya, my little one, my love, I am dying without you.

Paul

80

[Paris] 5 May [1930]

Monday

Gala my friend, finally, here's your answer to my long, sincere letter of eight days ago. I spent the day yesterday with Cécile and my mother. It seems to be understood that I'm taking her to Switzerland, to Montana, that my mother will pay for that, too. Cécile looks healthier. She has to see a specialist tomorrow. A four- or five-month stay in Switzerland will certainly do her a lot of good and she'll come back stronger than before she was diagnosed as ill. Don't worry about that. In children, these things can disappear without a trace if caught in time, but it's absolutely necessary to interrupt her studies. I still have Fr 300 and this time it's the bottom of the barrel. Nothing to hope for from anywhere. I gave Pierre back his Picasso, he's returning me my pieces. I couldn't pay. And I've received a tax summons on the rue Becquerel as well: Fr 960. What to do?

It's going to be impossible for me to retain this apartment for you. And you don't say a word to me about that. Why not tell me exactly what you think. Take up my long letter again, the one from eight days ago, to answer me comprehensively. The larger part of my letter spoke of our common situation. You answer it only with absolutely vague and conventional pronouncements: "Rest absolutely assured," "yours absolutely," etc. . .

Allow me to question the seriousness of your illness and the reason that prevents you from returning here. I do believe you would rather live anywhere than with me. Please understand me, my little girl, I don't reproach you for it and above all I wish you to live your own life, to be happy. But why kid one another? Eight days ago I took the step of telling you the whole truth, convinced that for me it was the best way to get out of it without too much damage. I must admit that I don't believe in your violent desire to see me. It's all very well to tell me that you don't want to spend more than a fortnight in Switzerland. But what is wrong is not to say frankly that, furthermore, you don't want to spend a fortnight in this damned apartment, or in Cannes or anywhere else, with me. And personally, I think that that would be totally out of the question. Your answer today to my long, pessimistic letter is really inadequate. Consider that I have some right to speak to you like this, for, other than the worst kind of practical problems, I am enduring that of a home which I wouldn't have were I as free as you, that of a home which I populate with you and which makes me dream endlessly of dying, of escaping, and which I don't escape so as to spare you all the worries that I am burdened with. Think too, that you have already admitted *truly loving* others than me. Know that I have no delusions. And, in all respect and fairness, speak to me frankly, bravely.

How much time have you spent here since October? And you try to console me by saying you'll drop by occasionally this year. My Gala, please consider that, under those conditions, it would be much less hard on me to take a simple hotel room and to have no more than a few books indispensable to me (and even then!). I'd give you everything else. I'd work. In any case, I'd live a little. Think that our roles could be reversed. And when I saw you, we would love one another no more nor less than now. Otherwise, it will end badly, very badly, in mediocrity, amidst all the nastiness of practical life. Is that what you want? Think that eight more days will pass before I get an answer to this letter, eight unendurable days. Everything could still work out if you are truly willing to understand our situation and to know what you want. And don't slip into being kind—which would certainly have unpleasant consequences.

Yours, only yours.
Paul

Don't hesitate to wire, if need be.

I've already written you that Noailles can do nothing more for me. Nor can anyone else. I've done all I can to fail most ridiculously. And my mother no longer owes me anything.

81

[Paris, 6 May, 1930]

Tuesday, 6 P.M.

If only you understood how I love you, how sick it makes me to give you pain. Why isn't it mutual[?] A new letter from you. I'll speak to you about it, I'll answer it when I see you, face to face.

My little one, I miss you. After last night's letter, to have some peace I took two luminals and slept until 5 o'clock in the afternoon. Everything is so painful to me: a gramophone tune, your dresses in the closet, a declaration of love in a book or at the movies, everything here, all you whom I adore.

Be serene and strong. Since you are loved. You do not have my torment. You must be faithful. All is pure within me, because of you.

As for Cécile, and it's *not at all* serious if she's gaining strength (believe me it's *true*), everything's arranged for Switzerland and you won't need to go there, since I'm going *with my mother*. If only you knew, but you do know how I've wanted you to be happy.

Char received Fr 5,000. Now we're safe from all those dirty little necessities.

As for me, I think I'll manage. Don't come back especially for me. Take care of yourself. But even so, answer my letter of yesterday carefully and frankly. My darling, my whole life, my whole life.

All of me.

Paul

And I may manage to sell some Company stock. I'll take care of it.

82

Envelope: M. Salvador Dali, in Cadaqués, Spain (Gerona)
Postmark: Paris VIIIe, 5 July 1930
Sender: M. Eluard Grindel, Hôtel de la Poste, Cernay-la-Ville (Seine-et-Oise) France
Arrival Stamp: Cadaqués, 7 July 1930

Saturday noon

My dear little Gala, you see, I am in a lovely cafe.[1] I've just come from the Bank where I deposited Fr 33,000 in cheques which Lagrange remitted me this morning for my remaining stock. Next Tuesday, he'll remit Fr 68,000 from the current accounts. And my mother owes me another Fr 10,800. There's our fortune. From that, I'll have to pay about Fr 6,000 in rent, Fr 4,000 to Ascher[2] and Fr 1,000 to Mantelet, for the dressing table. There's also about Fr 1,500 owed to the carpenter and Fr 1,000 to Dali. Consequently, we'll have Fr 98,000 between us.

I was very much hoping to find a telegram or a little note from you at rue Becquerel, which Odette has not yet left, I don't know why. You shouldn't leave me without word. I think of you constantly.

Here is Cécile's address. Write to her. She's very happy and is taking pictures.

Mlle. Cécile Grindel, Ker Envel
Avenue de la Concorde, in La Baule (Loire-Inférieure)

Cernay-la-Ville is a magnificent spot, but a little far from Paris. I had to leave this morning at 6:30 to be in Paris by 8:30.

I've written to Rott explaining that I don't owe him anything more.

I'd really like to go to the Solomon Islands or to New Guinea. Tell me what you think. I must say that I'm still dragging around a great, sad dream, to which my current life is poorly adapted.

I hope you'll receive this letter sent to Dali. Did you see Buñuel's talking film? Tell me. Everyone's seen it but me, and Buñuel's left

for three months.[3] The review's coming out Monday. For issue no. 1, there will be only a few luminescent copies.[4] Write to Crevel, whose address is:
La Moubra—Montana (Valais) Switzerland.
My deepest, deepest love.

Paul

Eluard-Grindel, Hôtel de la Poste
Cernay-la-Ville, Seine-et-Oise

83

Letterhead: Au Rendez-vous des Artistes, Hôtel de la Poste, Cernay-la-Ville

Saturday [12? July 1930]

My dear little Gala, I'm happy to get your letters and to learn that you're already settled in and resting. It's been really cold here for two days. And I've a good mind to pop over your way.

I was in Paris on Tuesday and Thursday and I'm really fed up with it. On Tuesday I finished settling the stocks. My mother owes me 30,000 instead of the 10,000 I figured by mistake.

Thursday, I sold the black skull box (just the box) to a friend of Keller's: Fr 4,000. That's not bad. The skull is worth twelve and maybe fifteen. And I've made three deluxe subscriptions: Keller, Colle[1] and that friend. That brings us up to ten. We'll try to make five more. I hope Dali received the review, which I sent in a sealed envelope: two copies.

Tell me if you want me to send you some money. In any case I'll be sending Dali his Fr 1,000.

Tell me what you think of the review. I especially recommend Valentin's article, "On ne vous le fait pas dire." It's magnificent. Read it all well.

I await, or rather we are all impatiently awaiting Dali's article. In issue no. 2 there will be a regular column by Maurice Heine:

"Chronique de Sade," an article by Duchamp on chess, a long article by Valentin, an article by Frois-Wittmann, the psychoanalyst, and some wonderful poems by Péret on Foch and Clemenceau.[2]

Char is still at Isle-sur-Sorgue. But he'll be coming back here soon. You could write to him anyway.

New Guinea? I'd love to. I'm thinking about it, but what difficulties.

I'm thinking of you. Please explain how I might possibly come to see you with Nush[3] for a few days. Perhaps I could stay not far from Cadaqués. Anyhow, if you don't think it's quite feasible, tell me.

My deepest love.

Yours.
Paul

My very best to Dali.

84

Letterhead: Hôtel Robinson, Agay, Var
[around 15? July 1930]

My dear little Gala

I was taken up by my changes of address—three in eight days. It's a very beautiful spot here, with a beach at the hotel. The weather is lovely, but there's some wind. It was the dog days in Paris.

Valentin's here with René Char.[1] I'm waiting for Char. We won't stay long, because it costs Fr 70 a day. It's too much. I'll go I don't know where. Everywhere I drag with me my anxiety and my ignorance of everything. As soon as it seems right, I'll go to Sitges[2] with Nush and probably Char. Don't write to me here, but at rue Becquerel. Before leaving Paris, I was working on business right up to the last minute, I don't think there are any problems left. Odette has gone.

I'm happy that you like the review. Speaking of which, the emblem on the cover represents the conjunction of Saturn and Uranus.[3]

PAUL ELUARD

My concept of you, of our love, is becoming more and more mystical and despairing. I love you to the deepest and the highest points within you. There is a possession which none can undo.

The old wolf who, after having loved and fought you, the old wolf will live and die for you. The old, useless and awkward fool. You are reborn with your loss. But the old fool doesn't see that there's anything to lose. Except that which is bad. My darling, Gala, Gala, Gala, the beautiful and *forever* beloved, and borne aloft.

Au revoir. I kiss you all over.

Paul

Yes, I'll do what I can to get Dali's painting. Send him my best.

85

Letterhead: Hôtel Méditerranée, Cannes
Friday, 1 August [1930]

My Gala, I received your telegram with your instructions about Dali's second painting. Understood, I'll do as you wish. I'll write to Keller.

Char arrived the day before yesterday. I'll come to see you with him. I'm distressed by the delay in my trip. Other than that, I look wonderful and wait 'til you see how I'm dressed! I dream of you every night. Tell me whether for you, as for me, nothing can replace our love. I'm often very afraid. I love you passionately, terribly.

I have the room here which we had last year. I'm not like you, I am sensitive to our memories. I see you naked in this room and I cry over those three weeks spent so happily here with you.

Tomorrow I'll send you some journals as well as the *Revue de Psychanalyse* in which there are two very good articles, one on Napoleon and one on surrealism. I've been paddling, I'm learning to swim. I'm also getting back to work. Doesn't Dali have any ideas for issue no. 2[?] It needs something sensational, other than the usual articles. Write me well and fully.

LETTERS TO GALA

I kiss you as you know, very deeply, all over. You are my friend and my love.

> Yours forever.
> Paul

86

Letterhead: Hotel Méditerranée, Cannes
[3? August 1930]

> Sunday

Time goes by monotonously, curing oneself, taking short walks and sleeping a lot. I'm sending you a fat package of journals: the *Revue de Psychanalyse* in which you should read Frois-Wittmann's article and the one on Napoleon; the *Nouvelle Revue Française* which contains a text by Rigaut and a text by that little prick Victor Crastre on Rigaut's suicide—all these publications, and the choice of Victor Crastre to humiliate us.[1] This issue of *N.R.F.* is a veritable challenge.

For issue no. 2 of *Surréalisme a.s.d.l.r.,* if Dali would like, aside from his article, to draw up some little notes on various subjects, they would be most welcome. I'm sending you some stories by Duvernois, whom I like a lot and who is beginning to be recognized as the great writer that he is (by Gide, for instance). They were recommended by Char. At the moment I'm reading *Les Soeurs Hortensia,* a wonder.[2]

I saw *The Cameraman,* with Buster Keaton, here. I hope you'll get to see it one day.

Also saw Mack Sennet [*sic*]: *Alice aux Galeries,*[3] which is an astonishing comedy, surrealist through and through.

I dream of recovering, and of going to see you.

Understood for the Dali painting. I'll write to Keller.

I'm going to see Picabia[4] tomorrow.

Please be nice: write to me as you've been doing, often and clearly. I adore you, you know! I live through you.

I kiss you all over.

Yours forever.
Paul

87

[Cannes] 7 August 1930

My darling little girl, we're leaving tomorrow for Marseilles, where we'll stay a few days. I'll go see a doctor. What I have isn't serious, it's just overexertion, it can be cured in a few days and, I hope, for my arrival in Cadaqués. Then we'll go to Barcelona, whence I'll write you and where you'll send me a letter and instructions on the closest spot to Cadaqués.

Could you wire me—Grindel, General Delivery, Marseilles—the name of the hotel where I stayed with Goemans last year. It was good and cheap. Do it at once.

Indeed, you must take good care of yourself, and, I believe, not go swimming. And I'm afraid that the Mediterranean air is no good for you.

Char and I will each bring you a *very* pretty gift, one that is very novel for you. Guess, the first is red, you put it on the ground and it whistles. And the other is soft, blue, white, and red, and you salute it.

My mother complains that you don't write her. But discretely. She's in Vichy, at the Hôtel Rivoli. I hope you received the journal issues and book.

All is well as to money. Don't worry.

And I love you as you can imagine, my beautiful, ancient and ever-youthful wife.

I love your descriptions of paintings!! It's pure Gala. I'm sending you a great little drawing.[1]

I kiss you all over.

Ys. frvr.
Paul

88

Envelope: Café de la Rambla
Sender: Grindel, Hôtel Royal, Furnished Rooms, 22 Calle Carmen, Barce(lona)
Addressee: Mme. Grindel, Cadaqués (Gerona)
Barcelona, [August 1930]

Saturday night

Gala darling, here are the photos. There's one other of you, a little blurry, which the photographer passed over but which I'll have printed.

This morning, we (I) bought you a pretty little phonograph, very powerful, and twelve lovely records which we'll bring you next week.

As for money, you can have some. I'll go to the Crédit Commercial on Monday and find out. In any case, I have some on me and I'll be able to give you some next week.

I retain an enchanted memory of yesterday. You are so beautiful, and the sea and the rocks suit you to a tee. Our best to Dali from the three of us.

As for you, I kiss you as you know.

Paul

89

[Paris, 26 August 1930]

My darling little Gala, a note in haste. I've had much to do. I went to four doctors before I could see one. They're all on vacation. He says it's not microbic, that it's a simple and very benign urethritis, that it's not contagious. It's already clearing up under care.

Other than that, I have one enormous dental abscess that's wearing me out.

For the supplement I wrote an article on Rigaut's suicide. And some notes.

Received the Dali. The notes are being translated by Berlitz. I'll get them in a while.

I'll be sending you the Fr 2,000.

Char is bringing an Andalusian woman back to France.

I'll write you more tomorrow. When are you coming back[?] 8 or 10 September would be good. I love you awfully.

Paul

90

[Paris] Wednesday, 27 August 1930]

My dear little girl, I telephoned my mother. Around 5 September she's going by car to La Baule for two days. She'll drive us there and we'll stay on a few days after her. Consequently, would you like to be back by then? I'll work everything out and will be at rue Becquerel for your return.

Other than that, I'm doing better. It's pretty hot here.

We're not doing the Supplement, but issue no. 2 straight off. Dali's notes are quite brilliant. Perhaps we could accompany them with a photo of a Dali painting, 4 pages of drawings on one page, or one large, handsome drawing, very complex and a little erotic but not too. But it's a rush, rush, rush. The issue is coming out 15 September. I'll give Moro[1] the article to translate. With Breton, I'm writing a long, five-part article on Man: conception, intrauterine life, birth, life, and death.[2] Not bad, but what work.

What heat! Write me or wire me that it's agreed, that you'll come on the 5th. And then write to Cécile that we'll be near her around the 8th.

I love you, you know. And wait 'til you see how I'm working. I kiss you all over.

Paul

Thank Dali for his very pretty drawings. Have him send us the photos of the painting by return mail.

91

[*At the end of the letter:*] Eluard Grindel, Hôtel Regina, Avignon (Vaucluse)

21 Oct[ober] 1930, Tuesday morning

Gala, last night I thought of you until 3 A.M. Then I went to sleep to dream of you.

I feel very alone, and yet I search endlessly for reasons to hope. Where is the time when all I sought were reasons to despair? Having Nusch by my side when we decided to divorce prevented me from grasping the kind of isolation I would have been subjected to.[1] For I don't think I'll ever be able to live with anyone, Nusch no more than another. I have loved you, Gala, for too long, I lived with you for too long, for too long, whatever you might think, I conformed entirely to your desires, your dreams, *your nature*.

I hope to be able to preserve for you the mirage of caresses, of desires, of optimism, of immortal love that you need—and to which, alas, you got me addicted as well. I laugh gently at the idea that I wanted to take with me (??) all that I love. That's a slip of the pen, my eternal Gala, my excuse for living; I meant to say: *leave with you* all that I love: and the Easter Island fetish and the black skull, and the *Départ du poète*,[2] and the Lautréamont manuscript. And the postcards too, if I didn't need some entertainment, some mechanical preoccupation (I can see you laughing!!). I'd come to see you, you, all that I love, surrounded by what I have loved only because you exist.

I don't know if I'll stay here. It's dismal, and no postcards.

Char came to see me yesterday afternoon.

I'd like to go to Marseilles for two days. In any case, you can write to me here, I'll be back. They'll keep my mail for me. Open any letters that might arrive at rue Becquerel, and let me know about anything that can't wait.

I adore you, I kiss you awfully all over.

Ys. frvr.
Paul

PAUL ELUARD

I wired Cécile that you would come to see her Thursday. Char just arrived. He sends you his greatest respects.

92

Telegram:
From: Marseilles, 25 October 1930
To: Mme. Grindel, 7, rue Becquerel, Paris 18e

Received your marvels. Wire me as soon as you receive mine. Kisses. Write no more. Be back soon.

Love.
Paul

93

Postcard
[Lausanne, January 1931]

Tuesday 6 o'clock

My beautiful little Galotchka of all time, I'm in Lausanne, on the shores of the lake "that bathed the weakness of my sixteenth year," at the moment when I was about to meet you, when I was about to see you appear. I am an old man. I'm not too well. I've been looking for cards. I found a few, but nothing exceptional.

Tomorrow morning I'm leaving for Montana (Valais), the Hôtel du Parc, where you must be sure to write me. Char shouldn't go via Basel if he wants to join me.

I saw Nusch at Mulhouse, very sweet. I don't think I shall ever find a better companion. You see, I'm so afraid of being alone. I am so weary, so poor.

The weather is very beautiful. Snow everywhere.

If you see the opportunity to sell something at any price, sell, because the quarterly rent is due on the 15th and I'm afraid of falling sick. I've broken my cough.

[unsigned]

94

[Montana, January 1931]

"If I had accepted that, I would be putting all this at the mercy of those pirates of high finance, all these provinces, these rivers, these shores, these hills where our flag waves, and for my own glory, so as to be blessed in the homes that would no longer have been crushed by the tax, for money, the money that would have been partially mine, for my own pleasure. Yes, for my own glory and pleasure! ... Are you asleep? ..."

"I'm not asleep, but move your hand, it gets on my nerves when you stroke me when I'm not aroused."

"I placed my hand on the breast of my country, and my country answered as you did. It gets on its nerves to be loved when it's not aroused..."

(Binet-Valmer: *Prosper Bourguillard, impuissant, Président du Conseil.*[1])

Char arrived this morning in a pretty bad state, but elated by the cold and the sunshine.

I completely agree with you for a response to that kind of intolerable provocation, like that last article on Barbusse that I read and which completely disheartened me. Who is Interim? Parain or who?[2] Be sure to send any news on *L'Age d'or*, if there is any.[3] And on everything. I hope to be back soon. I'm seeing a doctor tomorrow. I miss you.

                        Paul

I'm writing to Aragon.

PAUL ELUARD

95

Postcard: "*Crossing a crevasse*"
[Montana, January 1931]

A beautiful card which Char saw first. Very enjoyable. At 5 o'clock, the doctor. I'll write you straightaway.

> Yrs. frvr.
> Paul

Also to be examined upside down.[1] It's all there.

96

Letterhead: Montana s/Sierre, Grand Hôtel du Parc, Chalet Saint-Louis
[around 10 January 1931]

> Sunday night, 9 o'clock

I received, my best darling, your express letter of yesterday (though with only Fr 3-worth of stamps) only tonight. Listen, my little girl, anything you could do will be fine. I've just wired you to that effect. I hope you were able to sell something, for yourself as well.

I love you, you know. I'm coming back in any case on Friday or Saturday, and I'm *very* sad not to be seeing you before you leave. *Wait for me if you possibly can.* I'm living alone with Char in the little chalet marked X above and we (I) speak of you practically all the time. I've been telling him all about Clavadel, the war, Bray, etc. . . But hush . . . you don't like nostalgia. If you leave before my return, leave me a tuft of your hair with the keys. I adore you, you know, it will be sad for me to go to rue Becquerel if you're not there. I'd come back much earlier, but that's a bit of a shame. This stay is short enough as it is.

When I got your letter tonight, I really felt like crying at the thought that you're leaving Wednesday and I'm returning Friday or Saturday. Anyway, don't delay your leaving if you're very tired. Above all I want your health, your well-being. NEVER DOUBT THAT. I adore you.

I'm impatiently awaiting the lovely postcards. Be easy: I'll divide them up scrupulously, you know that. I have about 150 fairly unequal cards, but twenty or so that are very pretty, and old. Those which I sent you were very well chosen (the nicest) from among the newer ones. I hope you appreciated the cat, the balloons, the crevasse, etc. . . I'm in a hurry, I want this letter to go out. I adore you, my so youthful child. Everything you do will be fine, just fine. And take anything you want, you know you can. If you sell something, deposit it to my account at the Crédit Commercial, no. 722653 (Grindel). I hope it's still open. There must be Fr 50 in it. If that's not feasible, put it somewhere in the apartment.

Leave me the key to rue Fontaine, the keys to any dressers in rue Becquerel where I have some clothing, the key to the window. Don't put anything away, I'll do it.

But the best . . . the best . . . would be if I could see you, even for an hour before you leave. You know, I could come back Friday morning . . . anyway, let me know.

I adore you, I kiss your eyes, your hands, your breasts, your sex.

Yours forever.
Paul

Best to Dali. Char sends his best to you and Dali.

If you're interested, there's an article in the *Nouvelles littéraires* on *L'Immaculée Conception*.[1]

I paid 5,000 for the mask with mother of pearl. Sell it at the same price. Sell the green-eyed mask for at least 4,000. The totem on the dresser: Fr 5,000. The largest one: 7,500. A minimum price, I believe, otherwise it might be better to sell something else.

97

Postcard, humorous: "May you have good fortune."
[Paris, January 1931]

Wednesday

My dear child, my adored Gala,

I'm back in Paris where, I too, am missing you. I can't find the papers you were asking for on rue Becquerel, Odette had cleaned everything up and sent it off to you. I picked up some insurance money: Fr 3,300. But I have to pay a Fr 258 electricity bill for you. That way, I'll deposit Fr 1,500 for you in the bank. I'll keep the Fr 100 that remain from another sum. I'd rather not have to hold on to such little amounts, but I myself am very, very broke.

I'll give Portier[1] a call, because I think our pieces have been sold.

Here are three lovely cards. I've had news of you through Mme. Hugo,[2] and by the note you sent to Char. I love you awfully, forever.

Ys. frvr.
Paul

My very best to Dali.
Our blurb for *La Femme visible*[3] was published in *Cahiers d'Art*.

98

[Paris, 27 January 1931]

Tuesday, midnight

finally, a letter from you. There was nothing for 8 days. I was worried.

Very serious things are happening here. To start with Noailles is calling for the negative and the 3 copies of the film, to have them destroyed.¹ No question of it, of course. Too serious. We'll look after it, rest easy. Above all, do nothing. *Have faith.*

I had a fight with Apple. Gone. Good riddance!

Other things have happened that I can't explain to you by letter, too complicated.

My health is still shaky.

It seems to be worked out with Aragon. He gave in, persuaded of the risk he was running.²

Write to me often and date your letters.

Money matters are less and less promising. If you knew how I'd love to do you that favor. Anyway, I'll try, and I hope it can all be worked out within 48 hours. It has to be.

I have about a hundred postcards that I'll bring you soon, if the money comes through. Here are the nicest 3, in my opinion. Tell me what you think of them. But there are others that aren't bad.

I'm afraid you might have been incautious sending me cards. It's barely possible. Well, never mind!

I do hope I can get to Cadaqués. If I can dig up Fr 2 or 3,000, I'm leaving. Understood for the stove. I love you, I'm thinking of you. *La Femme visible* is getting dreadful publicity. But right-minded people find the book extraordinary.

Why didn't Dali put people's names in his dedication? This way, it won't be talked about, or else badly.

I love you, I'm thinking of you awfully.

Paul

99

[Paris, 29 January 1931]

My little Gala,

I'm depositing Fr 2,000 in the bank today, from my mother.

We were able to trade with Sadoul 200 of the most beautiful cards in his collection, but there was only one thing that tempted him, and that was a Dali painting. I promised it to him. Dali can do it, and Breton and I will each give him a gift of Fr 1,000. Forgive me, but without those 200 cards his collection ceases to exist. And furthermore, he's a very sweet and very unhappy boy. Other than the 3 months you know about,[1] he is tubercular and is going to Switzerland and has just found out that he's had syphilis for 6 months.

Did I do right? I did it especially for you, who didn't have any cards from Nancy.[2] If not, sorry. I'm sending you the nicest card in the collection, which Gala earned, and another that she wanted. There are many other very beautiful ones. Moreover, Breton and I found more. That makes about 300 cards I have for you, my beautiful Gala.

I'll bring them to you, for as soon as I have any money, it will be to come *see you* (my only desire).

Nothing to be done with Gaffé[3] as to the manuscript, not for anything. I'm a little concerned about the fate of the cards you sent me.

I love you. Only you. I kiss you all over.

Paul

100

[Paris] 2 February [1931], in the morning

My Gala, I really don't need to be scolded right now about not loving you and not paying you any attention.

I didn't write to you before I was sure that you were in Cadaqués. You left on the 16th. On the 21st I received a card from Barcelona that didn't say when you were leaving for Cadaqués. Then silence until the 26th. Your first letter. A registered letter was sent out to you (addressed to Dali) with three very beautiful cards, on the morning of the 27th. Another registered letter (also addressed to Dali) on the 29th, with two magnificent cards. I have the receipts. What do you want? You ought to stay in manageable countries. It's the same old thing every time. And wire. And, once again, date your letters.

I'm struggling like a condemned man to scrounge up a few pennies. I deposited Fr 2,000 at your bank. Today, I'll deposit another Fr 800 out of 1,000 received. I'm keeping Fr 200 to take steps toward finding some money, and to wire you later. If I haven't wired you it's because I hadn't the money to do so.

No, my little girl, my only, I adore you, believe it. You can always be sure of it. If you only knew how much I want to go to Cadaqués. And to find you some money, a lot. Nothing can be sold. I'd so like to bring you your cards, too. The ones you sent us are magnificent. But don't send any more. Keep them. Wait for my visit. I'll see about getting the marriage authorization. But you should have done it when you were in Paris. It would have been easier and more certain. How you complicate your own life! I'll always love you, be sure of that. I kiss you all over,

Paul

When you send me a registered letter, like the one I got this morning, only put Grindel. You know very well that "Paul Eluard" won't work. Here's another letter from you [sic],[1] turn the page.

Write often to Cécile—she's bored.

Finally, my one and only, my priceless one, you've received my first letter, and you'll be receiving the second. Thanks for the green and red cards, which are magnificent and exactly to my taste. But Breton needs some—how shall I split them?

The art nouveau piece that you're sorry about was not all that good, in the end. I went back to see it and didn't take it.

Char has left.

I don't have the clippings for *La Femme visible*. I'll tell you about them. But it's not that interesting. It'll have to wait a bit. I'm going out in a minute, but since you're comforted I won't wire you. I'm economizing my Fr 200, because without them I couldn't even go out to raise more. Last week I went about on foot and didn't smoke. I'll probably have some cards and photos soon, all very indecent and filthy and about thirty to thirty-five years old. They're from an uncle of Lucienne's husband.[2] But what state will they be in? He papered the walls of his room with them.

I went to Montlignon yesterday, saw our very sweet Cécile and gave her a lovely book. Saw Mireille, Lucienne's daughter (eighteen years old), who, along with some other young people from Lyon, is really a great admirer of Breton and me. My very best and my thanks to Dali.

This card I'm sending you is taken from my own collection, as a gift to you.

AH! IF ONLY I COULD GO TO CADAQUÉS.

101

[Paris, February 1931]

Tuesday

My beautiful beloved,

here's the marriage authorization. I hope it's right.

I'm out of luck at the moment. They came to cut off the electricity at my place this morning, supposedly because of I don't know what missing permit that I'll have to try to get.

Money is awfully short. I saw Ratton yesterday, and he's offered to hold a sale of my pieces and Breton's early in May. On request, he'd advance me Fr 10,000. At least I hope so. It's a risk that must be taken. Bellier will be his auctioneer. The colonial exhibition will be on at that time and he thinks that'll help.

What should I do?

The situation's getting worse and worse. Nothing's working.

In any case, a sale wouldn't go too well at the moment. But we must consider that for the few salable pieces that we have, there's a far greater number that we can't sell so readily. And will the price of artwork recover? It's just as much of a risk not to sell now.

Anyhow, tell me what to do. I'll listen to you.

I'm demoralized. I would so have liked to come see you in Cadaqués. And yet, I'm spending nothing. I ride the bus. I'm spending Fr 30 a day on living expenses.

But the few debts remaining to me are crippling. And nobody wants anything, even for free.

My darling, in any case don't let it get you down, I'm struggling to raise myself from the dust and I think I can manage it.

We'll have to resign ourselves to a loss, but we have to get out of it.

I still haven't deposited the aforementioned Fr 800 at your bank. I hope to do it tomorrow.

In all I've deposited 2,000 there.

I adore you. You are my only light, my only goal in life.

Ys. frvr.
Paul

102

[Paris, February 1931]

Wednesday

My beloved little child,

I'm writing you in haste. I'll write you again tomorrow, for tonight I'm seeing Gaffé to sell him the Picasso. Elsewhere, I came into Fr 10,000 on account (I'll deposit 5,000 at the bank for you tomorrow, perhaps 8,500 if the Picasso is sold) for the sale of our pieces taking place in June along with Breton's pieces. Ratton, Keller, and Carré as appraisers—Bellier as auctioneer. We'll get Fr 5,000 on 15 April (2,500 for you). I've been working for two days, transporting the pieces.

I'll know tomorrow whether I can come see you. I'm worried that I'll only be given a passport for Switzerland.[1] I'll wire you.

I'm very concerned over your fate. Why shouldn't you come back?

I'll write again tomorrow.

Valentine Hugo, who would be driving me, has passports for herself and the car.

Have confidence in me. I love only you.

I *must* know the exact date of your return to France. As soon as possible.

I kiss you all over,

Paul

PAUL ELUARD

103

[Paris, February 1931]

>Friday

A quick note and a card. I've just deposited the whole Fr 1,000 in your account.

I am still without electric light. And it's snowing. Cadaqués. Gala. Gala. My beloved. Money and I are somewhat back in touch with each other again.

And I wrote a poem that I'll send you tomorrow. And I adore you. And you keep me alive and not alive for all eternity.

>Paul

Things are working out with Aragon. Send him and Ella a card, 5, rue Campagne-Première, Paris (14e). He's old and in utter despair.

104

Letterhead: Grand Café de la Bourse, Place de la Bourse
[Paris, February 1931]

>Saturday

My Gala, my only, it's getting no better. Yesterday, too discouraged, I "played hookey." I spent the night at rue Becquerel. I met your ghost there, the ghost of our life, of our whole, difficult life, so full of tears and caresses, so full of you. You should have a red cloak, black stockings, red gloves, a red mask, your hair streaming, your head thrown back, naked beneath your cloak and I dead to all else, to all that is not you, my true life, the love I have for your sweet and simple eyes, for your kind and lovely hands, for your breasts that are even more sweetly disturbing than your pubic hairs, than your sex that I adore.

My beautiful head, my tiny little head, little skull in the palm of my hand, Gala, my divine Gala, my whole life, my death, never will I return to rue Fontaine, the day resembles you too much and the night has too much of your scent, I love you, I love you, my child, myself, Gala.

[unsigned]

105

[Paris, February 1931]

Wednesday

My little Gala, all the meadows, all the grass, I've returned to rue Fontaine but I haven't left you. I'll never leave you again. There is no longer any other woman but you.

Thank Dali for his calligraphy.[1]

Think of me.

Don't write to me in little envelopes. They're delivered late.

The Portier sale made Fr 4,000. I hope to deposit your 2,000 early next week. It's certain, even.

I'm sending you a poem truly written for you. You'll know it from my last letter.

I adore you. I kiss you all over.

Ys. frvr.
Paul

Woman with whom I have lived[2]
Woman with whom I live
Woman with whom I will live
Forever the same
You should have a scarlet cloak
Scarlet gloves a scarlet mask

PAUL ELUARD

And black hose
Reasons and proofs
To see you quite nude
Nude purity oh precious frills

Breasts oh my heart.

106

[Paris, February 1931]

Thank you, my beloved child, for the two cards, especially the one of the woman, which I love. Your letters give me enormous pleasure. I had just been dreaming that night that Nusch didn't want to go to Tahiti, where we were all going, when I received the letter in which you suggest that we all go there.

Since it's so hot, why don't you send me some photos of yourself, naked. I have much need of them. I'm eager to see you, for I have not aged. I am as young as springtime before your beauty, before your naked spirit. I'd like to see that galligraphy.[1] I deposited Fr 2,000 into Dali's account: profit from the Portier sale. Bellier won't sell the drawings. He wants us to take them back.

Write to Char, at the Hôtel des Trois Moulins. He's very depressed.

I want you to write me without clothes on, and your letters to be rubbed all over your body.

I can do anything you might ask of me. With animal delight.

Brotherly greetings to Dali.

[unsigned]

107

[Paris, February 1931]

Monday

I spent two nights at my mother's. Last night there was a broad strip of moonlight in the room and I saw you, really saw you, completely naked and your legs spread and possessed by two men, in the mouth and in the sex. And you were tan and very beautiful. And even now, at the memory of it, I can't help thinking that you are the embodiment of love to me, the most acute embodiment of desire and erotic pleasure. You are my whole imagination. And this afternoon while I am alone, I imagine that you can give of yourself, your body's daring in the service of your mind's delirium. And very gently I jerk myself off.

Why haven't you printed those nude photos of yourself[?] And I'd like some in which you're making love. And I'd make love with you in front of Nusch, who could only play with herself—and anything else you'd want.

You are a marvelous wellspring of imagination and freedom. And I adore you.

I think I'll leave for the south at the end of the week. I have to, because I've been having asthma attacks at night—for as long as two hours. I saw Philippon in Montlignon, and he gave me some medicine.

I'VE QUIT SMOKING. It's pretty rough.

I have my passport for Switzerland and England. That's better.

All my regards to Dali. Write me at length. I endlessly stroke your sex with mine.

Paul

108

Postmark: Lunel, Hérault, 27 February 1931
Addressee: Mme. Grindel, Port-Lligat, Cadaqués, Spain, (Gerona)

I forgot to ask you to confirm by wire whether or not you'll be having your flows next Wednesday.

If you don't, that's wonderful, if you do, never mind, but you know that I love you and that I'll take great joy in seeing you anyway. It might also be just a question of a day or two. Anyhow, wire me. It's not important, but I prefer to know ahead of time instead of wondering.

[unsigned]

109

[Lunel], 28 February 1931

My beloved Gala,

I've got yesterday's letter from you. We'll do as you wish. I'm wild at the thought of you. It would be great to go see Crevel, and Char as well. Finally, Avignon for the two of us, for your beautiful eyes.

This afternoon, I'll know whether or not "my country" is holding me captive within its borders.

I'm thinking only of you. I've been filing your cards. They're not too bad.

I adore your sex, your eyes, your breasts, your hands, your feet, your mouth

and your thought, all of my Gala.

Freedom makes me faithful.

Paul

Will Dali be coming? Give him my best. I'd like it, but the car only has room for three, alas! Well, we'll see.

110

Letterhead: Mas de Fourques, Lunel (Hérault)
[early March 1931]

Friday

Do you believe that the reality of feelings is opposite to that of dreams? In that case, you love me awfully. I think only of you, I can't do anything else, I'm delirious at the thought of you.

We won't be seeing one another before Wednesday, I'll have the answer on my passport tomorrow. I am humiliated and sad to be henceforth a prisoner in France. What a dirty trick! Otherwise, you'll come. I'll pay your passage to Perpignan, for instance. "Your passage" is badly put, since Valentine will come to fetch you, but your stay. I dream of it—awfully.

I've done three poems, and I'll do more by then, for your pleasure. I love you, I'll always do whatever you wish. I lay at your feet, in adoration. I'll do whatever you like with your sex, your breasts, your eyes, your hands. You are the perceptible and the sensual universe, where all beauty shines forth, where the world, the whole world becomes a charm, and through which all the world's charms are funneled. I adore you, my only sunshine. You are mine forever.
GALA.

[unsigned]

111

Postmark: Douarnenez, Finistère, 17 July 1931
From: Eluard Grindel, Hôtel Saint-Ronan, Locronan (Finistère)
Addressee: Mme. Grindel, 7, rue Becquerel, Paris, 18e

Monday

My darling little girl,

Received your second letter this morning. *You must write me often.* We'll leave[1] here tomorrow for sure, for the Île de Sein if the weather isn't bad. For somewhere else if the rain keeps up. I'm glad that Dali took my paintings to be framed. Thank him very much for me. And tell him to ask the framer to deliver the paintings to rue Becquerel, to the concierge, with whom he should leave the money to pay for them. Because that way, as I'll be in Paris before you, I can pick them up.

I'm sending you the poem which will be the last one in my book, *La vie immédiate*.[2] Tell me if it seems adequate to you? And to Dali as well? I'm doing very well.

Naturally I would have preferred for you to go to France instead of to Spain, since then I would certainly have come to see you. Or else go first to Spain and in a month or 5 weeks cross over into France. Anyway, do whatever's best for your health, and never think that I am not entirely yours, just as when you first appeared to me, that I will ever cease, night or day, to dream of you as of all that I have on Earth. You my only, I kiss you all over,

Paul

[Locronan] 17 July [1931]

My little darling, we're in a very ancient little village 6 kilometers from the sea (Tanguy's village). It's great here, the food is wonderful (Fr 35 a day). Why aren't you here? I dream of you night and day. The weather was too bad to go to the Île de Sein. It's still very cold. I keep telling myself that you're going to go away to some far distant country that is forbidden to me, and for a long time. Your departure was too hasty. I saw too little of you. And I miss my beautiful Gala whom I know so well. I'm concerned for your health. Have you seen the doctor? What does he say? You must write me often. I must know if the harm they did you has truly passed.[3] Be very careful not to choose a spot that wouldn't be good for you.

I am a very sad man. For nearly 20 years I shared a secure life with you, despite the knocks. It was my whole life. Life for me now is entirely vain. The life of one defeated.

But don't be pessimistic. I have grown wiser. Sadness is a millstone. I don't know anymore.

The tensing of your features, the strength of your eyes, all of that supports me.

I don't want it to be lost.
We'll surely see one another in September or October.
The main thing is for you to take good care of yourself.
There are so many things that will bind us forever. I live only for you, for the idea that you not be unhappy.
Tell Cécile that I love her deeply because she has your eyebrows, your eyes, because she's a girl, your girl.
When it's sunny we'll go to the Île de Sein. Write to me here.
Be confident that I love you as on the very first day, and that my life belongs to you. My Gala.
Send me all my mail.

[unsigned]

CRITIQUE OF POETRY[4]

It's understood I hate the bourgeois rule
The rule of cops and preachers
But even more I hate the man who hates it not
As I do
With all his strength

I spit in the eye of the man who's smaller than life
Who of all my poems does not prefer this *Critique of Poetry*.

112

Postmark: Quimper, Finistère, 18 July 1931
Addressee: Mme. Grindel, 7, rue Becquerel, Paris 18e

Saturday

My darling little girl, thanks for your letter. Understood for the passport. But it's infuriating and sad, since with your stays in Spain ... My love ... The weather is atrocious. We'll leave Wednesday for the Île de Sein unless it's still as bad. Otherwise, we'll head inland or to the south. I'm in a hurry to send off this letter.

PAUL ELUARD

You mustn't be sad. But simply accept that I fight against Cadaqués and the foreign countries that are to keep us apart. Obviously, those countries have some advantages and especially for you who don't like France, but if I am not to have a passport any longer, what will become of our relationship[?]

I love you, don't write me here after Monday at the latest.

Let me know ahead of time and by wire if possible the address where you'll be.

I think of you constantly.

I never forget you for one minute and I'll never be without you. I kiss you all over.

Paul

Ah! If only I could see you before you leave! Best to Dali.

113

Postmark: Audierne, Finistère, 24 July 1931
Addressee: Mme. Grindel, Hôtel du Portugal, Vernet-les-Bains (Pyrénées-Orientales)

Friday, 8 A.M.

My beloved child, my precious Gala, the boat only leaves here on Fridays and Tuesdays. It leaves the coast to get here on Wednesdays and Saturdays. So your letters must arrive in Audierne on Friday and Tuesday nights.

Paul Eluard-Grindel
Hôtel Marzin
Île de Sein (Finistère) via Audierne
I'm in a hurry to get this letter off on the boat.
I'm doing very well. It's very sunny. I'm eager to hear how Vernet is.
Everyone sends their best to Dali and to you. I adore you.

Ys. frvr.
Paul

114

Postcard: Île de Sein. The "Little Pig Rock." Port Entrance.
Postmark: [Finistère], 6 [August] 1931
Addressee: Mme. Grindel, Hôtel du Portugal, Vernet-les-Bains (Pyrénées-Orientales)

Monday

Since you write me that you're leaving for Cadaqués around the 20th, I'm leaving here tomorrow with Valentine and will be in Paris the day after. In any case the weather's very bad. I'll come to see you in a few days. I'll let you know by wire. I hope you're getting used to the altitude and that you're already stronger.

Sadoul and Breton, who are staying here, send you their very best, as well as to Dali and Crevel.

Myself, I am ys. frvr.

Paul

You haven't told me what you thought of *Critique de la poésie*.

115

[Paris, around 20 August 1931]

Saturday

My beautiful Gala, I got back all right yesterday, but pretty tired. I was very moved by your letter, very happy. But how did you manage to find another Fr 500? I, too, am overjoyed that I was able to see you, overjoyed by those few days, so good, so marvelous through your beauty, intelligence, and grace.[1]

Char arrived this morning. He didn't go to Vernet because he was penniless. Still just as sweet, very well.

I had terrible nightmares last night. I woke up and wakened Nush by calling your name out loud. Bathed in tears. All night long I dreamed that I was feigning madness and that I would never again be able to sleep.

At last, the weather's brightened for a few hours.

Aren't you in Cadaqués? I'm sending this letter there, on the off chance.

Dali's poem had great success with Aragon, last night. I read it out loud myself, and that was the least of the oddities.

I'm going to have your postcard framed.

Char sends you his very best.

As for me, I'm ys. frvr. I kiss you endlessly.

Paul

116

[Paris, late August/early September 1931]

My beautiful Gala, I'm glad that you're sleeping better in Cadaqués. I'm eagerly awaiting Dali's questions for the survey.[1] I'm writing in a hurry. Couldn't Crevel make a fuss with Viot[2] to give us some money[?] I have Fr 1,000 to get me to 15 September. Have him explain, too, that I'm stuck in Paris because of it. And I'm truly unable to ask him myself.

Since I returned we've had December weather. The fire's been lit and we can't go out, it's raining so hard. Char's book is coming out at the end of the week under the title: *L'action de la justice est éteinte*.[3] Aragon sent his poems to the printer under the title: *Persécuté persécuteur*.[4] Read all this to Crevel and Dali. As for an article by Viot, it would be better if Breton asked him for one, on a specific subject. Here's Breton's address: Hôtel du Levant, Castellane (Basses-Alpes).

Have Crevel write to him with Viot's address.

Tell Crevel that his letter did me good. I'm sending you some transcribed poems, one of which you don't know.[5] It's nothing great. What do you think?

I'm quiet, I don't go out. It's 4:30, I'm still in pajamas.

Do you like these two cards? The woman is pretty. How is the thinking machine? Tell him, and Crevel, that I love him with all my heart. *Au revoir*, Gala, my beautiful darling woman, ys, frv.

Paul

Send a card to Unik:[6] Hôtel des Marronniers, 10, bd Joffre, Reims (Haute-Marne).

117

Postcard
Postmark: Reims, 30 August 1931
Addressee: M. Salvador Dali, Port Lligat, Cadaqués (Gerona)

"Beauty treatments"[1]
Best to the three of you.[2]

Paul

my regards to you

P. Unik

118

[Paris, early September 1931]

Wednesday

My beautiful Gala, I am impatiently awaiting the heralded photos and questions.[1] Has Crevel told Viot, convinced Viot that I am truly without money and without means to get any[?]

On Sunday I went to Reims to see Unik, who's very sweet and is doing some really fascinating things. Write to him. Yesterday and the day before I was in bed with a bad cold, which is better today. I'm working a lot. Will send you some new poems soon. Herewith some news which will cheer you up, I think. I'm thrilled by it. An idiotic death.[2]

I don't think that Breton has received the promised letter from Dali. He must have support for No. 3. He needs it badly.[3]

I'm going to do the general catalog for Corti. Can I announce a new book by Dali? In that case, wire me the title—or send it express. Paris is sad. But I'm in a great fever of work. I've paid Fr 1,285 in insurance (Eaubonne, rue Becquerel and rue Fontaine). You'll owe me Fr 500 out of that. I'm sorry, but the bill left me with Fr 100 and Fr 1,000 in debt. If you could get it to me, one way or another, I'd appreciate it.

Forgive this letter. I'm waiting for your long registered letter. Believe me yours forever.

your Paul

Always tell me what you think of my cards. Thanks for "You've got a good eye." I write on all the particularly erotic pages of my albums.[4]

119

[Paris, early September 1931]

A quick note, my Gala, could you ask Crevel to please write to Mme. Cuervas[1] and to the old spinster to make no approaches to the ambassador or any other official about my passport. All things considered, it would be insufferable and might give occasion for justifiable recrimination toward me. *It's very important.* The Spanish government is behaving in such manner that any such steps are unacceptable to me.[2] I'm counting on Crevel to make it very clear that I want nothing from these people, that I refuse.

Received Dali's questionnaire, which I'm sending to Breton. Aragon thinks it's great, except for the last question about the vampire.[3]

I'll write you again at length tomorrow.

Ys. frvr.
Paul

120

[Paris, 11 September 1931]

My darling little Gala, I'm worried, I've had no letters from you. What's going on? I'm working like a slave in the Anti-colonialist Exhibition, in the Soviet pavilion.[1] It will be very good and very useful for us.

I don't think we can risk the responses that Dali's questions would provoke. And it would be most impolitic. The time has not yet come. Anyhow, we'll discuss it again when you return, that is to say soon, I hope.

Write to me. You know I can't remain this far from you unless you write me often.

Best to Crevel and Dali.
I think of you constantly.
I love you awfully.

Paul

121

Postcard: The tomato—missile of protest.
[Paris, September 1931]

My beautiful little Gala,

the weather is marvelous here. If only it would last until your return when you'll be here.

I wanted to send you some poems but was afraid this letter would reach you too late. I'll give them to you when you get here. I'm still working at the exhibition. I take breaks on Thursdays and Sundays.

Be calm. When you get back, you won't find me changed toward you. Always just as loving, my fine Gala.

Breton read us the first two chapters of his book. It's very important and I think it will put us once and for all on the path to dialectical materialism.[1] I love you, I'm still yours.

> Ys. frvr.
> Paul

122

[Paris, November 1931]

My darling little child, I'm pleased that you've written me. It makes the bad weather more bearable. You know I think of you constantly, of Our life which is not finished, which will only finish with the two of us. I'm sending you the poem that will be at the top of my next book. I'm writing a lot. I'll send you some poems when I've brought them up to snuff.

Dali's text, or rather what I take to be a text fragment, seems to me, and to Breton, to be quite incomprehensible. I imagine Thirion collaborated on it. Don't tell him. The sentence about diurnal fantasies and the residue of conjugated dreams and reality considerably misinterprets Breton's formulated idea, and makes the much more significant work he had planned impossible to write.

If Dali has no objections, there may be a chance for Breton and me to revise the text entirely. As it stands, the fragment is unpublishable, being obscure and above all poorly expressed. I'm wiring Thirion to call me today, and he'll pass on our objections to you. For I imagine that Thirion inserted two or three tangents into this text that make it unworkable. Anyway, I think that when he knows our objections, Dali can only agree with us. And the best would be for us to revise this preface ourselves.[1]

My darling child, the weather is awful. But you never leave me. I think of you all day and a good part of the night, my eyes open, reliving that which we lived.

Take care of yourself. I adore you. Ys. frvr.

> Paul

What have you become why this pink and graying hair[2]
Why this brow these torn and tearing eyes
The radium wedding's great misunderstanding
Loneliness pursues me with its spite.

123

[Paris? late November/early December 1931]

My poor, darling little girl, I am both sorry and relieved that the doctor has located the source of your discomforts. If the other doctors whom you consulted didn't discover this fibroma, it's because it isn't very big and won't need to be removed. It seems that it is neither a bloody nor a dangerous operation. You'll have to go to a good clinic, where one is more comfortable, in every particular, than at home. You must also find a very capable specialist. And I'm sure that afterward, your condition will return to absolute normal. Moreover, I'll naturally pay half the expenses. But it must be done under the best possible conditions. That way, then, it won't present any danger and, really, the most minimal discomfort. And we can rejoice in the idea that afterward, your life will no longer be ruined by these perpetual discomforts.

I love you, my darling Gala, my dorogoi, my precious little girl. Never doubt it. Nothing of what exists between us can be erased. I want your well-being, and be sure to tell yourself that I am always ready to sacrifice everything for you. I'm living in a wholly pessimistic way, but it's our love that gives me the courage to do so. The sentence is much better, altered that way. I'm sending you back the text.[1] We'll speak of all this again on my return, which is not far off, despite the bad weather, but I've got no more money. Besides, I hope we can always revise the text in proofs. For now, for your entertainment, I'm sending you a few little poems, insignificant but all of the same color (black and red, phosphorescent).[2]

I've done some long ones which I'll send or bring you.

PAUL ELUARD

Give Dali my and Breton's best.
As for you, I kiss you all over.

                       Ys. frvr.
                       Paul

124

[Paris, around 30 January 1932]

                       Saturday

My beautiful little Gala, nothing more significant than my exhaustion, my poor health at the moment. I'm spending tomorrow night in Montlignon with Cécile. Maybe I'll end up making my mother keep her promise, and I'll leave. Buñuel, Tanguy, Max Ernst, and Giacometti went to the first meeting of Revolutionary Artists last night.[1] There were 100 people. They had a pretty good reception. But we're not shot of all the problems that Aragon created for us.[2] I haven't reapplied for my passport yet. I'll do it next week.

I am absolutely penniless. But that's not the worst of my worries. Alas!

I'm sending you a very interesting article by Maurice Heine.[3]
Write me concisely, clearly, at length.
I think of you constantly.
I kiss you awfully all over.

                       Ys. frvr.
                       Paul

125

Postmark: Paris IX, 12 February 1932
Addressee: Mme. Grindel, c/o M. Salvador Dali, Port Lligat, Cadaqués (Gerona)

Thursday

My very lovely body, my very lovely name, my eternal love, I've been a bit exhausted these last two days, that's why I didn't write yesterday.

Insults against us were published in *L'Humanité,* and we're meeting tonight to work out how we should and especially how we can react.

My mother, whom I see fairly often, no longer has to worry about sending me anywhere. She's penniless. Incidentally, I'll be reapplying for my passport to Spain some day soon. Honestly, it would be much simpler if they gave it to me.

Write me concisely and at length. My best to Dali.

I'll write to you tomorrow in detail about our progress on Aragon.

I kiss you awfully. I penetrate you, I jerk off for you.

Paul

126

[Paris, 2 February 1932]

Thursday night

My beautiful little girl,

Since you left my life has been in great disorder. I'm bored, I hanker after you. I'm seeing my mother on Saturday and I think I'll agree to go off somewhere for a while, as I'm depressed and weary. Aragon and the other three are called up before their Party tomorrow. I'm afraid they might be asked to renounce surrealism!!![1] Buñuel is in Paris.

Everything's going bad for Surrealism. I'll write you where we stand tomorrow night. We've sent out 2,000 flyers for Aragon. We've only got 25 signatures to date. Don't be surprised if I don't write much. I am becoming more and more incapable of it.

When will we get out of this mess that Aragon has dumped us in?

If things were to get very bad, how many would remain to us, what could we do?

I love you truly. Inhale the clean air, open your lovely eyes wide.

[unsigned]

127

[Paris, 3 February 1932]

My darling, beautiful little Gala,

you're wrong to be sad on my account. When I write you that I love you as you love me, you should understand that "I hope you love me as I love you." How could I not have reason, I too, to despair[?] Think. I no longer have the material means to join you, nor to rest, nor even to work at what came a bit more naturally to me than anything else.

There was a meeting last night, without results. We're expecting that Aragon and the others will be expelled from the C.P. I don't think they have any chance left to save themselves.

There are to date 130 signatures for the Aragon Affair, and an article by Vautel.[1] And more are coming. But not from anyone very well known.

There's a big article by Renéville in the *N.R.F.* (I'll send it to you) in which much is made of Dali and the rest. Breton responded lengthily and very well. We hope it will be published.

I'm working without enthusiasm on some mediocre, though indispensable things.

A long, 20-page article in *Échanges* in favor of *Capitale de la douleur*, and viciously against *L'amour la poésie* and surrealism. I'll write a reply and ask that it be published.

I'm exhausted. My mother's chickening out about sending me to a Sanat[orium], says she first needs to raise some money.

Well!

Give all my best to Dali.

And you, doubter, remember that your life, your health,

your well-being are the only reasons for living that remain to me.

Without you on Earth, without all that has always united us, nothing else would exist.

Ys. frvr.
Paul

Did you get the Aragon papers[?]

128

[Paris, 6 February 1932]

Monday

My beautiful little Gala,

thanks for your letter and the clippings. Starting today, I'll write to you every day, for you are all that keeps me connected to life, though from so far away, alas!

Work is beginning to trickle off, but so is any sign of money. Some old debts came up and I am penniless once again. Moreover, my mother's chickening out, says she'd be happy to send me off somewhere, but that she'll need to find some money in order to do so, etc. . .

Anyhow!

We're up to 150 responses for Aragon, but the most famous people are Giraudoux, Reverdy, Paul Fort, Jules Romains, etc. . . Picasso is asking to consult his lawyer before signing. He's afraid of being deported. Not bad, is it! If he doesn't sign, we'll denounce him, attack him violently.[1]

Last Friday, our four friends in the C.P. were summoned and asked to sign a commitment to denounce and fight surrealism. They refused, so they were told they would be smashed along with surrealism. They're going to be expelled, and I think that tomorrow or by Friday at the latest we'll be reading some fine assaults against us in *L'Huma[nité]*. They're claiming that surrealism would prevent them from forming the Association of Writers and Artists. Not bad, is it?[2]

Dali should send me some photos and some text *very soon* for a new issue of the Serbian review.[3]

Char is in Perpignan and I hope to come see you. Here's his address: Hôtel du Lion d'Or. Perpignan. Pyrénées-Orientales. Write to him at once. He is really very sweet and his devotion is at the height of his affection for us. I love him deeply for loving you so much, my happy–unhappy little beauty. I'm only really close to people who love you.

Now, a very important request. If you really want to console me for our separation, and to help me, write me more concisely, taking more time to do it—once in a while—as I do today and often.

I saw a naked Arab dancer in a film who looked like you. What longing it gave me for you. I love, I adore your eyes, your mouth, your breasts, your ass, your legs, your sex, their color.

Your spirit, I have remained what I was when I first met you, but more disheartened, more, much more sad.

I love you, my Gala.

> Ys. frvr.
> Paul

129

[Paris, around 10 February 1932]

> Saturday

My beloved little Gala,

I'm really very pleased with the lovely photos you sent me. Also, thanks very much for the Fr 200 in this morning's letter.

Breton is writing a manifesto by himself, to answer the people who, from the left (*Huma*) to Gide, are saying that we're afraid for Aragon.

That, I think, might clarify the situation.

LETTERS TO GALA

Char's presence is very helpful to me right now. He's an angel. I'll send you an article on *Ris donc Paillasse* by a clown.[1] Quite sensational. I still love you attentively, scrupulously. I kiss you all over.

Ys. frvr.
Paul

She is not there.[2]

The aproned woman watches the rain at the windows
The clouds are staging a battle of wits

A featherweight little girl
Made to hold her tongue
Is playing on a broken couch
Silence has its regrets

I have followed the walls of a very long street
Some stones some cobbles some greenery
Some earth some snow some sand
Some shadows some sun some water
Visible life.

Not forgetting she was there
Strolling through a large garden
Pecking at a white bramble
The snow of her laughter sterilized the mud
Her bearing was a virgin's.

Paul Eluard

130

[Paris, late February/early March 1932]

My beautiful, my only,

I'll probably leave Tuesday morning for Grimaud with Nusch. My mother's driving us there. That doesn't remove the worries over money, the spiraling debts. I'm sort of counting on you to sell something. Forgive me.

I'll wire you my address as soon as we're there.

I'm sending you Breton's booklet in haste.[1] I think that a break with Aragon is to be feared. I haven't seen him in a fortnight. Sadoul and Buñuel are supporting him and we might lose them too. Unik and Alexandre are wavering between us.[2] How many of us will be left? There will be a covered edition for sale, on stronger, ordinary paper.

But I find this bible paper, so light, opaque, and so supple, to be really very lovely. 800 copies of it are being sent out.

As soon as you get my address, you'll tell me what you think of the pamphlet.

It's time for me to go. I'm as bad off as it's possible to be.

I think of you constantly.

I love you.

Ys. frvr.
Paul

131

[Paris, late February/early March 1932]

Monday morning

I'm writing you a quick little note from the Orsay station, where I'm waiting for Char.

On Saturday night I went with Cécile to see the French version of *The Threepenny Opera,* which she liked very much. As did I, incidentally.

I'm glad that Char is back. Perhaps he'll be some help to me.

Your long, well-written letter received yesterday morning, I reread it constantly. Write often like that.

I'm going to send you *Locus Solus* and *Impressions d'Afriques,*[1] which you probably don't have. I'd like to find *Playboy of the Western*

World for you. Your readings seem very serious to me. Aragon is drawing very gently to a close.

If he's expelled, he'll abandon everything—us included (he says so). If he's not, it comes to the same thing. Well, well! The end is sure to come.

Act as if I hadn't told you all this. But Surrealism must continue to develop normally.

Best to Dali.

I love you. Ys. frvr.

Paul

No new poems.

132

[Paris, early March 1932]

My mother's taking us tomorrow morning. I'll send you my address as soon as we're there. This penniless eve of departure is poisoning me. I can't even have a prescription filled, nothing. I have Fr 2. It's idiotic and irritating. Anyway, I hope for a fortnight's rest. Breton too.

The break with Ara[gon], Buñ[uel], Unik, Sadoul, and Alexandre seems to have been effected. Sadoul alone had the courage to write a parting letter to Breton.

Char, too, is in the blackest, most atrocious misery. Unable to remain at the hotel, he agreed provisionally, and at my insistence, to stay at rue Becquerel. Otherwise, he was on the street. I hope you're not angry, my little one. While you're not here it's of no importance, and I gave him the strictest and most strenuous guidelines. Make me very happy and accept it without being angry at all.

I am sad, sad—very unhappy. I miss you too much, too much—

I've been unfair to Nusch, who is so sweet. And I'm withdrawing into my solitude. I don't make love anymore, ever. I could only enjoy it with you. Anyway, don't be alarmed. I've still got a lot of courage.

PAUL ELUARD

Until a few days from now.
I kiss your sex at length.

> Ys. frvr.
> [unsigned]

133

Letterhead: Hôtel Beausoleil, Grimaud (Var)
[15 March 1932]

> Monday

My beautiful little Gala,

the warm weather here allows me to hope that it's the same in Cadaqués. My mother left us this morning. I'm already very rested and I'm barely coughing. I weighed myself (74 kg). And you? You must rest well.

I think you've had word on Aragon's current behavior. He had a note published in *L'Humanité* in which he entirely disavows Breton's pamphlet, any rumors surrounding his name on that occasion, and he adds that any communist must consider the pamphlet counterrevolutionary. So the bastard has finally unmasked himself. Sadoul is following him. I don't know whether Buñuel will follow him, but I'm afraid he will. Unik is against *Misère de la poésie,* but has stated to us that he will never disavow it. Unfortunately, the attitude adopted by Aragon forces us into a great intransigence.

I got *L'Humanité* on the road. I wired Crevel, Char, and Péret at once, to draft a manifesto in solidarity with Breton and denouncing Aragon's dishonesty. They're working on it.[1] That whimpering filth, who threatened us with his suicide, etc. . . , that coattailed flunky of "Senile Moscow,"[2] that helmeted counterrevolutionary deserves no pity. Have Dali wire Crevel to insist as I did on the necessary force. So, surrealism will be a good deal stronger than before. Remaining: Breton, Ernst, Crevel, Char, Tanguy, Tzara, Thirion, Péret, and I. Giacometti is not too sure. What I'm sorry for in all this is Unik, whose poems, honesty, enthusiasm, and critical faculty I liked very much. I'm staying in touch with him. Dali should write to him (25, rue des Petits-Hôtels, Paris Xe) to ask him what his position is. He admires him, and such an approach might move him.

Breton must have left Paris on Friday or Saturday.

You and Dali might perhaps send a card to Péret (who is still writing wonderful poems). Here's his address: Benjamin Péret, Hôtel Livingstone, rue Livingstone, Paris 18e.

I'm drunk on serenity. But this sunshine, this sea, and this hotel, where I stayed with you just a year ago, make me suffer from not being in Cadaqués. If you stay there a good while longer, I'll sell anything at a big discount, but I'll come visit you for a time. Or else you'll come back to Paris, which is better.

I have to pay Fr 2,000 I owe at the end of the month. I don't know how to raise it. Couldn't you sell something significant to Noailles, for instance. Because afterward, I'll have Fr 1,300 in quarterly rent—and a bunch of little debts. My mother's paying for me here (Fr 40 isn't much).

Anyway, write me at length. What's Dali doing? I'm slipping very slowly into work. But I've truly lost the habit.

I love you as you know I do, forever and always as deeply.

Paul

1,000,000 greetings to Dali. He's not forbidden to write to me.

134

Letterhead: Hôtel Beausoleil, Grimaud (Var)
[March 1932]

My beloved little Gala,

I'm writing you in haste. Herewith a note for Breton.[1] I received your long letter. As to Char, be patient. I taught him well enough. He gave me his word that no one could be as scrupulously tidy as he.

And besides, I'm terribly attached to him. He's such a good friend. Before I left, he shared the little (very little) money that he had with me. And he likes you so much. And I love him for all his affection for you.

I'll write you more tomorrow. Ys. frvr.

Paul

135

[Grimaud, around 20 March 1932]

My darling little Gala,

I'm very sorry that you're leaving Cadaqués, right during the good weather, and where life is so much easier for you.

Your letters at the moment are sheer delight. All you say finds an echo within me.

It's lovely out.

Let me know by wire two days before you leave, so I can write you at length in Paris.

If my mother sells her house, I'll have her take ours at 150,000.[1] I'm counting on it. On what date do we have to make the Fr 1,300 interest payment on the mortgage?

In a letter to come, I'll send you a long surrealist text that I like.

I've suddenly realized that you might think that I don't want you to come. *And it's the opposite*. Only, I was worried about the expense, and that you would push forward your return to Paris uselessly. I'll stay here 'til the end of the month, because I think my mother will pay until then. She was very proper with Nusch, but she called her *Madame,* at arm's length.

I'm feeling better. Just some asthma attacks and palpitations.

Philippon says it's not dangerous and that it will prevent me from becoming tubercular. It's fattened me up. I weigh 74 kg. MY GALA—NAKED—BEAUTIFUL.

I wanted to write to Dali. Tell him it will be some day soon. I was quite willing to do that preface, but I'm not sure I can. Perhaps, if I can't, I'll manage to write a long poem about him.[2] Anyway, if I fail, he shouldn't hold it against me. I have been more and more unable to write. I'm sending you two poems written in Grimaud.[3] I hope you'll find them briefly entertaining.

I hope that, above all, Dali has written to Crevel to insist on the force to be given to the pamphlet against Aragon. I'm afraid that oratorical precautions will not be sufficiently taken.

Your boy.

Paul

136

[*To:* Dali] Hôtel Beausoleil, Grimaud (Var)
[March 1932]

Tuesday

My very dear Dali,

if I don't write you more often, it's that I write everything I want to tell you to Gala. I hope that she shows you everything that might be of interest to you in my letters.

As for the ultimatum I gave to Unik (whom I hope to save) concerning his relationship to Aragon, the former, while entirely condemning Aragon, answers me: "And you, what about your relationship with Dali . . ." and quotes me several long passages from your letter to Buñuel, of which I approve. I answered him very categorically by a long letter, in which I tell him that if Buñuel repudiates *L'Âge d'or*,[1] I would consider him responsible for so completely ruining "Lion Cheval dormeuse"[2] for me, etc. . . I ask him to show my letter to Buñuel who, it seems, has been deeply "affected" by your attitude(!!). All that I know about the Association of Revolutionary Writers convinces me that it will founder in a gentle tide of mockery. Our tract must have been published. I hope it will be forceful enough. I told Gala how utterly incapable I feel of writing a preface for your exhibition. In any case, give me a fortnight to try.

I'm so sorry that you're leaving Cadaqués just when it must be turning beautiful. And Paris is so expensive!

I'm expecting Valentine and Breton today.

We must prepare a sensational No. 5.[3] I've written a short surrealist text, *Beaux Arts,* which won't displease you, a short article on mosaics.[4]

I hope you haven't left Cadaqués.

Yours with all my heart.

Paul

I'm doing a poetry anthology.[5]
Mightn't you have one or two fairly short poems?
I can't put more than 80 to 100 lines from each author, at the very most.

137

[Grimaud, around 23 March 1932]

Monday

My Gala Dorogaya,

I've worked hard these past two days. I wrote a manifesto against Aragon under the title *Certificat,* which I alone am signing. It will be printed tomorrow evening by a small press in Saint-Tropez. I hope you'll be pleased with it. There's some mention of Dali in it, by the way. The Paillasse manifesto really didn't satisfy me. It was full of mistakes and lacking forcefulness. This one is of a higher tone and of a calculated violence from which Aragon will not recover. It is written in a sentimental style, does not bring politics into play but perfectly reveals, I believe, the man's treachery and baseness. It ends with Lautréamont's sentence: "All the waters of the sea would not suffice to cleanse a stain of intellectual blood." Like Breton, I have also answered the inquiry into desire.[1] We sent the questionnaire to Crevel for his answers, as well as to Char, Ernst, and Tzara. Breton's answers are magnificent. Did I tell you that we greatly appreciated Dali's[?] Mine is very different from those two, but I think you'll like it. Anyway, I'll send it to you in a forthcoming letter.[2]

My greatest hope is that my mother will sell her house and buy ours. I wrote to Delamour[3] to find out the date of the interest payment. If my mother were to take our house, it might be preferable that she make us monthly payments, for example Fr 3,000 a month, which would allow us not to spend it all too fast. And on Fr 1,500 a month, with what Dali makes, you could certainly manage to live for a while. Me too. You're wrong to despair about money matters. I believe that things will always work out for us. What does poverty matter, so long as you can live more or less as you wish, and youthful and beautiful and healthy.

And you are sure that I love you. You write me letters that I adore, letters in which you are quite entirely my Gala, my same little girl as always.

I kiss you awfully all over. I love you forever.

Ys. frvr.
Paul

Response

1.2.3.4.5. The principal desire of men, in the society in which I live, is to possess. Leaving aside the passive reaction of those who seek poverty, I claim solidarity with that class of men who would abolish private property, and I believe that it alone is capable of lending full validity to the lofty desires that are mine.

The noblest desire is that of fighting all the obstacles set up by bourgeois society to the realization of man's vital desires, those of his body as much as those of his imagination, these two categories, moreover, being almost always deeply intertwined and mutually determining.

6. Indeed, passion symbolizes for me such a totality of desires, in quality as much as in quantity, that I very often have

trouble relating it to the simple concept of desire. The desire to be happy, to be unhappy, to relate to another individual, to lose one's own individuality, to outlive oneself, to die, etc. . . .; all that goes into it makes me overvalue it too much to have a clear idea of it.

7. Man can never entirely destroy the walls that were imposed upon him in his childhood. For him to develop freely, as a child he would have had to have been raised by children.

Paul

Here, for your entertainment, is a copy of my response to Ristitch's survey. I think my "certificate" will be ready tonight. I'll send it to you at once.

I'm working on the preface to your exhibition. It will be a poem, but actually a preface poem.4

Yours, the both of you, as well you know.

Paul

138

Postcard: Grimaud, the Hôtel Beausoleil park: "Cacti of Mexico." [Grimaud, March 1932]

My beautiful, darling Gala, how grateful I am for your lovely and loving letters. Don't torment yourself over material concerns, there's no tragedy involved, there never will be anything tragic about it. I am convinced that things will always work out. I don't know if you'll be coming with Breton and Valentine. Here, it's as bad now as in Cadaqués. The entire plain below Grimaud is flooded. The road is under water. If it rains any more, cars won't be able to get through. But if you were to come, we would be returning to Paris afterward. I'd rather you didn't return at once, that you take advantage of the good weather that can't fail to be on the way, that you rest up a good deal. But you know how great is my temptation to see you after an absence. I have only one photo here

with me, the one of the two *Pierrots* in Clavadel.[1] I can't look at it without immense uneasiness, a great wave of passion for our life together. But I want you to be happy and you are and you will be.
I love you forever.

[unsigned]

139

Postcard: Grimaud, rue des Juifs-les-Arcades
[Grimaud, late March 1932]

Thursday

Valentine and Breton have reassured me. You had written, "we're leaving the 20th," without saying of which month. Apparently it's of next month. Myself, I'm not sure when I'm returning to Paris. I have enough money for another 5 days, but not to get home. But I think my mother will want me to stay a while and will send me a little. Anyhow, I won't stay more than 8 or 10 days. As soon as I'm home, I'll get down seriously to raising some money. We're going to need quite a bit. I think we have yet to pay the quarterly rent for rue Becquerel on 15 April.

Forgive me for talking of such things. But trust me. Believe that I love you, madly, awfully, that I don't want you to have any worries—under any circumstances I love you. Never doubt that.

Ys frvr.
Paul

We're having lunch at the Noailles's.

PAUL ELUARD

140

[Grimaud, late March 1932]

Thursday

My beloved little girl,

here is the preface poem for Dali and the tract for Aragon.
If Dali doesn't like the poem, he should have no qualms about telling me.
In any case, as I would like to have your opinion very soon on these 2 things, write to me at once. Because I'll probably be leaving here Tuesday. If you write on Saturday I'll get your letter. Otherwise wire me and write me in Paris so that the letter will get there by Wednesday or Thursday. I'm in a hurry, I'm doing the mailings. You'll have some tracts to send out.
I kiss you awfully all over.

Ys. frvr.
Paul

141

[Grimaud, late March 1932]

Wednesday

My beloved Gala, we're leaving tomorrow morning. I hope we'll be in Paris tomorrow night. We're traveling third class so we'll have Fr 300 left when we get to Paris. But I'll get onto finding the money foretold in the cards. I'm anxious for you, above all.
From Paris I'll send you the poem on Tanguy[1] and three others for you.
Herewith, a few *Certificates* which you will be so kind as to send on to Spain.

Let Dali rest easy as to Buñuel, Unik, Alexandre, Sadoul, Giacometti. There is no question that anyone among us will keep in touch with them. We wouldn't tolerate it. We'll do a magnificent No. 5. Miró's letter is not funny. He's afraid we're going to heckle his "ballet *russe*."[2]

I think we'll be very glad to see one another again, my little dorogaya; I dream of seeing you naked for a long time, and your eyes will be naked and your sex will be open to me.

We will never really leave each other.

I adore you infinitely, forever.

Paul

142

Telegram
Postmark: obliterated [late March 1932]
From: Grimaud
To: Cadaqués

Returning to Paris. Write to rue Fontaine.[1]

Love.
Paul

143

[Paris, early April 1932]

My only little one, I've had much to do since returning to Paris. On top of it, I came home without a penny, I'm looking; every day, from morning to night, I've had a headache; it is horribly cold and snowy. On top of that, I had to finish my book within a few days to submit it to a publisher asking for a book of current poetry by Tzara, Breton, and me.[1] And I have a cold.

It's because of all this that I haven't written you. This accumulation of ills, concerns, and worries has caused me to break the good habit I had adopted of writing you more or less every day. But rest easy. It hasn't changed me.

Yesterday, I worked with Char at rue Becquerel (which is not messy at all. Char cleans with the vacuum every day, and dusts!) I like rue Becquerel very much. I feel your presence there. And it's a lovely location. One is comfortable there—calm, clean, lucid.

I did indeed receive Dali's poem and wrote him a letter about it. It's very beautiful, but I think that, for my anthology, I'll take some fragments from the *Grand Masturbateur.* I'm waiting for Dali to see with him whether we can make any cuts.

I'll try to be back for the quarterly rent. But it's very complicated.

Anyhow, the day draws near, my dear *Madame,* when I shall come to visit you on the rue Becquerel. Chaste, eyes lowered and legs well spread, you will straddle me as I sit calmly on my chair, and you will delicately engulf a cock that, for you, is six inches long and as hard as an eagle's beak. I love your whole tanned body, down to its tiniest places. You drive me wild, you bewitch me.

Paul

144

[Paris, around 15 April 1932]

Perhaps you will have left by the time this letter gets to Cadaqués. So much the better. For I'm more than ever ready for you.

I had the greatest trouble paying my rent. I hope we'll manage to pay yours. Then everything will work out, as always.

I've been working very hard these past days to finish my book, which is to be published by *Cahiers libres* in June, with a large book of poems by Breton and one by Tzara. In a 12-franc edition.

I've done another two poems which I'll read to you soon.

This book, too, will be all filled with you. I prefer it to the others.

Soon we'll be together and, as we haven't lost our taste for one another, we'll take pleasure in each other.

I dream of your breasts, of your eyes, of your marvelous sex.

> Ys. frvr.
> Paul

145

[Paris, around 10 July 1932]

> Monday

My beautiful little Gala,

I came home four days ago and it was only today that Laporte[1] gave me your two cards in which you tell me that you hurt yourself. Poor little girl. It's deplorable for you to injure yourself this way. After that fall in Cadaqués, I was so afraid that you might have broken something! Poor little darling. When are you coming back? I've finished my great poem and I want to publish fifty copies of it on Japanese vellum. Corti will buy them from me.[2] But Dali will have to agree to doing me a line drawing that can be electrotyped, and especially that can be reduced, which means that *the lines mustn't be too fine*.[3] As the whole *end of the poem* speaks of many women (I'm sending it to you[4]), I'd quite like the drawing to show several naked women.

I saw Laporte, who wants to bring out *Babaouo* very soon.[5] So he'll need the photos for the displays right away. I've forgotten the theater's address. But still, there'll be time enough if you come back. I'll have cards made up with: "Courtesy of Salvador Dali, absent from Paris." I'll do the publicity.

Send the drawing registered, in strong cardboard, to Grindel, 42, rue Fontaine. Paris.

The drawing shouldn't be too big.

Have you received the English review[?][6] They're going to make a book out of it, in French. Then it will have to be published in

Catalonia and in Germany. Breton has *definitely* broken with Valentine, who's trying to bide her time in the hopes of one day being on a friendly basis with him. All of this was brought about by a new affair of Breton's, an affair, furthermore, that turned immediately sour. All of this strictly between ourselves. *Top Secret!*

I think Cécile's coming back some day soon.

Corti wants to do the edition!!! He's jealous of Laporte!!!![7] Breton's decided to see as many people as possible. But even so he's very, very low. Send him some cards, but make as if you know nothing either about Valentine or this whole business.

What a muddled letter. I'm doing a little better, only my kidneys hurt. Come back soon. Press Dali for my drawing (the lines fairly thick, several women, among whom Gradiva, the others naked, wouldn't be bad).

I caress your poor little head, nevertheless so lovely and alive. Write me. Ys. frvr.

Paul

146

[Paris, July 1932]

My poor little Galotchka, this whole business of injury and serum has me upset. Why didn't you ask to be anesthetized with a series of injections[?] In any case, the only remedy is potassium or sodium iodide, I'm not sure which, I'll ask and wire you the answer. That's what I was given when I returned to Montlignon from Luchon, and it cured me. Only depuratives will cure you. As for Valentine, I don't understand what you say about the magazine, etc... Everything has been definitively and brutally broken off between her and Breton. But my position between her and Breton is very difficult. I'm going to give notice. That one room is impossible.[1] Breton is in a bad way from every angle: emotionally and materially. Nusch is looking for work. She may get a job as a model. As it's pretty well paid, that will remove, for her as well as for me, the painful feeling of material dependence.

Thank Dali for the drawing, which I am impatiently awaiting. And tell him that I love him truly—and deeply.

[unsigned]

147

[Paris, late July 1932]

My darling Gala,

I should have written you sooner, but I was a little too shocked and depressed by Dali's drawing for my poem. I have often thought that he wouldn't understand much about it, but to this extent! The surrealists to whom I read the poem and showed the drawing either burst out laughing or protested. If, in illustrating his own poems, Dali made a general use of humorous cocks, alright. But that is not the case (see, for example, *L'Amour et la Mémoire*). My poem bears no relation to his caricature: coat rack-phallus-heron in a straw hat. I prefer the *Lion-Cheval-Dormeuse* that was sacrificed.

When I write a poem for Dali, I try to keep his paintings in mind. Except for yours, the women's names would have to be changed. I could care less about Matilde, Ellena, Dullita.[1]

Tell Dali that I am not angry, but sad. I know that, in accordance with his principles, he will draw, or try to draw, some satisfaction from it. I accept Dali as he is. I would not wish him to be even remotely otherwise.

Tell him that I believed myself authorized to take an unfinished drawing that he had given me and which I like very much.

I hope that you are entirely better now. I was very, very moved by your last letter. Nothing's going very well here, neither health, nor money—nor morale.

I am more and more inclined to believe that it won't last long. Everything hurts me, everything cripples me.

In any case, always be sure that you are infinitely precious to me.

Ys. frvr.
Paul

PAUL ELUARD

148

Postcard: Mona Lisa lucky charm (collage)

My precious little Gala,

I'm giving you three of my card albums that I brought to rue Gauguet.[1] Crevel will bring you a little box of them for your amusement. I'm leaving Thursday for Castellane, whence I'll wire you my address on Saturday.

I'm going to send you the luxury editions of *Babaouo*.

I've reapplied for my passport to Spain. I'll know Tuesday whether I can go there in September.

The English issue is coming out around 17 August.

I'm thinking of you more than ever. You are the only refuge in my entire life.

I kiss you all over.

Paul

149

[Paris, first days of August 1932]

Monday

My beloved little Gala,

I'm glad to have had your letter. This very day, I'll bring some postcards to your place that you'll find when you get home.

Dali was very wrong not to send *Babaouo* to Laporte.

I'll do it.

I gave one to Savinio, who's leaving. He still has a boundless admiration for Dali. He'll do some articles. Other than that, it should be given to no one before the end of September.

Nothing new. I dream of you every night. Our life goes on.

I love you.

Paul

Here's Cécile Grindel's address: The Orchard, Tring Avenue, Ealing Common, London W.5. England.

150

Postcard: 1900
[Paris, first days of August 1932]

My beautiful little girl,

I hope all is well and that you're not bored. If you drop me a line on receipt of this card, I'll get it before Thursday, the day I'm leaving.
As soon as I get where I'm going, I'll send you my address.
Think of me—I am thinking of you.

Paul

151

Postcard: 1900, illustrated by R. Kirchner
[Paris, 4 August 1932]

Wednesday

My beloved Gala,

I'm leaving tomorrow morning. I'll come to see you in September.
Here's my address: Paul Eluard-Grindel
Hôtel du Levant
<u>Castellane</u>
Basses-Alpes

I love you, I kiss you all over.
I'll write you at length from there.

[unsigned]

PAUL ELUARD

152

[Castellane, early August 1932]

Tuesday

My beautiful, darling little girl,
I forgot to tell you that the night before I left, I went to rue Gauguet. Your whole entrance hall was cleared, and two workers were doing work on the ceiling. I hope you had been warned about it. It seemed to me that great care had been taken with all of the things that had been moved.
If I come to Cadaqués in September, where I hope you'll still be, I will naturally be alone. I feel as if I could work more and better in your company than elsewhere. And then, I'll have you—under any circumstances—everywhere.
I adore you, my Gala, I jerk off as I imagine you naked, or making love.
Be beautiful, be calm, I love you as ever. You are my only life. I love you. Write me often, even if little, but often. I kiss you all over.

Ys. frvr.
Paul

153

[Castellane, August 1932]

My wife, my great beauty,

I didn't understand your compliments on my capacity to appreciate people. Alas! In any case, I'm as bored here as anywhere else. It's even become impossible to take a book to bed with me to fall asleep. One must regret nothing. This sadness dates from my birth. My love for you is not salvation, since there's nothing to save, but it remains the only peaceful, certain, eternal thing. My first and my last thoughts are for you. Everything is so strange compared to that, so futile. All the rest is lies, more or less necessary lies. My connection to it is merely dialectical (hi hi hi!!!) in relation to your existence. Without you, I would only believe in death.

I *stubbornly* hope that, finally getting my passport, I'll come to see you in September.

What about money? Though I'm not paying for my stay here, the expenses of leaving and travelling were high.

Anyhow, try to put me up.

Castellane is hot and I'm getting a tan.

I am worried about your sunstrokes.

Write me often. Give my best to Dali and Crécre,[1] who are angels.

Ys. frvr.
Paul

Nusch, Valentine and André [Breton] send kisses to all three of you.

154

Envelope: Grand Hôtel du Levant, Castellane (B.-A.)
Postmark: Castellane, Basses-Alpes, 18 August 1932
Addressee: Mme. Grindel, Port Lligat, Cadaquès, Spain (Gerona)

Last night I dreamed of you continuously. I suddenly remembered that I still had an apartment that I was renting for Fr 200 a year. I hadn't any means of living left. It was Gonon's[1] old place on the rue des Lions. I thought that Gonon could certainly give it up. I had lent it to him without any commitments. We found ourselves there. It was very poor, very low-ceilinged, but very clean, quite pleasant. You were in a big armchair, near the fireplace. Right next to you, I was sobbing. You had come back. We were going to live together forever. The dream of our youth was to be relived. We had a lot of books, paintings, especially engravings. And I went out to buy food and drink. I looked through the large stores for what you like: little fish, fruit.

Then, I was writing to Nusch. She was there. She asked me to whom I was writing. And I answered: "To little Gala." This morning, I am immersed in OUR life, deeply immersed, in the conviction that I behaved badly, that I wasn't careful enough not to lose you. I'm sitting here waiting for the miracle that will return us to one another, for we belonged to one another, for we belong to one another, for we always will.

My little Gala, in any case do not despair of life. I'd do anything for you to be happy, for nothing has changed in my love for you. I'll share with you all the happiness that befalls me. Be sure in any case that never for a second have I believed us separated.

You are still my wife, for eternity.

For your entertainment: in *Gringoire* there's an article by Marcel Prévost, in large measure about me, in which he cites *Nuits partagées* and claims to have understood that it's about a man and a woman who still love one another and see each other after a separation—etc.

[unsigned]

155

[Castellane, late August/early September 1932]

In the village gala, feasts are quite common.[1]

I'm leaving, we're leaving here [in] two or three days. So don't write me anymore. We'll stay three or four days near Avignon. Then I'll go to Laporte's for a few days (near Toulouse). Then to Cadaqués!!! I'll be there between the 8th and the 13th.

My Gala! I'll write to you regularly.

Ys. frvr.

Paul

156

Eluard Grindel, c/o M. Laporte
Letterhead: Château de la Chapelle-Lauzières, Saint-Paul-d'Espis
  (T. & G.)
[September 1932]

Tuesday

My beautiful Gala,

since I've been here, I've had a very bad headache (four aspirins a day and I can't shake it).

I should have written you two days ago so you would hear from me before leaving for Barcelona.

The weather is unsettled, rain, sunshine, and I'm in quite a bad way from it.

Anyhow, perfectly listless. It's not serious, but annoying.

The Laportes are nice. I don't know how long I'll stay here.

I'll write you more tomorrow or the day after.

Ys. frvr.
Paul

157

[Passy, 23 January 1933]

Monday

My beautiful, darling little Gala,

finally, here I am in the snow and sunshine—and yet again in a sanatorium.

They want me to keep to my room for a fortnight. They always start that way. I don't think Crevel will be too pleased.[1] Anyhow.

I'm a little bit under my mother's thumb, but I'm resting. The food is very good and it's only Fr 100 for Nusch and me.

Arriving in the snow reminded me of Arosa, and made me exceptionally jittery for a day.

As soon as I'm a bit calmer—in two weeks—I'll write you a long commentary on *Comme 2 gouttes d'eau*. How did you like it?

Tell Dali not to forget my lovely, empty frame.

The exclusively French clientele in this sana[torium] is monstrous. Some young seminarist types, two vicars, a few wealthy young girls, and their conversations—I hear them—I understand them. Blissful, honeyed Arosa, with your marvelous female patients. That's telling you!!

I'm still quite weak but not coughing and consequently shall recover rapidly. I already have a very new poem to write, on that which is no disgrace to poetry.[2]

Write me nicely. When Dali has nothing else to do, have him send me some tiny little obscene sketches, to purge me for a while of the nurse and of two or three patients who fly indefatigably in the blue sky of universal shit—in Passy. I love you, think of me, of us.

Tell me, as far in advance as possible, when you're leaving. Because before you leave I want to ask you to run an errand to Corti's.

I love you forever, forever.

Paul

Give me Tota's[3] address—I have to thank her.

158

Postcard: Passy: Hôtel du Mont-Blanc
[Passy, late January 1933]

Friday

My lovely dorogaya,

very glad for your letter. I was examined and x-rayed again. Nothing but some old, scarred-over stuff—many of them, but healed ones. As of today, I can take an hour's walk. Crevel's coming in two or three days. But say nothing to *anyone, anyone,* because it might be very serious, and behave toward him as if I hadn't told you: he's got bacilli, four per field. He's desperate, because things could get excessively dramatic with this operation. Anyway, once again, behave absolutely as if I had told you nothing. Perhaps he'll write to you. You'll have your poem upon its genesis in Spain.

Would you go to Corti's—if you can buy things from him without paying—and pick up the following reviews: *Nouvelle Équipe—Esprit* No. 3—and *Le Phare de Neuilly*—which you'll send me as printed matter. Without saying they're for me, because I've already ordered some books from him and I'm afraid he'll think I'm taking advantage, since I don't pay for them.

Thank Dali for the gifts he's planning. It consoles me for the clientele here, which is beyond belief. I'll write you again soon.

I love you. I kiss you all over. Ys. frvr.

[unsigned]

159

[Passy, 29 January 1933]

Sunday

My dorogaya, Galotchka, my life,

your last letter made me happy.★ If you always write me like that, I might be somewhat able to forget that I won't be seeing you again for months. What a complicated, *absurd* life. What an unlikely understanding there is between us. Last night, in my dreams, I proposed marriage to a woman who looks like you and is staying here. When I say she looks like you, it's indisputable. From afar it's fantastic, but without the marvelous expressiveness that is yours, and older, which, when you see her close up or talk to her, makes her a caricature of you. And yet, those are your lips, your hair, your eyes (but without sparkle), your nose (but without that sweet,

★ Don't put Fr 1.50 on your letters. Haute-Savoie is in France, little girl.

funny little tip), the facial profile (slightly less narrow), the shape (less delicate) of your body. All in all, as you see, *your monster*. But quite a shocking monster, and, for me, quite disturbing. Especially as she's with two guys: an uninteresting little old man, and a young one who looks like Beer[1] (from Arosa), but in a better looking, more striking version. In my dream, your double turned down my proposal. We were near a *metro* entrance, at night. I was seeing her for the first time. Then, I was entering my room in the dark, went toward the bed, thought I saw two people in it and had come into the wrong room, when someone called to me, the false Gala was in the bed, naked, alone. I caressed her, she was extraordinarily soft, warm and yielding, very arousing. Still in the dark, I went toward the windows to close the drapes. On the other side of the street there was a large, very modern building, unadorned: 10 floors, 100 windows. At each window there was a seamstress sewing a white dress on a machine. All of them dressed in white, all making the same movements.

◆

I had another meeting with your double. With whom I was very much in love. Without making any connection to you, without once thinking of you. A meeting in a large, very vulgar ballroom. The idea, then, that it was a sham wedding, without a bride, with the idea of tempting the woman who was at another table, very poorly, to drink. At my table, political figures such as Léon Blum, Herriot, etc...

Suddenly I find myself dressed as a Renaissance nobleman. A suit and a beret of royal blue shading my eyes. People are fighting. Gentlemen beat the air with their swords (they are not swords, but scimitars, in this shape: ⚔). At the moment when I'm leaving the room, one of them throws himself upon me from the other room, his sword drawn, but a draft slams the door, into which he sinks his sword. As the sword gradually penetrates the wood, I see him dying, as if struck by the blow that he gave to the door.

Another meal. Rehearsal of Poe's story (*Professor Tarr and Dr. Feather*),[2] but with a majority of sensible people who are convinced that the madman is rational and that a sane guest completely mad. To convince them that they're wrong, as the supposed madman has just behaved despicably, I suggest to the supposed doctor that his patient's head must be cut off. Suddenly, the patient is Laporte. The bogus doctor, delighted, takes a large knife and approaches Laporte, but the guests, understanding their mistake, subdue him with napkins tied end to end. I wake up.

Crevel's arriving Wednesday. I think that, at least during the time I'll be with him, my supervision won't be useless to him. He really needs some time under a strict cure. We'll try to reassure him, but it's a pretty tiresome affair. Let's hope that it really is on the ruined side. That way, it might clear up.

I'm delighted with the decisions on *Maldoror*. But shouldn't Dali have a contract[?] Forty plates rack up a lot of expenses and a lot of time. Are they engravings or lithographs?[3]

Received today the first Fr 400 promised by Corti for *Gouttes d'eau*. One could not be more (pleasantly) surprised than I was. Anyway, my fine, beautiful, eternal Gala, I'm thinking of you. When I'm a little calmer, I hope to work a good deal, especially for you.

I'm impatiently awaiting Dali's drawings. Thanks for all the promises: drawings, painting, book. I am honored and moved. Nusch sends you her regards.

I kiss you all over. Ys. frvr.

Paul

160

Letterhead: Grand Hôtel du Mont-Blanc, Passy (Haute-Savoie)

8 February [19]33

My darling little Gala,

the thought of you never leaves me for a instant. I dream almost every night. I've written a fairly long poem (70 lines), quite funny and two or three passages of which seem to me to be inspired by Dali's painting.[1] Tell him that.

I am particularly happy that you're coming back in April. Other than that, last night, sleepless, I was tormented by the thought that the apartment on rue Gauguet might be in Dali's name—and the house in Cadaqués? I positively can't accept that (allow me to speak this way. I have a right to, since it's for your good—and I have wanted and want only your good above all, you know that). Think, my little girl, that if Dali were to die,[2] you would have nothing. His father could take everything from you, everything in his son's house—and all YOUR paintings (and thus *mine*) would strictly belong to him. And the thought of that is unbearable to me. And if he found out that you had taken the least item, he could have you convicted of theft. That's the danger of not being married. Consequently, you must get married,[3] or else Dali must consult Fourrier (78, rue Laugier) to draw up an acknowledgment of what is yours and mine at his place in Paris and in Cadaqués. It would be too dreadful. It seems the father has disinherited the son,[4] but the son cannot disinherit his father, nor his sister. It's immeasurably serious. It would be unfair in any case that the half of all our paintings that is mine should become Dali's father's property, and your half as well. No negligence is permissible. The simplest way would be for you to marry under communal law. Or else, for Dali to acknowledge on notarized paper that half of all that is in his house, except for his paintings, belongs exclusively to you. Forgive me these worries, but it is essential to get this squared away at once. Think, you wouldn't even have the right to take your own dresses.

I should have liked you to send the reviews I asked you for, especially *Nouvelle Équipe* and *Esprit* No. 3, if you can take books from Corti's. Also, buy three or four copies there of *Gouttes d'eau* on green paper, because they'll soon run out and I have none left.

Once again, get married. And don't hold this advice against me. You know I love you and that above all I don't want my tiny little girl, my little Russian from Clavadel and from everywhere and forever to be unhappy. And she never shall be as long as I live, by God!

Dali's drawings are marvelous. When he has some tiny ones, put them in an envelope. Many thanks. I'll copy out my poem to send to you. Give me the exact date of your departure so I can write to Cadaqués if necessary. Crevel is well. We're happy with the review (5–6).[5] We're working on it. These numbers have to be super-surrealist. I've regained some strength here, but unfortunately I still feel rather strongly that I couldn't be in Paris—at all. Tell Dali that I have nothing but respect, admiration, and affection for him.

As for you, my little darling, my beloved little child, I kiss you awfully all over. Ys. frvr.

[unsigned]

161

[Passy, 10 February 1933]

My Galotchka dorogaya,

received your note about the insurance. Don't worry about it. I'll pay it and cancel.

I wrote you a long and serious letter two days ago. Watch out for it.

I dream of you every night.

Here is the *title* of my poem (which I'll send you).

"The light extinguished when, by chance, I do not choose the little green horse and the little red man, the two most intimate of my hypnotic creatures, I inevitably use my other symbols to complicate, clarify or disturb as much as possible my recollections and my sentimental aspirations."[1]

This rather long title makes the poem much more interesting.

In any case I love you forever.

Paul

Fine for Kochno, as long as the piece is exclusively surrealist.[2] Tell me?

I hope you're feeling better. When are you leaving?

Date your letters.

PAUL ELUARD

162

Postcard with glued-on fabric flowers
[Passy, February 1933]

Here, my dorogaya, is a card for your collection.
Today, a tubercular Jewish gentleman took us to Chamonix.
I'm sending Cécile a curious little box of chocolates as well as a card like this one.
I'm fairly happy with my long poem. Yesterday, for the first time, I tried to smoke a Camel. It immediately made me very sick: sweats, nausea, palpitations. I must be completely poisoned. Write me. Tell me fairly ahead of time when you're leaving. Clouds, no snow.
You are my little Gala. I speak of you endlessly to Crevel.

Ys. frvr.
Paul

163

[Passy, around 10 February 1933]

Here's the poem.
By the same mail I'm sending you a book which I found very funny, and a journal that has some lovely photos.
I'll write to you.
I'm writing another strange poem. Crecre has no more bacilli, he's pleased.
Tell Dali that I love him very much. Send me some little drawings in your letters.
I positively love you.
I want your tranquility and well-being above ALL.

Paul

LETTERS TO GALA

The light extinguished when, by chance, I do not choose the little green horse and the little red man, the two most intimate and brutal of my hypnotic creatures, I inevitably use my other symbols to complicate, clarify, disturb, and mingle with my sleep the final illusions of my youth and my sentimental aspirations.[1]

What has she left of herself
Of a morning in a field
Of one of her mornings in a field
Of one of her eldertree mornings
What is left

That which I want
An armor
The one I selected in the ruins
From the most chiseled of dawns
An armor like a thicket like a star
Like the glow of a pearl
The breath of light

An armor beneath a tree
A fine tree
Its branches are streams
Beneath the leaves
They drink at your sun spring
While the fish are singing
The tedious days
By this everyday tree
I am the master of my four wills

Then a woman in a red rose collar
Red roses that one opens like a shell
That one breaks like eggs
That one burns like spirits

Still beneath the tree
Like an irresistible magnet

PAUL ELUARD

Despairing
The flame hunted by the sap

Sometimes fragile sometimes strong
My gifted benefactress
And her delirium
And her love at my feet
And the baskets of her eyes from which I will not fall
My smiling benefactress
Is beautiful limpid in her armor
Laden with glass
Or with iron
She dreams
She dreams of whom
Of me
In the cloth of her eyes who dreams
Me

♦

Her hands are lithe
Real gleaner's hands
Spun with swords
Broken by dint of pointing the awful sempiternal morning hour of work

Hands for lovingly holding a bouquet of thornless red roses
And this buffalo herd
My four wills
This sunlit woman
This bursting forest
This brightening brow
This vision in rag-embroidered bodice
A thousand rags on waves of dust
A thousand silent birds in the night of a tree

It would be fine to think of other feasts
Even parades stripped bare defaced and bloodied by the grimaces of masks can despite all attain a reprehensible serenity
And what passerby just offside at the crossroads of a polite smile would not stop to greet with a flash of the hand the rude belly of spring.

♦

A laundry basket on the wing tenderly subsides
Its corollated stem bends toward its shattered knees
Held in sway by no color kneecap
And with the ripping of a lace
It disappears
Along a road of flesh

To drink
A great bowl of dark sleep
Down to the last drop.

Paul Eluard
Passy (Haute-Savoie)
10 February 1933

164

Envelope: Grand Hôtel du Mont-Blanc, Passy (Haute-Savoie)
Postmark: Passy, 21 February 1933
Addressee: Mme. Grindel, c/o M. Salvador Dali, Cadaqués (Gerona) Spain

Tuesday morning

My little dorogoy,

I'm very bored without news from you. I sent you a book and a poem in Cadaqués. I highly recommend the book. This kind of story, and the personality of good Schweik will please and amuse you. The first volume, which I've just read, is a masterpiece. If this genre of literature were always of such quality it would be bearable. The author was a dog thief, dead very young of hunger after the war, on a roadside. The books were written during the war, which indicates the most intelligent kind of courage.[1]

Received a letter from Breton that we find rather alarming. I wish Dali would give me a detailed account of his thoughts on the situation we're in. I was in favor of Breton's *nominal* direction of the A.E.A.R. review. I think it would have allowed us to shrug off all our "political" proclivities and to support an aggravated surrealist activism elsewhere. For at the same time, I was led to believe that publication of Nos. 5 and 6 of our review was certain. Breton's last letter put that publication in doubt. Breton writes that he does not feel up to seeing Laporte, a real pain in the neck, that he's depressed, etc. . . Furthermore, Schira [*sic*],[2] whom I don't know, has offered him the directorship of a "high class" review, but with Bataille and Masson, at the least, as collaborators.[3] Breton says that he postponed his answer. I believe that our collaboration with those scoundrels, our worst enemies (another violent article by Bataille has just been published in *La Critique sociale,* attacking our recent books—Crevel and I being specifically targeted), would be fatal to the group we constitute.[4] It would be infinitely less dangerous to collaborate on *Europe,* on the N.R.F., a solely promotional collaboration, with all its advanatges and risks. I am also rather mistrustful, having very few details, of the surrealist ballet by Kochno, a White Russian.

If in reality we are forced to make more and more concessions, we should avoid the arbitrary and make them all. We should give each man his freedom, or rather his freedom to err (and there will be no more collective surrealist action). We are not strong on political spirit. We'll be even less able to connive with the *bourgeois* than with the others. Dali, with Breton, is certainly one of the most important pivots of our common solidarity, and I really wish he'd make an effort to figure out, quite objectively, how we are most likely to be able to *maintain* what we are, what we have done, and everything we want.

Various signs make me believe that our activism and our situation at the A.E.A.R. will not always remain as bright as they are, but little matter. We will have done everything we *had to do,* we will have demonstrated our good faith, our good will, contrary to what is forever being insinuated about us. I know that Dali does not share my ideas on this duty, this *necessity,* but most of us do. And because it is so indeterminate, and most of us are so casual about nailing it down, it is essential to leave no one hanging in the balance, unsatisfied, malingering.

It's time for the mail. Write me. As to Dali, I love him deeply. I hope he does not doubt that, nor my passionate interest in everything he does. Without him, as without Breton, surrealism would die.

And you tell him, too, what efforts I have to make to write such a letter.

I have a bad headache every night. And kidney pains. Write me. Tell me what you think, both of the poem and of Schweik.

I kiss you awfully.

Ys. frvr.

There's a radio receiver here, and on Saturday night it informed us that "M. André Gide, who is leaving for the U.S.S.R., will be received and escorted there by the French writer Louis Aragon." *Verbatim*!!!

A lovely couple.

[unsigned]

165

[Passy, late February 1933]

Sunday night

My beautiful little Gala,

finally, a letter. I was afraid you hadn't received my poem and the book. I have the second poem (60 lines), but unfortunately there's a little something missing at the end. As soon as the something is in place, I'll send it to you.

Don't let Dali worry. My idea is to send you nothing that other people have seen first.

I'm sending you some magazines brought (and read only by) Tota, who arrived two days ago. Crevel is pleased. Nusch will be leaving on Wednesday, and I around 10 March. I think we'll live at Montlignon until 15 April, because the idea of staying on rue Fontaine again frightens me. Keep writing to me here until I tell you not to. I hope Dali will answer my last letter.

PAUL ELUARD

Crevel's novel is taking on phenomenal proportions.[1] On my advice, he went back to work on it, with the happiest results. This book, which in its first version I didn't much care for, finding it rather gratuitous and useless, is now wonderful. At every turn of the page one discerns all the reasons that made Crevel write it.

My delicate little dorogaya, if you want to make me happy, and console me in my misery, develop a good habit: always answer me by return of post, and following line for line what I tell you in my letters. You'll see how much easier it is than improvising. And that way, we'll have short but real conversations.

I dream of you almost every night—and every day too. I love you. I'll try to send you as many things as possible. I kiss your breasts, your eyes, your mouth, your hands, your sex.

      Ys. frvr.
      Paul

If Dali has some little sketch lying around, send it to me in a letter. It entertains me, and I'm collecting them.

I reopen my letter. I've finished it, here it is. I'm glad that you like these poems. Both of your opinions are most important to me. Everything you think of them touches me.

Poetic objectivity exists only in sequence, in the chain of all the subjective elements of which the poet, until further notice, is not the master but the slave.[2]

  A war of guides and rovers
  Against the grain of fear
  Against the grain of counsel
  Far from any tangible shore
  To flee the health of seas
  Hope in the first steps
  To flee the inhuman banners
  Storms of flaccid gestures

LETTERS TO GALA

With great empty bodies
The labyrinth of stars
The oceans of milk of wine of meat
The waves of fur the waves of rest
The sand in its bed
To flee the boats and their craft.

◆

Shattering morning in sleeping arms
A russet-haired reflection that won't return
Pointed breasts friendly hands
Offering of the self by whiplash
The diverted foam
Cuts short the sentence that rises to the lips
That makes for the heart
That crumbles in a vintage laugh
A blinding laugh.

◆

Among the bare trees forlornly rowing
Toward the spring
Lightning-armed awaits a bodily caress
The reaping smile heads held high eyes raised
The smell of sound
The explosion of time fruits always ripe for memory.

◆

Even when we are far from one another
Everything connects

Play the echo's role
That of the mirror
That of the bedroom that of the city
That of each man every woman
That of loneliness
And it's still your own role

And it's still mine
We have shared
But you vowed your role to me
And I vow mine to you.

◆

PAUL ELUARD

And your hands of rain over hungry eyes
Blossoming nourishment
Pointed out glades where a couple was embracing
Ringlets of fine weather lizard springtimes
A dance of glowing mothers
Snub-nosed and precise
Of laces of needles tufts of sand
Storms denuding all the nerves of silence
Diamonds birds between the teeth of a bed
And of a great innocent writing I love.

♦

So many idle dreams
So many budding windows
So many unripe women
So many child treasures
And justice pregnant
With the sweetest marvels
With the purest reasons
And yet
The happy in this world make the devil of a noise

Laughter to hang oneself with
Tears to scoff at death
Eyes and mouth like wrinkles
Stains of virtue everywhere
Everywhere shadows at noon.

Paul

166

To Dali:
[Passy, late February/early March 1933]

Just this little note, my little Daris, while waiting to write a long answer to your letter, but I'll wait until I get home, around the 15th, so as to be better apprised of our situation.

LETTERS TO GALA

You're well aware that, under any circumstances, I agree with a revival of a more intense surrealist activism, but along with that we must take into account all of the political aspirations held by a majority among us. And besides, if they were given free rein they would reinforce surrealist experimentation, and would allow the concurrently free exercise of experimental surrealism.

I am provisionally in favor of this separation of the tasks of surrealism.

I'm sending along something that may not displease you.

Here are some illustrated magazines. And the end of the second poem as well.

Tell Gala to write me and that I love her.

Very affectionately yours.

Paul

To be added on to the end of the second poem I sent.

◆

Honeyed wreath that wastes away[1]
The flaming arch uprears
Enough of flying to the shameful aid of yesterday's images
Woodland perfection the sun's delicate manger
The medals of love amelt
Faces that are crumbs of hope
Tomorrow's children this evening's sleep
And gambling oaths and absurd words
Everything bears black wounds

Even the woman whom I miss.

Paul

167

Envelope: Grand Hôtel du Mont-Blanc, Passy (Haute-Savoie)
Postmark: Passy, Haute-Savoie—, 6 March 1933
Addressee: Mme. Grindel, Port Lligat, Cadaqués (Gerona) Spain

PAUL ELUARD

My little lark, my sweet almond, my dorogoy, maya crassiva[1] Galotchka, thanks for your letters. Everything you tell me I am thinking too, on awakening in the morning, on going to sleep at night, and every minute I hear your name within me: Gala, which means: I love Gala. I have loved you for twenty years, we are inseparable. If one day you are sad and alone, I'll be there. Because, despite the desperate turn my life has taken, I do not want you to be forsaken. Forever yours. If we must grow old, we will not grow old apart. I am a damned pessimistic idiot, but I live for you. If I were to renounce life, you would be the cause, or rather it would be my desperate love for you that killed me. My only greatness is in your happiness, in your life, in the plants you grow, in your games, in your coquetry, in "your" affairs. My eternal Gala, when I was mean to you it was that I was always unsatisfied, unsatisfied, insatiable. Happiness in love, what a joke.

I'm as proud as a king from what you tell me of my poems. You know yours is the only praise that moves me. For you, I shall return to work at once.

I don't know if you enjoyed Schweik. On the off chance, I'm sending you the first volume, as well as a gangster story that passes the time pretty well. You must have got the end of the second poem, which finishes it pretty well, I believe.

Your long letter gives me unheard-of strength. Don't forgo those Fr 500 for my sake. I'll leave around the 11th. If you can send them, send them to Montlignon, to M. Eugène Grindel in a crossed cheque. I'll be penniless but I'm beginning to learn to do without. Don't deprive yourself for my sake. I'd rather be the one helping you. I hope that one day I'll have enough money again to share it with you. You should count on that.

I'm leaving in any case, as my health is less than brilliant. I've got bad pains in my kidneys and head, I'm on a diet and drinking water. I have to consult a specialist. I've lost weight. The doctors here are barely adequate for the lungs and won't demean themselves to care for anything else.

Nusch left last Wednesday and Tota yesterday. Crevel will leave with me. He's doing better and he has to go home to publish his book. But he'll come often to Montlignon. You still have enough time to drop me a line as soon as you receive this letter. Then: 22, rue des Écoles. Montlignon (Seine-et-Oise).

Tell Dali that we will certainly answer his survey.

They won't be x-raying my kidneys, stomach, and intestines until tomorrow. I'll write you as soon as I know the results.

I often send little things to Cécile. She has a vacation in April that she'll spend with me. She adores us. And it's deeply sincere. She unites us in a great, impassioned respect.

My little child, be good and merry. So long as I love you—and I will love you forever—you have nothing to worry about. You are my whole life. I kiss you awfully all over.

Paul

My very best to little Daris.[2]

168

Letterhead: Grand Hôtel du Mont-Blanc, Passy (Haute-Savoie)

8 March 1933

Last night, I was among a group of soldiers who were guarding, at bayonet-point, some female prisoners in a kind of fortress. I saw you in the middle of the women. You were dressed very shabbily and carrying a package beneath your clothes. I motioned to you to drop your package and to get out and, my gun under my arm, we tried to escape. The fortress gate was closed. We had to go back. Then I thought of the great gate where the officers were. Still accompanying you, we went back through the women. I told a woman sentry that I had to bring you to the commandant. The sentry gave me a note for him. Trembling but impassive, I passed by the guards, the officers. Having crossed the gate, you started running. And I stayed in that dismal place. Watching you run moved me, made me cry. But you were saved.

♦

The fortress had become a grammar school, but even more dismal, more prisonlike. One of my companions, a very strong man, was going to leave. I begged him on my knees to take me with him. He was on the verge of consenting when a very stylish priest tapped him on the arm, saying: "Let it go." He left. I remained alone.

I felt that I wouldn't be able to bear this captivity. The boredom was overwhelming. Not even one day would pass before I went completely mad. I discovered an alleyway that had only one shop on it, with artwork—souvenirs which seemed marvelous in their miserable state, and a few pitiful books, among which: *The Three Postures of Nudity,* whose cover was decorated with an engraving showing a naked man over whom leaned two naked women, and a sort of hardbound "grammar book" by Saint-Pol-Roux: *In Russia with My Visionary Camera.* I paid the woman five francs instead of the stamped price of Fr 3.50. I opened it. I imagined that I could learn Russian and thus make my captivity bearable. I opened it to a page that read: "The Russian word for God is translated from the Breton word, *boeuf.*"[1] I couldn't understand a thing. And the boredom returned, more consuming than before, like an atrocious physical pain, a burn. I grimaced before mirrors, I cried, I drooled. In panic, I thought: "In a few seconds from now I shall be mad—lost." I started to jump, to dance, then calmed myself by going down on all fours and crawling very, very slowly, waddling...

I woke up feeling fairly optimistic. No bad impression left from this dismal dream. Last night I was very pessimistic. I've been in bed since yesterday, as I have a cold. And I'd rather not return coughing to Paris. I've checked my cough with the syrups that Grellety-Bosviel gave me. Rest assured that I'm returning to see kidney and stomach specialists. The doctors here tell me that my lungs are in perfect condition. Rest assured that I'll stay in Montlignon a lot. I'll send you a poem soon.

I love you awfully. You are my Gala forever.

[unsigned]

LETTERS TO GALA

169

Postmark: Passy, Haute-Savoie, 12 March 1933
Addressee: Mme. Grindel, Port Lligat, Cadaqués (Gerona) Spain

Sunday morning

Maya dorogaya Gala, I am not leaving, we are not leaving here until Wednesday because I had the flu. I was in bed for two days and I'm a little tired. Especially my head, in the morning. Tell Dali that we'll answer his survey. Also tell him that I've replaced the two lines he didn't like:

"Among the bare trees forlornly rowing
Toward the spring"
by
"The length of walls bedecked in decrepit orchestras
Dandling their leaden ears toward the day
Lightning-armed [. . .]"

It goes better with what follows: the sound, etc. . .

Correct it on the mansucript. Dali's remark could not have been more to the point. I am deeply grateful to him for telling me what he likes, what he doesn't like. I have unfortunately seldom been given the honor of having my writing examined with such care and frankness. His criticism, for me, is the most authoritative of all. I'll write him which are my two poetic objects.[1] But first, let him know that the most living poetry of the moment is him. And I know more about that than most.

And I say this *despite* and *because of the reservations* which his poetry inspires in me, like love, like life. The thought of all that Dali does is motivation to me.

I'll be in Montlignon Thursday. Write me there. I dream of you every night. Last night, I quite exhausted myself deciphering for you a very obscure manuscript written by Tanguy and me.[2]

PAUL ELUARD

I love you, I kiss you awfully all over. You are my little Gala forever.

Paul

170

[Montlignon, 21 March 1933]

Tuesday

My darling Gala, infinite thanks for the check, which will be extremely helpful to me. I'm staying in Montlignon. I think we've found a two-room flat, with bathroom, kitchen, on the fifth floor (elevator), very sunny, with a little balcony on which we can put a recliner, on rue Legendre, near place Clichy. In any case, I won't move before the 15th.[1] I went to the doctor, for I've lost weight. He says I seem to have diabetes (sugar). I'm going to have a blood test. If it's also found in the blood, I'll have to go on a strict diet. But it could be that that's making me so tired.

As you can see on the back, I'm speaking in very bad company tonight.[2] I wasn't very partial to them. No one is very fired up. But what's happening in Germany is so serious! Dr. Apfel was tortured and killed himself. Dead: Brecht, Erwin Kisch, Ludwig Renn, etc... and all the others, constantly beaten and tortured.[3] Aside from that, the A.E.A.R. couldn't be doing worse. We planned out the two issues of *Surréalisme a.s.d.l.r.,* 50 contributors. It's great. Have Dali begin thinking about what he'll give us. We'll be publishing many experiments. Dali can have two pages of illustrations. In the body of the text, we'll do a line reproduction of Chirico's painting, the subject of some experiments.

We're also going to prepare a Swedish issue.[4] This afternoon, Breton, Crevel and I are going to see Schira [sic] again, who's giving up on Bataille. Tomorrow, we're preparing the surrealist exhibition (the catalog) etc... etc... As you see, we're not idle. And letters!!!!

Don't think for a second that I've forgotten you. I love you. Here is the final poem.[5] Perhaps it doesn't seem finished. Tell me. I'll add a long surrealist bit to it.

[unsigned]

171

[Montlignon, 23 March 1933]

Thursday

My darling little child,

this morning I went to have blood taken for a sugar test. Because the doctor, a good doctor, thinks I have diabetes. I would almost be glad to find out that I do, because maybe then they can eliminate the cause of my ruinous exhaustion and so many discomforts.

(my pen is awful)

I'm waiting for Breton to go to Picasso's. Skira's review would work if it weren't for Bataille, who recently wrote some scurrilous articles about us, and specifically about Crevel. If only he would take the initiative of a public reconciliation, things might work out. I hope so.

Two nights ago, side by side with Gide, I read a declaration drawn up by Crevel and myself, in which I declared myself speaking not as a member of the A.E.A.R. but in the name of surrealists the world over. A very forceful declaration in which I recalled our activism since 1925. The declaration was greatly applauded by the hall (2,000 people), but not on the podium, where an impressive coldness began to be felt. Malraux, who spoke after me, attacked us. But without much success. Then a German (a friend of Aragon and Thirion), Kurella,[1] stated that the surrealists, *among whom he counted many friends* (which had a very good effect, since he didn't mention any of the other speakers), were mistaken, that a united front of intellectuals was desirable, feasible, etc. . . .

In any case, I don't think we're close to knocking the A.E.A.R.[2] on its ear. Enough is enough, already!

The weather's beautiful. Montlignon bores me stiff. I'm having great fits of independence. These past few days, I have been on the verge of flying the coop several times. But it would have been a pretty lame flight, as I don't have much strength. I even escaped twice, but they caught me immediately. My Gala, my whole life, I am weak, weak. Without you I'm vegetating, without my love for you I would die. My little Gala, Gala, Gala. . . .

And then, an apartment was found for me, on rue Legendre, near the Rome station, right near place Clichy. Two rooms, kitchen, bathroom, and terrace where we can eat, on the fifth floor (elevator), in the sunshine above the courtyard. I'll move around the 15th of next month. Keep writing me in Montlignon.

Strength, strength! and all would change. I've lost 10 kilos in 6 months—and nothing in the lungs.

Here's Breton.

Tell little Darys that I love him well. I've recopied and distributed his survey. I'll answer it. Read him any parts of my letters that might interest him.

Crevel's book is on the way.

I adore you forever.

Paul

172

[Montlignon, around 10 April 1933]

My beautiful little beloved, your letters comfort me. You're an angel.

I have been rewarded for the good taste I showed in never ceasing to love you. When you come back I'll visit you often. I'll spend days and days there. I'll write poems there. I'll go to the movies with you, etc. . .

You are for me like a source of air, a branch of cherry blossoms. I love you. Your presence does me more good than everybody else's put together.

I've done a lot of work for my move. Not finished yet.

For the review (2 issues), I'm putting the finishing touches on the

Experimental Research on Irrational Knowledge and I'm going to write an article on it. It's the devil's own work. All our texts have to be together by the 15th. Heine's going to give us a wonder. It doesn't seem to be working with Schira [*sic*]. We put our good will into it (considering Bataille, etc. . .) but he's only interested in Breton's contribution, in the form of his article on Picasso.

And I'm the only one considering the review's pecuniary potential. Seeing as Laporte . . . !!![1]

How useful your Fr 500 were! Up to now.

The A.E.A.R. is just about done for. Nobody's bothering with it anymore. Went to see your landlord about the two bookshelves. He was a little worried about your unpaid rent. Anyway, he let me take them. Apparently you told him that someone would pay for you. Who? I asked Laporte, who wasn't in the know.

I go to Grellety-Bosviel every week. Very sweet. The sympathicotonia (a sickness of the sympathetic nerve), caused by aerophagia, is treated with sedatives: sedobrol, bromide, valerian. He's searching around, varying the medications: Pancrinol, various glandular extracts, etc. . . I am more and more exhausted. Perhaps I have inactive encephalitis. I am shaking more and more. He has hopes of finding the cause. Anyhow, it's not serious.

Cécile is on vacation for 8 days. She is beautiful and loves us. She has a lot of your personality, but she's not as nervous as you.

Sunday morning—Crevel and Tota are coming here to lunch. Drop Crevel a line.

In his preface to Arnim, which is very long and of great importance to surrealism, Breton cites Rimbaud, Lautréamont, Cros, Nouveau, Jarry, Apollinaire, and *Dali*.[2] I'm pleased for him.

These 2 issues of our review must come out. If necessary, I'll ask Noailles for some money. Seeing as Laporte. . . !!

Give my apologies to Dali. I've too much to do. This survey and my article will take up 10 pages of the review. You're mentioned in it.

Tell him I love him well.

I've just learned at the last minute that Terry[3] has sent André a check.

I kiss you all over with delight. I love you forever.

Paul

173

Paris [April 1933]

My dear little Darys,

Minotaure is coming along. Bataille, whom we've seen several times, will publish in the 1st issue, in which he speaks very well of surrealism. In the 1st issue, articles by Breton, Tzara, and yourself. But you must send in your article: the preface to the *Angélus* might be just the thing.[1] Also one or two illustrations for the preface.

It is necessary for Skira that your text should be *in no way* porNOgraPHIC [sic]. Work it out. It's urgent. Send to Breton.

Only, this mustn't deprive us of your best work for the review *Le Surréalisme a.s.d.l.r.* We're putting out two issues of it. We'll probably cut back on the illustrations (8 pages in all, instead of 12). We can only give you one page in it. Only, *top secret,* say nothing of this to anyone, even Laporte, there will be 90 pages of text. We'll need a text of 4 or 5 pages from you, at the most, on the *Angélus* if you like, and some notes for the columns. We have 50 contributors. And some unpublished wonders by de Sade and Lenin. Nothing political.

I'm working like a dog. I'm finishing up some games and writing an article. I'm moving house.

Tell little Gala that I love her very much.

The issues should come out 15 May. Skira's review on 5 May. All my affection.

Paul

174

[Montlignon, April 1933]

Tuesday

My beautiful Gala, my dorogaya, I'm going back to Grellety's today. The medicines he gave me haven't done me any good. I'm growing more and more exhausted. Let's hope he ends up finding the cause of this exhaustion. I should tell you that we—Tanguy, Gabriel,[1] and me—have all moved out of rue Fontaine. Rue Legendre is being set up slowly, but well. Write me: *M. Paul Eluard-Grindel, 54, rue legendre, Paris (17e)*. I go by there every day. I have considerable work: 1st, the commentary on the survey for the review; 2d, the press review; 3d, the first two long poems for the review; 4th, an article for *Minotaure,* Skira's review, on a portrait of Baudelaire by Matisse (3½ typed pages). And on top of that, all the money matters with Laporte, which are fairly difficult. Aside from that, great news: M. Bataille has been kicked off Skira's review. Which strengthens our contribution to the latter: Breton, Dali, Tzara, Crevel, and me. Our politicking was good. Did I write you that the doctor said I must have a "spicule" on the brain, going back to my membrane fever at 12 or the beginnings of meningitis I had at 2. I must also have had encephalitis lethargica. This spicule consists of a sclerotic patch. It rather diverted me. And I have had a very sane reaction to the idea: never have I considered myself so intelligent. We are awaiting Dali's contributions to *Minotaure* and our review with the greatest impatience.

Last night, you were very hard on me. You made me go through underground passages filled with delirious robots and wild bulls. But I got myself out of it, I met up with you and we managed to find a restaurant where they served very rare meat.

I love you. I'm waiting for you, counting the days. Cécile is like us. And beautiful, beautiful.

I deeply kiss your breasts, your mouth, and your sex.

Paul

175

[Montlignon, April 1933]

My Gala, things aren't going great. Life at my mother's is unbearable. The woman provokes me constantly. What misery to be dependent on her like this. It's a continuous humiliation for me.

Moreover, I can hardly deceive myself any longer on my possibilities for making a living. The days are getting darker and darker. Forgive me for discussing such depressing stuff. I was clearheaded enough to save you from this mediocrity. But it has sapped my courage, all my courage, everything has lost its color. I had a dramatic sense of life—it's decaying. My youth is leaving me and it's instant death.

At last word, I don't have diabetes, but, according to Grellety-Bosviel, problems of the greater sympathetic nervous system. I have to go back to him in eight days.

Will I have the strength to flee? Probably not. For you I composed, I composed the happiness I wanted for you. Your letters are miraculous. Be sweet a little while longer.

At the moment there is that sort of deplorable, false security: the new apartment. A sinister joke. I've adapted to it like a tire to a nail. Anyhow!

Write me at length, often.

Yours forever, my only truth.

Paul

176

[Paris] Thursday, 28 April [19]33

My beautiful Gala, my dearly beloved, I keep thinking you should be back any minute. Perhaps you won't receive this letter. In which case, I would be seeing you, you would be speaking to me, you'd be at my side. Moving into rue Legendre is painful, my mother proving particularly ungenerous. She bought me a cupboard and a gramophone. Enough to make you laugh. And yet, I'm not having fun. I'm desperately pursuing my youth, without catching it. I'm living with Nusch in Montlignon, for how should we eat otherwise? When you're not here, I only set my heart on being alone. Nusch is sweet, easy, but the thought that she would have no means of subsisting if I left her makes me horribly stupid. And yet, and yet! Our relationship is becoming more and more friendly, less and less amorous. It is paradoxical, having been unable to live with you, to wish to live with another. A paradox that takes away all my freedom, ages me, that makes me view a woman's proximity to me, and women's company in general, as a last resort, as the *most miserable* of necessities!

I've done a lot of work putting the finishing touches on the irrational experimentation. I've written eleven pages like these, which Breton and Crevel find *very* good. I am also giving the review the first two poems. The 2 issues will have 104 pages instead of 72 (55 contributors). But there's already enough text for 120 pages!!! Skira wants his texts Sunday. My article on Baudelaire's portrait by Matisse. Title: *Baudelaire's Mirror.* I'm getting to it.

We performed Dali's experiments, which were fascinating. We're expecting his contribution to *Surréalisme a.s.d.l.r.* It's urgent, urgent. Nobody had a penny to wire him to hurry. All the texts are already at the printers. Crecre's book is coming out any day now.

We did the Swedish number, which had to be short, with some old texts. By Dali, we took the text on artworks published in the review, and the *Short Critical History of the Cinema.* The Swedes, apparently, know nothing.

The surrealist exhibition at Colle's won't happen until 20 May. The 2 issues will come out then, as well as Achim d'Arnim and the Swedish issue. Crevel's book will have come out by then.

Breton spoke to me *confidentially* about Dali's ballet. Altogether admirable, but likely to make a number of people faint. No dances, which will not enthrall the Russian Dancers.

Write me, 54, rue Legendre. I go by there every day. I kiss you awfully all over.

Ys. frvr.
Paul

PAUL ELUARD

177

[Paris, August 1933]

Thursday

My paramount Gala,

I wrote to Dali two days ago. I've a lot of work at the moment. I put a German song by Marlene Dietrich into French (for a record). It's very stupid, of course. But it will pay. So much per record sold. I'll see the lady at the end of the month, for the pronunciation. She might be useful to me, to allow us, Nusch and I, to make a little money. Don't talk about it. I'm signing as Folantin, the hero of Huysman's *À Vau-l'eau,* a very pessimistic gentleman who ends up preferring filthiness to nature.

Did a poem for the book on Man Ray (the chapter on female nudes), in which Breton's photo and mine will appear.[1]

Later, we're bringing the survey text to Skira (finally completed by Breton!!).[2] It's a little more difficult for the 32 pages of poetry. We are hostile to the fact of becoming the historians of poetry. Leave that to others. An anthology would almost be better.

Still miserable. I'm gradually giving up the idea of going to Belgium. My mother's becoming a monster. If she leaves me here all summer and penniless, we'll have to take Cécile back from her. That's all she deserves.

My health is getting worse and worse. I've had some very bad nights. Never a true rest. And such dreams! Always this choking, and the awful desire to cry. Always YOU!

My little darling, I'm nevertheless happy that you are free of Paris. And that our situation is not too precarious.

If Dali writes to Skira, have him insist that as many postcards as possible be published. And have him object to the idea of making us write about dead poets. It would be better, yet again, to have poems by the dead and by the living.

I love you as you know I do,

forever,
Paul

178

54, rue Legendre [Paris], [around 15 August 1933]

My darling Gala,

I'm leaving today for Belgium and England. At noon, I'm seeing a boy to whom I hope to sell Skira's 2 books,[1] the remaining number of which he is giving up to Breton and me. It would be too perfect. And otherwise I'll try with Gaffé.

I'm in a hurry. Don't write me for a few days. I'll forewarn you of my return.

I was ill.

Don't worry about this business with Cécile. It was a threat to my mother, who this way will pay for my trip and afterward certainly for a little vacation.

Will write you at length from Belgium.

Ys. frvr.
Paul

179

Letterhead: Grand Hôtel des Colonies, Brussels [17 August 1933]

Friday

My beloved Gala,

this trip is finally over. Not too soon. I succeeded here in selling for Fr 4,000 the Ovid's *Metamorphoses* illustrated by Picasso that Skira had given to Breton and me. Unfortunately, we only get Fr 1,200 in cash, the rest in 4 months. Anyhow, it's always like that. I'm leaving tonight for Ramsgate. Mesens[1] is coming with me. I'll be back in Paris Monday or Tuesday. Thus, you can write me there. I've been living here at the expense of Mesens, Nougé,[2] Magritte. It's been cold, I'm coughing. I'm tired.

My mother will give Nusch and me enough to spend three weeks in the country. I need it. I've lost a lot of weight. I've got less strength than ever. I'm letting myself go. Unable to write. I'm losing any hope of going to Cadaqués.

My Gala, your daughter must be impatiently awaiting me. We'll write you.

The fellow who bought Ovid's *Metamorphoses* from me is interesting. He's coming to Paris in the second half of September and wants to buy a Dali. Shame I don't have mine. Tell me what we might do. Without going through Colle, of course.

Tell Dali I love him well.

And you, my whole, my entire life

Paul

180

[Paris, early September 1933]

Saturday afternoon

My beloved little Gala,

TO BE READ SLOWLY, ATTENTIVELY
TO BE READ AND REREAD

Here is the serious letter. I beg you, I beg Dali to pay the strictest attention to what I'm about to tell you. Issue No. 3 of *Minotaure* could mark our success in that review, toward which Breton and I spend all our days working. Breton is making desperate efforts to that end. You know how we have to fight, especially with Tériade,[2] for every detail. I am firmly decided that all of Dali's plans for issue No. 3 shall be scrupulously, rigorously put into effect. But Dali works tranquilly—a lot, to be sure, but in the calm of the open air—and for himself. I commend him for that, but I ask him to consider that we, on the other hand, we have not a minute to ourselves. Every day without exception, we spend an average of two or three hours at *Minotaure,* on detail work that never seems to get further along, since we are constantly running up and struggling against Skira's blundering on the one hand, and on the other against the inertia, the concealed and dissimulated ill will of Tériade. And you can help us, I'll tell you how later on.

These are our positive results:

1) This issue will be 84 pages long, without the survey, which is 16.
2) The postcards will make up a booklet of 16 pages (over 100 cards reproduced). We'll have a *secret,* 4-page supplement printed of the "impossible cards." Several color reproductions. The page setting is done. It'll be shot at the beginning of next week.
3) Breton's article on automatism will be 8 pages long with many reproductions.
4) Péret's doing a highly illustrated 5-page article on robots.
5) Tzara's doing an illustrated article on women's hats.
6) Piaget (a professor specializing in child psychology) has been asked for an article on verbal automatism in children.
7) An important English astrologer has been asked for an article on "excessive details in the drawings of mediums and astrology."
8) Asked a specialized astrologer (a retired lieutenant colonel) for the horoscopes of Rimbaud and Lautréamont (without giving him their names).
9) Brassai will publish three pages of graffiti and wall stains, with a note by him.
10) Three pages of Dali's engravings.
11) Dali's article on art nouveau.
12) two pages of faces in ecstacy, one of which by Brassai.
13) Asked Frois-Wittman for an article on modern art and psychoanalysis.

This is what we were able to avoid, *which was not necessarily avoidable.*

A[1]. An article by Tériade on spontaneity and the absence of models for painters. Large color reproductions.
A[2]. Reproductions of works by Borès, Beaudin, Roux, and Masson (serious).

B. An annotated article on Roussel by Leiris (not serious).
C. An article by Reverdy on the relationship between poetry and art (*fairly* serious).
D. Reproductions of sculptors' studios (Laurens, Maillol, Brancusi, Giacometti). Which is not serious if we manage to push through the involuntary sculptures, a page of 4.[3] I am just about the only one to defend these involuntary sculptures *tooth and nail*. Support me, insist. Breton is lukewarm, doesn't find that they can be attractively reproduced. It's a great shame that the photographs are bad, because I know how difficult it will be for me to have them redone. In general, I have to admit that Brassai does not show much enthusiasm for anything that is not his photography, his own work. Couldn't Dali do a few new sculptures in Barcelona and have them well photographed himself, either by Man Ray or by a photographer[?][4] It's *essential* in order to fight the nuisance of the other sculptures. Man Ray will probably be in Cadaqués next week. You should make use of him, either by buying him plates, or by telling him to present the note to Skira (in any case, Skira prefers to have notes sent to him, since he's penniless at the moment). Likewise for the art nouveau. Next week, I have to have a regular photographer photograph all of your rapturous texts, if I don't forget, each one separately, to bring them all down to the same size. For I'm sure that Brassai's photography is useless. Very annoying, since I need some cards for the postcard pages. I also have to have Brassai (who insists it's not worth the trouble) redo a photo of my art nouveau head. We won't find any better.

I believe it will be *impossible* to push through any of Dali's paintings, or those of any other surrealist, in this issue.

This is what I need from you, what would be helpful (I ask you not to neglect a single point):

1) To come back as soon as possible, because Breton and I will probably be leaving around the 8th for a fortnight, and when we return, it will already be too late to change, to fight all the dirty tricks that won't fail to be played. We'll be out of strength. It's obviously a great shame that I'm leaving, but if

LETTERS TO GALA

I don't I'm afraid that I'll fall ill in the autumn or the winter.

Therefore, and since you ask me, I advise you to come back by the 27th *at the very latest*. For the whole issue will be at the printer's on 1 October. And imagine how much work we'll have, Breton and I, at the end of the month, with the results of the survey (to be sorted out, put in order, and annotated), as well as with our own articles and that of Péret, which will probably have to be redone from top to bottom.

2) We ask Dali to write his article and all his texts immediately, as clear and as *best* he can, since, if he's not here, it'll be very difficult to work out in French. And not too long, but highly illustrated.

3) To send Skira some photos of his involuntary sculptures himself (very important). 4 at least, 6 would be better, we'd choose among them.

4) To send as soon as possible all his (complete) documentation on art nouveau. Once the blocks are made, we can rest easy.

5) To obtain (very important) a lovely, one-page contribution by Duchamp, such as, for instance, *The Bride Stripped Bare* (or something else, drawings), a page we could render in facsimile. But above all, no articles on chess.[5]

6) To answer our survey at once, as briefly as possible, but well.

7) To send Foix[6] one of the two issues of the Swedish review I'm sending you. Just show the other to Duchamp, that's enough.

8) See to it that the famous Spaniards (Foix must have the addresses) receive all the survey material, which [I] will send you next week.

I may be forgetting some things, but in any case, be very careful with everything I haven't forgotten. We must go the limit. And what would work best is if Dali were to send as many things as possible, the ones that are attractive and definitive. In No. 4 we'll print some Dali paintings in color, some Max Ernst collages.

Bye.

My beloved little girl, I'll probably go to Colliure, and thence to see you, to kiss you, to take you, my lovely, my Gala, my first and last.

[unsigned]

PAUL ELUARD

181

Postmark: Paris, 17 September 1933
Addressee: Mme. Grindel-Dali, Port Lligat, Cadaqués (Gerona), Spain

My Gala forever,

no, I won't be going to Cadaqués. At the moment, I'm in Montlignon with Cécile. It's the only rest I will have had.

You are the only being in the world whose compliments move me (this in regard to the poem on Man Ray). These past few days, owing to some unusual circumstances, I have been brought back to what I was with you, a few years ago—dreams, life, yearning. Your gardens. I too, my little child, love you awfully. You shouldn't doubt it, Galotchka. I am in exile, You are forever my mental homeland. You must believe me: my fidelity to you is unshakable, despite all appearances. I'd die for it. Behind all that I do, there is you, there will always have been You.

I rejoice for your early return. We'll take advantage of it. Cécile will also be very pleased.

I love you, my dorogoy. I kiss you all over.

Ys. frvr.
Paul

On the back, some information for Dali.

You shouldnt' be upset with Brassai. He's very sweet even so. Except for the head, the art nouveau photos are magnificent. He'll reshoot the head. Impossible to use (postcard) photographs of heads.[1] Dali would do better to send us those he's already succeeded in doing, and they'll be reshot one by one, so as to have the faces all of more or less the same size and tone. It's a large work for Brassai and Breton and me. We'll make one beautiful page of them. As for the rest, everything's going very smoothly now. We're working nonstop. Skira is still in Switzerland.

And Dali's answer to the survey, Duchamp's? And Duchamp's contribution? Everything is in a rush, a rush.

A thousand greetings to little Dali.

182

[Montlignon, around 20 September 1933]

My dorogoy,

did I tell you that in Tériade's article there will be a Dali painting in color[?] But as we want to print a *small* painting and there's nothing left here, we're very much counting on whatever Dali brings with him. Only, it's in *a rush*. If you return before him, as I hope you will, bring anything that might work that way, as well as the etchings. When you get here, send me a *pneu* [pneumatic express letter] (Breton's telephone is cut off).

All is going as good as can be at *Minotaure,* except money—none. But Skira says it'll work itself out. We have 4/5 of the issue, which will be half as big again as the 1st.

As Dali will figure 6 times in the review (survey answer—art nouveau article—faces in ecstacy—involuntary sculptures—Maldoror illustrations—paintings in color), which is too much, it will be necessary, in my opinion, to give an impersonal (editorial) tone to the commentaries on *Faces in ecstacy* and the *Involuntary sculptures,* and not to sign them—or else to have Breton or me sign them???...[1]

I'm waiting for the faces in ecstacy to get to work on that page. I'm in Montlignon with Cécile. But I go to *Minotaure* every day. We'll be taking up almost the whole issue

Survey (12 typeset pages)
Postcards (16   "   ")
Péret: Robots 7   "   "
Breton: Automatism 10 "   "
Tzara: Hats 3   "   "
Heine: Sade 1   "   "

Lacan: —2   "   "
Giacometti: sculptures 3   "   "
Brassai: walls 2   "   "
Dali: Art nouveau 5   "   "
" : Lautréamont 3   "   "
" : Faces in ecstacy 1   "   "
Brassai: "   "   " (very beautiful) 1   "   "
Man Ray: color plates 1   "   "
Horoscopes: Rimbaud. Lautréamont. 2   "   "
Piaget: on childhood 3   "   "
Dali: Involuntary sculptures 1   "   "

<u>73 pages</u>

the rest consisting of 16 pages on sculpture by Reverdy, 8 pages on painting with Miró, Dali, Picasso, Braque, etc... by Tériade, and 4 pages of documents on Raymond Roussel.

I'm waiting for you. I dream of you. I kiss you awfully.

Ys. frvr.
Paul

183

[Paris, early October 1933]

Yesterday, Sunday, I went to Montlignon. With Cécile, who's back at school now, I spent a long time looking at her photos of you, of us. I know that the past is nothing to you. To me either, except for ours. It's a terrible neuralgia. The present is so little. Please believe that I'm not trying to create for you something you don't feel, but please know that, were you to vanish from me, it would be the end of my life, my whole life. My whole life I've been connected to you. Nothing I do is distinct from you. You are my whole, my whole life.

Yes, I'll go see a doctor. But I'm feeling somewhat better.

How, why do I live? Only because I have had, because I still have the living thought of your existence. Secretly, my whole life's blood hangs on that thought, my beautiful little Gala. I'm very melancholy. Wintertime. Night falls an hour earlier.

Don't think me too abominably sentimental.

I love you.

Paul

184

Paul Eluard-Grindel, c/o Mme. Fossat, 14 rue de Massigny, Nice, (Alpes-Maritimes)

[First days of February 1934]

My beautiful darling Galotchka,

after many difficulties, we're finally moved in. The room costs Fr 250 and the meals are virtually free (Fr 5). Despite that, the pathetic amount my mother gives me probably won't be enough for me to stay here as long as I'd like. You're going to have to make some desperate efforts to sell something: *a painting or a sculpture* (the bird, for instance, is very salable), at any price, of course. Don't you have a collector among your acquaintance good for Fr 1,000[?] Because if I could find Fr 500, I could prolong my stay here by a fortnight at least. And that's not insignificant, because the weather doesn't start warming up until 15 February.

If you go to Brussels, speak to Mesens about the Mallarmé-Matisse that Vriamont[1] had had reserved (3,000).

You know, I'm dragging out a life of bitter thrift here which, compared to the prodigal life I once led, has somewhat changed my landscape. Nevertheless, I have a peaceful room, sunshine, I'm resting and I think I am able, and I want to work as never before, rabidly and stubbornly. I'll send you everything I do as and when I do it.

Has Salvador received an answer from Donoël and Stile [*sic*]?[2]
Has the large painting been well received?[3]

Write me nice letters, as you know so well how to do.

I'm looking for art nouveau pieces for you, since Nice must be full of them, judging by certain cafés and theaters.

I love you. I kiss you awfully all over.

       Ys. frvr.
       Paul

185

[Nice, first days of February 1934]

              Tuesday

My beautiful little dorogaya,

before receiving your letter, Tzara and I had each sent one to Breton, in which we expressed our regret on the violence of the attacks to which Dali has been subject, and that we did not feel it possible to continue surrealist action without him. I had been surprised to see to what extent Tzara values Dali, to what extent he admires him. We asked Breton to read our letters if there's a meeting (this between us: you must please let me know the effect these letters will have made). Nevertheless, I can't fool myself about the almost insurmountable problems which Dali's Hitlerite-paranoid attitude, if it persists, will engender. Dali *absolutely must* find a different subject of delirium.[1] It is too much in our interest, his as well as ours, not to break up. And the praise of Hitler, even and especially in Dali's scheme of things, is unacceptable and will engender the downfall of surrealism and our breakup. If Dali didn't support such theses, no one could honestly reproach him his caricatures of Lenin or his defense of the family.[2] Let him drop Hitler, as it is positively dangerous, and quite a few among us will support anything he does. As to the hatred, jealousy, incomprehension, and idiocy of which you speak, please believe that, even speaking for myself alone, my mind is perfectly made up. But it is useless to want to eliminate them. They have always existed, they have never done anything but change objects. They don't shock me anymore. The essential is to continue to support common action, without which any individual action will soon become vain, even noxious, because it will grow bourgeois.

Yesterday, at 6, we went to a demonstration of Nice civil servants, from whom, to tell the truth, we didn't expect much. Well, Nice is not so bad as all that. For over an hour, thousands of demonstrators managed to march through the main thoroughfares of Nice, behind red flags held by teachers from the grammar school singing the *Internationale*. Right up to when the mounted police were called in. Then it became magnificent. The soldiers had to defend themselves with clubs. They were overrun. A red flag that had been lost was retaken. Everything was smashed to pieces. For Nice, which was all prettified for its carnival, it was a veritable hurricane. All the stone balustrades were torn down, shopfronts smashed, all the benches pulled up, the streetlamps, the kiosks, the columns in the middle of the streets were demolished. At one moment I was very scared for Tzara (without passport), who was *very brave,* very excited, but had taken refuge with some demonstrators cut off from the others in a passageway where a wounded, unconscious policeman had been brought, and where they were arresting people and twisting their arms. We stayed until midnight. I received a club blow in the ribs that knocked the wind out of me, but which doesn't hurt too much.

Nusch says that if you want her to make a vest for Dali, you only need send her the wool (ask what is required at the store), and the measurements, with a drawing showing the exact shape.

Anyway, my little darling, don't be alarmed, don't be upset. As for money, it would be ideal if you could find even Fr 400 or 500, from anything at all, since I'm forced to eat on Fr 5 and it may not be too healthy.

I truly love you, I think of you constantly.
I've begun a long poem that you'll like, I'm sure of it.
I kiss you passionately all over.
Ys. frvr.

Paul

PAUL ELUARD

186

Postcard: 1900 "The old rake's Christmas box.2"
c/o Mme Fossat, *14*, rue de Massigny, Nice (Alpes-Maritimes)

[6 February 1934]

My dorogoy,

I'll write you a long letter tomorrow on current surrealist events. Breton brought me meticulously up-to-date. I think Dali will rather like this card. I have more. I very honestly drew lots. I won this one, the nicest, but I make it a gift to you.

Ys. frvr.
Paul

187

[Nice, February 1934]

Tuesday

My beautiful, darling girl,

I'm writing you quickly so that you get my letter before you leave. The one I received from you yesterday softened me all up, comforted me. It's a real shame that I can't speak to you, or to Dali. We'd get along better. Dali is well aware of how I value what he does. If I happen to balk at his political reasonings, I have nothing but admiration for *all* his painting and poetry. And almost all his ideas seem to me continually beautiful, surprising, and new, and I defend them.

I haven't written a single word about my stay here. Sad, sick, disorganized.

As for you, you must behave yourself and be healthy. And happy.

I'll return to Paris on 20 March, and if I can find a little money there, I'll go to Cadaqués for a few days.

I was moved by your offer of Fr 2,000. But, you know, you mustn't go without. I live so simply.

Tzara remains on Dali's side and is contemplating a protest on what constitutes modern art. Char has nearly come to the same conclusion.

Anyhow, I kiss you with my whole being. And I love you forever.

Paul

Regards to Dali.

188

[Nice, February 1934]

My little Gala,

I must say that your telegram reassured and comforted me somewhat. There was an affectionate tone to it which, since your last letter, I had despaired of ever hearing. What's the point of discussing it, my little girl[?] I am old, and such trials make me all the more insecure. I am given over to a fairly happy, but endlessly drawn out life. A life which shouldn't be mine—not exactly mine. A life on the sidelines. You know in any case, my darling little Gala, that I am now more than ever afraid of displeasing you, of annoying you. In this Dali business, I tried to act as artfully as possible. I defended Dali and will continue to defend him, while warning him all along of the inevitable consequences of his obstinacy. *I am well aware that he is not a Hitlerite,* but what can I say? I still hold some prejudices against certain ideas that Dali's working on today and which I'm sure he'll have forgotten tomorrow. As for me, I will always hold these prejudices. Please believe that I would hold them against anyone. I am quite happy to be thought of as a "humanitarian." I don't see why that should make you angry. And anyway, let's drop it. You are leaving and yet, face to face, my explanations would not provoke your anger. I am probably the only one to suffer in this business. And I am weary, weary of everything. Since your letter, I have been carrying around an absolute sadness and exhaustion. That's why I'm writing to you so badly. My head isn't clear. It's bad.

One day, my little girl, you'll have to recognize that all through my life, beyond all that I've thought, that I've said, that I've done, you have been there, you have been responsible, really responsible for everything. I have developed with you. I'll write you better the next time.

I kiss you awfully all over.

Yours forever.
Paul

189

[Nice, 7 February 1934]

Wednesday

My beautiful little dorogaya,

I haven't been told about what happened Monday night. But I am aware of the decisions that they wanted to make, of the proposals to expel Dali.[1] How can he still persist, knowing that his point of view is absolutely intolerable to all of us, in defending this lost cause? From whatever point of view that Dali takes, Hitlerism is, for me, all that is most detestable in the world. I cannot for one second bear that internationalism should be held up as Christian. That paradox is tripe. Whatever Dali may think, fascism, every type of fascism, defends the fatherland, the family, and religion. The racial theories are there only to idealize such a base cause. The only philosophy on which they are founded is that of the wretched Gobineau (I advise you to read the last issue of the N.R.F. which is devoted to him. What misery, what a dirty trick!)

Anyhow, since Dali persists, and since I judge that:

1) The fascists will be only too pleased to have a supporter like Dali;
2) This obstinacy is a veritable betrayal (objectively, it will give Aragon justification, for instance), I gave my proxy to Breton yesterday, who will employ it in the future as he shall see fit.[2]

I cannot possibly hear, without anger, such a defiance to what I have always believed.

My beautiful little Gala, you can well imagine, too, that it is not without immense sorrow that I think of this separation, perhaps already effected, since I am afraid of it complicating our already so tenuous relationship.[3] Yesterday I awoke, and strolled for hours with your ghost. You made my youth, you made my life.

I love you. Yours forever.

Paul

And it is not on the eve of fascism in France that I shall change.[4]

190

[Nice] 9 March [1934]

My beautiful little Gala,

I have received your letter with the bit of change that will come in very handy. I'm very grateful to you for it. I'm writing you this note in haste. I was worried. I even wired you at rue Gauguet two days ago.

Received a sad letter from Cécile. Jouc is dead.

I'll write you again tomorrow, at length.

Herewith two documents that will entertain you.[1]

There was an article on *Minotaure* in the N.R.F. (highly flattering of Dali: they say of him: "the discovery and discoverer of surrealism.")

My regards to Tchang and Dali.

And you I love frvr.

Paul

PAUL ELUARD

I'm leaving on the 20th. If you write me at once, you can still send it to Nice. Otherwise to Paris, 54, rue Legendre.

I may sell the Rousseau. What minimum, do you think?

191

Nice, 13 March [1934]

My beautiful little Gala, I hope you're feeling better and that you're completely settled in. We're returning to Paris on the 21st. Therefore, don't write me here anymore. I have a share ($1/5$) in a ticket for the lottery on the 20th. If I win, you'll have no more worries.

I have had no news from Paris from our "good" friends in a fairly long time. I'm starting to think that our inaction is shameful and I intend to tell them so. It is also my delightful intention (and one could not be firmer) not to allow myself to attend those café meetings any longer, so sterile, so childish. I'm completely fed up with them. If they can't be changed, we shall see what we shall see. You must find me gloomy, but I swear I'm like a bear with a sore head. Keep all this to yourself until I've determined whether there's anything to be done in Paris. I've worked very little here (2 fairly long poems). I'll send them to you in two or three days.

Too many things in this area remind me of our presence here together (in Beausoleil, in Cannes the "fine" Hôtel Méditerranée, in Nice). You are still my little Gala, the great, the strong, the true.

I kiss you all over.

Yours forever.
Paul

192

[Nice, 16 March 1934]

Saturday

My beautiful little Gala,

here's one of the two poems.[1] I'll send you the other in two days. Your last letter, in which you described your dream, gave me sweet pleasure. It was one of your real letters. Galotchka's words are all precious. I love them. You are ever my dorogoy, forever.

My mother gets here tonight with the car. We'll leave Tuesday to be in Paris on Thursday.

Write me immediately in Paris whether Dali is contributing to issue 5 of *Minotaure* (with what), to which I have been asked to contribute. If he weren't asked for a contribution, I would refuse them mine.

In any case, you can be sure (*but all this strictly between ourselves*) that I am returning to Paris with some very drastic plans.

I'll write you again in two days. I love you and caress you and kiss you all over. Ys. frvr.

Paul

Also, write me at 54, rue Legendre, what you think of the poem (and Dali too).

Regards to little Darys.

193

[Paris, around 27 or 28 March 1934]

Wednesday

My beautiful little dorogaya,

I've been in Paris for 7 days. We came back hastily, my mother left by car in the middle of the night, and we by train, because we had received a telegram from Valentine asking us to, Cécile having the measles in Fontainebleau. It's better now, and she's in Montlignon where she'll stay to rest for a month. At her age, great precautions must be taken. But anyway, she's doing very well and you have no need to worry.

I came back here, of course, to find work. Unfortunately for the others, I am not at all disposed to trouble myself for them. *Minotaure* is preparing a fifth issue. But I won't work on it unless they pay me. I'm sick of wearing myself out for things that I can better do without than eating. They're expecting Dali's article. It's understood, you can count on me for the reproductions. But send me photos, drawings, etc. . . . Likewise for a special issue of the Belgian review *Documents 34* of which Nesens and Nougé have become directors and which will have 56 pages of text and 8 pages of reproductions. The issue will be called *Surrealism in 1934* or maybe even *Surrealism in 1935*. They need all documents by 12 or 13 April at the latest. I myself will give them my longest poem.[1] This issue has to be very *up-to-date*.

I, too, think of you constantly and am impatiently awaiting your return. If you can return earlier, do so. I'm happy to see that Cécile, like me, adores you. We speak of You, our little Gala of all time, forever.

I could not be more appreciative of your compliments on my poems. Yours is the most precious, perhaps the only opinion. I love you, I kiss you all over. I dream of your body, delicate and tan and hot.

Ys. frvr.
Paul

I'll send you another poem in 2 days. It only lacks a title.

194

Postcard: 1900
Postmark: Paris, 28 March 1934
Addressee: Mme. Dali, Port Lligat, Cadaqués (Gerona), Spain

My letter has been sent. Tchang is visiting.
Everything is fine with *Minotaure,* except for a few minor details,

which I'll work out. I'll write you which ones. I'll need a large and very good photo of one of the latest paintings. Kisses,

         Paul

Arrived safely. Will write tomorrow.

         Very affectionately yours.
         Raymond Tchang

195

Letterhead: Hôtel Alexandra, Nice
[Paris, early April 1934]

My beautiful darling Gala,

no, I didn't leave the paintings at *Minotaure,* not for a second, and they're in perfect condition. You know very well that I am responsible and careful!!! (I am especially happy that you're coming back!!!!!!)

And I took some others for a big *Minotaure* exhibition decided upon 4 days ago at the Palais des Beaux-Arts in Brussels, where there will be some very important Picassos, Matisses, Derains, Braques, etc. . . . , and many Dalis. I set the insurance very high, I have the receipt. From rue Gauguet I took *Le Grand Masturbateur,* Chirico's *Intérieur Métaphysique,* a little Dali painting whose title I don't know (in which you are with the sea) and a large drawing: *Cannibalisme des objets,* a man eating a shoe, and a Tanguy. Breton lent his *William Tell.* There will be a beautiful catalogue. *Minotaure* will come out, very lovely. I'm working like never before.

I felt it was all right to take the responsibility of taking the paintings. Dali had to be very well represented. And there's nothing to worry about. You know, I have to do everything.

The secretary of the Palais des Beaux-Arts was here for 4 days. We have every guarantee. The vernissage will be held on 12 May.

The paintings will all be returned by 12 June at the latest for an *enormous* surrealist exhibition to be held in Paris on the 15th.[1]

Unfortunately, I'm lacking some recent photos of Dali for the special issue of *Documents 34*. I'm afraid there won't be enough time by the 8th.

The anthology is coming out this month.

I love you. I'm in heaven over seeing you again. Cécile too, who is still convalescing and who's waiting for you as she might a gift, the most beautiful gift.

> My Gala, I love you forever.
> Come.
> Paul

196

[Paris, around 20 April 1934]

> Monday night

My beautiful darling Gala, not writing to you drives me to despair, edginess at every moment. I'm awfully busy at the moment, with a thousand things that wouldn't get done without me.

Even Meissonnier's photo takes up a considerable amount of my time. Rights have to be paid, etc... etc...[1] And tomorrow or the day after, I have to go to rue Gauguet to photograph whatever of Dali's new work we find there, from which we'll make up one page of reproductions. My mother keeps letting me down. With her car, I could do a lot more, and faster. The anthology? I've broken off everything with Lely. I'm now making an approach to Mme. Bûcher. I think it'll work out.[2]

There's also politics, a survey on joint action that we're doing. Tomorrow morning, for instance, I have an appointment in Courbevoie at 7:30 to correct proofs. Then at 10 to Mme. Bûcher's. The afternoon, *Minotaure,* which is coming out in 10 days. Then with Man Ray, if he's free, at rue Gauguet. At night, a political meeting. It's like that every day. Without counting the doctor and the dentist, 4 times a week.

Even so, last week I managed to spend two afternoons with Cécile, who's doing very well and is at boarding school now. Her last year, I hope.

Dali's article is altogether magnificent. In Breton's opinion, too. But I wish we had some photos of his latest paintings. A real shame. For many reasons.

Did I tell you about the special surrealist issue of *Documents 34* (80 pages), which can include reproductions. It'll need a much shorter article than that of *Minotaure,* with 2 or 3 really sensational pictures. *Before 25 April.* I'm very much counting on Dali.

The *Minotaure* issue is going to be sensational. Other than Tériade and his frightful painters, nothing but surrealists. 1 page of Max Ernst, 1 page of Tanguy, one page of Dali. De Chirico's *Les mannequins de la tour rose* as a frontispiece, in color. As well as a Picasso.

Not having a title for the poem herewith enclosed greatly delayed my writing to you. Never mind, I'll give you the title later.[3]

The heat is stifling.

I am old.

                        I love you forever.
                        Paul

DON'T FORGET ME.

197

Letterhead: Barthelemy Vicens, import-export, 18, rue des Trois-Mages, Marseille

[Paris] 30 July 1934

My beautiful little Gala,

your letter pleases me a great deal. Better to have sunburn in Cadaqués than no sunburn in Paris. I just went to the Gare du Nord with my mother. I'll accompany Cécile to Folkstone, where she'll be spending her vacation. I'll stay there three or four days. We'll leave 2 August. I'll try to work. My book's coming along a bit. I'm hoping that by the return home in October it will be a legitimate book like *L'amour la poésie*. I want the N.R.F. to agree to publish it fast, within 2 months; otherwise I'll take it elsewhere.[1]

I spent three days with Cécile talking a lot about you, about my little god, about the excitable, pure, and pathetic girl you have always been for me. Now, after so much suffering and unhappiness, my only aim is to see you happy, in any case safe from my worries, my angers. You know, I shall never again do you any harm, never. Remember, I love you so much, believe me, it hasn't always been a bed of roses for you, but I've always loved you so, so much. You have dictated all of my poems to me. You should forget all my madness so as to remember only this: I dream of you every night.

I'll send you some poems in the next few days.

I kiss you all over. Ys. frvr.
Paul

198

[Brussels, August 1934]

My beautiful little Gala,

despite my asking Mesens to send the Rousseau and the Chirico back to my mother, he shipped them to your place.

I wrote to M. André to ask him to take them out of bond and hold them until my return—or else to have them held on deposit until then.

I told him that you would confirm my request. So could you drop him a line at once. (It's pointless, I think, to tell him which paintings are in question.) Do it at once, please.

I'd like to end this business quickly.

Herewith a clipping from *Les Nouvelles Littéraires* that will please you.[1]

I love you. Ys. frvr.

Paul

199

Postcard: flowers
[Brussels, August 1934]

Tuesday

My Gala, I'm leaving Saturday. Don't write here anymore, but to 54, rue Legendre. M. André has Mesens's paintings. I sent the return expenses (Fr 136!!!) A trifle! Anyway, it's all worked out.

I'll write you again at length in the next few days.
Ys. frvr.

Paul

200

Postcard: flowers
[Brussels, August 1934]

Tuesday

My Gala, I'm leaving, we'll be in Paris Monday night. We're stopping at Mulhouse to see Nusch's grandmother.

Write to me at 54, rue Legendre, whence I'll write you.

Ys. frvr.
Paul

PAUL ELUARD

201

Paris, Thursday [around 15 August], 1934.

My beautiful little darling Galotchka, I've been back from Belgium for eight days, Cécile returned from England 4 days ago, and we're staying with her in Montlignon at the moment—for her, and also for lack of money, even though I got Fr 400 from the Klee you had given me.

I'm waiting impatiently to find out if our little green Picasso has been sold. If yes, I'll send you half of what I get at once, or, if you ask me to, I'll keep it until your return.

I'm going through a melancholy phase, missing you greatly, memories that I can't seem to shake, and yet, that I would like to hold within me. . . . One day I shall certainly have to go live in your shadow, my beautiful sunny one. I'm living surreptitiously in your life, I see you waking up, rising, bathing, I see you in conversation, doubting, laughing or raging. I see you clean and naked, or tired, small, miserable, more touching still.

Cécile's becoming very beautiful. She's looking more and more like you. In early October, she and her grandmother are returning to rue Ordener.[1]

I've taken my book of poems to Gallimard, with the stipulation that it come out in November. I'm waiting for an answer. Did I tell you the title (hotly disputed among the surrealists, Breton and Char against, Péret, Man Ray, the women for):

LA ROSE PUBLIQUE[2]

Tell me what you and Dali think of it.

Our collaboration on *Minotaure* seems deeply compromised. Those people came to Breton and me *exclusively* for this issue, with a nearly full agenda, very scientific, boring, and quite reactionary. Nothing but reproductions of old French paintings—and quite probably, as they're savages, Virgins and Christs all over the place. A cover by Miro!!!!!

Promises that the double issue following will be what we want, but nevertheless we'll probably refuse to contribute. If only to see whether they're committed to us. If so, we'll stipulate conditions. Don't worry about anything.

It would have been good if Dali had *immediately* sent us two photos of paintings and appropriate text in French, because it's *very urgent* for a special issue of a Czechoslovakian review. But as always, subject to censorship.

Send Dali all my fondest regards, in which he should believe.

I love you and kiss you all over.

Ys. frvr.
Paul

A Spanish painter is going to arrange a trip to the Canaries for Breton and me (it costs Fr. 400).[3] A conference. But we'd also have to bring a print of Un Chien Andalou or, better yet, of L'Âge d'or.

How to go about it?

Answer everything soon.

202

[Montlignon, 20 August 1934]

Monday

Gala, my beautiful, darling little girl,

the fact that I'm getting married tomorrow has plunged me quite absurdly into the depths of melancholy.[1] Yet nothing will be changed in my life, except in that if I wanted to leave Nusch, being married I would have fewer qualms, since then her material circumstances would be more easily taken care of.

But every night I dream of you, you naked in the mountains with Crevel and me, you in Saint-Brice, etc. . . You rarely leave me, but I miss you more and more.

It must be said that, for lack of money, we have been in Montlignon for a few days and that, compensating for this charming family life, I have taken refuge in my memories and old desires.

PAUL ELUARD

Moreover, Galotchka, I shall in any case return one day to live near you, at whatever distance you like. I'm starting to get fed up. Life, poetry, women, great journeys, little walks—none of this is possible without the reassurance of seeing you, of your voice. I need your nakedness for the desire to see others, etc. . . . It's you who have made up my universe.

I kiss you all over.

Ys. frvr.
Paul

Herewith a photo which you can put in my next book, on 1 November.

The little Picasso has been sold, apparently. But we won't get the money until 15 September.

203

[Paris, August or September 1934?]

Wednesday

Dorogaya Galotchka,
I hope that you received Gradiva.[1]
I thank you for your cards.
We should have an answer this afternoon on an apartment on rue d'Artois, between Saint-Philippe-du-Roule and the Champs-Élysées (6,000). It's great, but will we get it. . . . ?
I'm doing well. I hope you're looking out for yourself and having fun.
I think I'll still be in London on 14 September.
Nusch sends you her fondest.
Kiss Dali for me.
I kiss you.

Paul

204

Postmark: Davos platz, 22 February 1935
Addressee: Señora Salvador Dali, Port Lligat, Cadaqués (Gerona), España

Davos Thursday

Dorogaya, I hope you received my card from Clavadel in good order. The place is larger now, but what hasn't changed are the paths, the view, the snow. It seems as if so little time has passed, so little. I really am joined to you forever.

As Nusch tells you,[1] I'm feeling better and am determined to live peacefully—that is to say, without pettiness, without useless annoyances. M. Skira was here last week. He had arrived Sunday. I bumped into him on the street Friday. Under these conditions, I will not contribute to *Minotaure* anymore. I am not lacking more important and *better paying* reviews to which to contribute. I am in any case determined (see above) not to put up with this kind of boorishness, from anyone, any longer.[2]

It appears the Rousseau has been sent back—to my mother. Tell me to whom we might suggest it. And how much? It's very serious. It's going pretty badly with my mother and I'm risking mild starvation when I get back.

I'll leave here on 7 March. So you can still write me very attentively. You must be better by now, rested and with time on your hands. You know, Zwemmer[3] hasn't sent *Le Lever du Jour*[4] back to me. I have no luck with my Dalis. And as I have no receipt and I fear great problems with Skira, perhaps you might write to him (A. Zwemmer, 78 Charing Cross Road, London W.C.2.) to ask him to send it immediately to Mme. Grindel, 3, rue Ordener. Paris. 18e. Your request will have greater weight than mine. But do it at once, before any serious problems arise between me and Skira. For the latter is a cad and I fear him greatly.

My other Dali is in Denmark. I hope to get it back.

I have refused to participate in the first conference planned, to say:

PAUL ELUARD

"Why I am a surrealist." I could only do it in a negative, almost dadaist way: "If I am a surrealist, it is because I am not . . . ," etc. . . It would be stupid.

My beautiful darling little Gala, by the time you get back I shall, alas, probably have lost my good looks, that tanned beauty which, when I look at myself in the mirror, gives me confidence in myself.

Write often to Cécile. It comforts her, gives her a change from my mother's company.

Crecre[5] sends you a kiss. He's sad, because he's been asked for his books for a Moscow library and he's missing the one on Dali.[6] Don't you know where a copy might be found[?]

I don't forget you for a single instant, I shall never forget you. I kiss your pure and delicate body.

Ys. frvr.
Paul

My very best to little Darys.

205

[Paris, March 1935]

Wednesday, 10 A.M.

My little child, my Gala, indeed, I've already quite exhausted myself since I've been back. In particular, I've come to recognize the danger of the slightest drop of wine or alcohol to me. But anyway, I have improved. My morale, especially, is better. Everything seems less gloomy, I am experiencing a fairly wide detachment from useless, petty problems. And I am applying myself to the belief that a new life is possible, disengaged from the routine and habits in which I have been foundering for too long.

I have to admit that it's beautiful here. Springtime always has the best influence on me. I am determined to eliminate, eliminate and eliminate all that is stagnant in my daily "intellectual" activity.

When are you coming back? Your presence and your advice

would be a very precious help to me. I think of you only with pride. We have lived well, *courageously.*

The weather is as sunny as the feeling I have for you, for our love.

And you know, I loved you fiercely and I didn't give you a bad life. Our love made us aware of ourselves, master our puerility, our innocence like that of madmen.

Now, I love you calmly. I have the complete assurance that I will no longer torment you, that you will be happy. Gala, my beautiful Gala, little girl, I shall die easy.

You need to write me good letters. The last was deeply satisfying. And I got the Fr 200. Moreover, it came in the nick of time.

Nusch is delighted by your friendly feelings for her. She is for me, as Dali is for you, an entirely loving and devoted being, perfect.

Another time, I will tell you about my relationships with our friends, relationships more complicated than ours, too complicated. I'm going to simplify them, brutally if need be.

Breton's coming back from Gers some time soon. I'll be curious to see the result of his stay with Ernst. I haven't seen him yet. He'll be leaving again for Prague, where he's giving his first lecture on the 28th.

There's also some question of a trip to the Canaries with him, where I have been invited, but I'm afraid too many people will be going there and I'm afraid of being obliged to avoid going, in order to have some peace and to keep my independence.

Apparently, Giacometti is starting to play the fool again.

Haven't yet seen Skira, who's not here. I'll only continue my work on his review if he redeems his boorish pranks on me. Everything else, etc. . . etc. . .

Tell Dali that I love him a lot.

> Ys. frvr.
> Paul

I would have liked to send you some poems, but I'm writing you from a café. You'll soon have some in print.[1]

PAUL ELUARD

206

Letterhead: Hôtel Paris, Praha
[Prague] Monday, 7 or 8 [*sic*] April [1935]

My beautiful little Gala,
I must tell you everything concerning this trip. I really wanted to take stock of our situation in this country. But as I had no money for the trip, Tota gave me Fr 1,000, telling me I could owe them to you. It will be Fr 1,000 paid on what she owes you, or else returned to her. So I'll do as you prefer: I'll pay it back in May, either to her or to you. I'll have it by that time.

This trip has been a revelation. There are a few really good people here: first, Nezval[1] and Teige[2]—two painters: Styrsky[3] and Toyen[4]—a very strange woman—they're doing magnificent paintings and collages—a sculptor—Makovsky.[5] But, though few in number, their radiance and their influence are so great that they are constantly obliged to rein them in, to discourage them. Their situation in the communist party is exceptional. Teige runs the only communist review in Czechoslovakia. There are one or two articles on surrealism in every issue. They were at the Writers' Congress in Moscow and defended surrealism tooth and nail. They are true poets, full of heart and originality.

Here are the results of our trip.

Breton gave three lectures in Prague: one at Manès (the art club that invited him) on "The surrealist position of the object, the position of the surrealist object," with slides (700 people),

a political one to the *Left Front,* which is organizing intellectuals and workers against fascism. I also spoke there, then recited some poems (350 people)

one to philosophy students: extracts from "What is surrealism?" (250 people—when Bergson only had 50.)

A lecture in Brno—on the object (500 people).

In Brno, he spoke on the radio for 3 minutes—in Prague, for 10. I read one of my long poems on the air. And as it was recorded on records, I heard myself immediately. It gave me a strange impression of sincerity.

Breton signed over 400 copies of the translation of *Les Vases communicants*. In 3 months, 800 of them had been sold. *Nadja* is coming out some time soon. *La Rose publique* (in translation) is coming out in September. I got Fr 400 on account. Also got 200 crowns from *Left Front* and 200 from the radio. Then, *Capitale de la douleur* is to be translated. Our pictures in the papers, highly flattering articles in the communist papers, interviews, I think that Prague is our gateway to Moscow. But according to opinion here, we'll have to wait a year. We live marvelously here. They don't let us spend anything. Delirious admiration and affection. On the street, workers recognize us from our photos. In the Jewish museum, the guard, a young student, thanks us for coming, etc. . .

A very curious city, as Apollinaire correctly described it. Crazy. Beautiful women, also very welcoming. . .

We're working on an illustrated *International Bulletin of Surrealism*, dated from Prague, in collaboration with the Czechs. We'll do one from the Canaries, then from England, etc. It will be very important.

The activity of the surrealists here is enormous. Nezval has written 50 books. He's one of the 2 greatest Czech writers. Endless conferences, theater, reviews. We're much more famous here than in France. I'm sending you the special edition on surrealism, quite funny, of a stupid review (for 1 April). In Paris, I'll show you a bunch of Dali reproductions and articles about him.

Write me in Paris. I'm returning in 3 days. We've been here over a fortnight. Breton's going to Zurich to give a lecture.

I don't forget you for one second. If you come here one day, they'll certainly tell you how often I speak of you.

I love you. Ys. frvr.
Paul

207

[Paris] 2 May 1935

My darling little Gala,

the thought of seeing you again on the 15th makes me happy. Six months without seeing you. That's much too much. You can be sure that I'll pay you back that Fr 1,000 when you get here. For I shall certainly sell, a sure thing, either a painting or my manuscript of *La Rose publique* for 2,000. Rest assured on that. Count on it.

Breton and Péret left 4 days ago for the Canaries. I was a bit too short of money to go with them.[1] I am patiently awaiting different times, enough money to eat. I'm sure it'll come. But for now, we're inescapably down and out.

By the same post I'm sending you some copies of the *International Bulletin of Surrealism*. There are others. Give these to Barcelona. Miravittles, Cassanyes[2] and Foix must have received it.

Be sure to save the publicity from Dali's lecture for me.

I'm awaiting you with such eagerness!!! Cécile too, you know. We'll stay together a lot, very joyously. I'm going to give you a lot of presents. You have many things to show me.

My little dorogaya, see you soon.

I love you, I kiss you religiously all over.

Ys. frvr.

Paul

I've given *Minotaure* a story in which *Appliquée* becomes *Amimère*[3] at night.

208

Postcard: "Rossetti—Dr. Johnson at the Mitre."
Postmark: London, 6 June 1935
Addressee: Mme. Dali, 7, rue Gauguet, 7, Paris 14e, France

For the first time, the museums are a haven for me. I prefer their comfort and luxury to the street. That surprises me, says he. But Burne-Jones isn't bad either, especially *The King Cophetua and the Beggar Maid* (the latter a perfect embodiment of my erotic ideal).

I'd like to see all of this with you. I am more invisible here than anywhere else. Shame I'm not a painter, so I could do your portrait. You'd see what kind of roles I'd have you play.

[unsigned]

209

Postcard: Mme. Tussaud's Exhibition London, Mme. Tussaud and her model of the sleeping beauty.
Postmark: London, 8 June 1935
Addressee: M. and Mme. S. Dali, 7, rue Gauguet, Paris 14e (France)

Saturday

I'm leaving. I'll be in Paris tonight. Unfortunately, I'm afraid I shall have to take to my bed upon arriving. Last night I had some bad bleeding from my ear.

Nusch will call you. I wish I could see you.
I kiss you.

Paul

210

[Paris, late July/early August 1935]

My Galotchka, my dorogaya,

your hand brings me luck.[1] I think I'm doing better. And I'm going to the country for a few days next week. M. Barr[2] stopped by: he bought Fr 2,000-worth of paintings from me, of which Fr 700 goes to you. Therefore, I can and *want to* give it to Ramlot or send it to you. For, besides, I have been offered (for Mme. Ocampo's[3] review) Fr 1,000 for a poem. I've sold Max Ernst's *La forêt* and *Les chapeaux* (collage) that were at your place, for Fr 1,400. And M. Pierre Matisse[4] is coming to see the old Chiricos. And it's going to work out with the surrealist documents (350 dollars), etc... It's phenomenal.

In secret from her grandmother, I gave Cécile Fr 100 for her trip.

PAUL ELUARD

And the book *Facile*[5] will be in photogravure. Etc. . . . etc. . . . That lovely hand!!

Ramlot still hasn't finished striking off, but it's only a matter of days now. I'm taking care of it.

Tell me, therefore, if I should give the money to Ramlot.

The collective manifesto will not appear in *Cahiers d'Art*. Zervos[6] wanted to cut it. We'll publish it as a pamphlet.[7] But it costs Fr 600. How much should I give for your share (Fr 50 minimum)?

I'll write you better in two days. I love you forever.

Breton sold Fr 4,000-worth of stuff (2 Tanguys and some minor documents) to Barr.

[unsigned]

211

Paul Eluard-Grindel, Le Hiquet, Montfort-en-Chalosse, (Landes), France

[August 1935]

A little note in haste, my darling Gala, to tell you the prices I quoted to Pierre Matisse, just so as there's no misunderstanding.

Le duo 25,000
Portrait de l'artiste (at your place) 6,000
Le depart du poète 10,000
Le torse aux bananes 9,000
Le grand intérieure métaphysique (at your place) 10,000
Petit intérieure métaphysique avec les objets de pêche 4,000

Breton is asking 15,000 for his very large canvas and 12,000 for *Le cerveau de l'enfant*. All of these are absolutely net prices for us.

We're very comfortable at Lise's,[1] who's very sweet. We're staying here until early September. If you were very nice, you and Dali would drop me a line here at once. What do you both think of the manifesto?

LETTERS TO GALA

(I'd rather be with you than anywhere else we'd get along very well, you know.)

My very best to Dali. I kiss you all over. Ys. frvr.

Paul

You'll have to tell me, for M. Barr, the fairest prices for your Chirico drawing (the *Napoléon 3* in pencil in the bedroom) and for your (very green) painting *Intérieure métaphysique*—which is very beautiful, you know.

212

[Paris, early days of September 1935]

Saturday

Galotchka, dorogaya,

I've been back for 2 days and I've adopted your daughter. But she's the one supporting us. In the south, I bought some paintings by a dead naif painter whose work is of great value.[1]

I'll give you one of them as a present: *L'Angélus* by Millet.

I was very pleased with your letter.

I'm going to see M. Matisse again. But I'm not very eager at the thought of parting with the Chiricos for any length of time. If there were war, we'd never see them again. And they're among our few salable things.

Anyway, I've an appointment with him Tuesday.

Cahiers d'Art is almost ready.[2]

I don't forget you a single moment. I kiss you all over. Ys. frvr.

Paul

PAUL ELUARD

213

[Paris, September 1935]

Gala dorogaya, my beautiful Galotchka,

when are you coming back? I hope you're thinking seriously about it. I really need to see you, even briefly, as is our habit. In Paris, you could certainly do as I do these days: stay quietly at home, have no appointments, nothing to do. It makes you optimistic, I've been doing it of late and have a renewed tolerance for myself. And so I dream of you, I love my books again, my paintings, I try once more to write poems.

Answer me at once: when are your returning? If you remain in Cadaqués a while, I'll send you a little Russian anthology of French poetry (quite poor, from what I understand) in which I figure. How much water under the bridge since Clavadel, when you taught me French poetry from similar books! hi, hi, hi!!!

In Montfort, at Lise's place, Man Ray had brought us an issue of *Harpers Bazaar* containing a magnificent color reproduction of Dali (fashion tips). Everyone was so excited that it was decided to send him a congratulatory telegram. It didn't get done, out of laziness, but the intention was good.

The *Cahiers d'Art* issue will be ready 2 October. My little book, *FACILE,* in a fortnight. Have you received a copy of *Nuits partagées,* with two Dali drawings, very well reproduced[?] It's lovely. And it's an especially beautiful text, one of the most serious, one of the deepest I have ever written about our long life, yours and mine. Dali's drawings fit the text marvelously.[1]

Dali would be an angel if he would quickly do me three little drawings (to be line-blocked) in black ink (on sheets approximately 12cm by 18 centimeters). They are being requested in Japan, with great insistence and kindness, for an edition of *Selected Writings of Paul Eluard*. But the book is in production and I'd need them at once, *at once.*

And the lines mustn't be too thin!!

In Montfort, I did 3 poems for the review *Sur,* which paid me Fr

1,000 for them. I'm sending you all three.[2] You know the extent to which what you think interests me. Tell me. And Dali?
The fair Cécile also misses you.
I love you. I kiss you all over.

Ys. frvr.
Paul

My very fondest to little Darys.

214

Postcard: [painting] Wather von der Volgeweide
Postmark: [obliterated]
Addressee: Mme. Gala Dali, 101*bis,* rue de la Tombe-Issoire, Paris
   14e, Francia
Madrid 6 February [1936]

Dorogaya Galotchka,

we're leaving Sunday for Cordoba, then Seville, then Valencia, then Paris, where we'll be on the 20th.

I gave 4 lectures in Barcelona and 2 here, one of which very well introduced by Gomez de la Serna (Ramon).[1]

Tota just called us.

We're having lunch today with Manuel Nuñez de Arenas, who once came to Eaubonne 10 years ago. I found a marvelous art nouveau head in Barcelona.

I can't wait to see you. Send my regards to Dali. I kiss you very, very. [*sic*] Ys. frvr.

Paul

PAUL ELUARD

215

[Paris] 31 March 1936

My darling little Galotchka,

no, nothing's wrong with Cécile. I saw her yesterday: she says that she's only had one letter from you. She's going to write you. I see her often, she loves you very much. You are both next to my desk, to my left, watching over me. I am on edge these days, a little unbalanced. I've also been drinking too much. Life wearies me. I'll never learn anything new again. Your last two letters did me some good. I'd like to please you, pamper you, make you happy—at least contribute to your well-being.

The *Cahiers d'Art* issue on objects is being prepared. We have the photos, except for Dali's, which Petitjean is taking care of. Dali will have to send his article soon. Lacking money, I don't think I'll be able to make my piece. Once more, I'm beginning to be completely without money, and I am in debt again. No news from America.

After having messed up the engravings for my little book, Picasso suddenly went away for a long time, destination unknown. The hope of many times Fr 500 went with him. He had given us a lovely watercolor.[1]

Except for my foot, which will have to be treated with electricity, I'm doing well. Write me often, I'll always answer.

Regards to Darys. I love you frvr.

Paul

No, there won't be war before long, but, on the contrary, the peace and prosperity that Darys proclaimed.

216

[Montlignon, April 1936]

Saturday

My beautiful little dorogaya,

your letter with the Fr 300 reached me on Tuesday morning, in the nick of time, as Cécile had just spent three days with me, since her grandmother was in Montlignon, and we wanted to take her out. She was delighted with her visit. I was very moved by your gift. You are the sweet little thing you have always been. Never be concerned by my moody behavior. I never pay much attention to yours. You have a significant place in my life. You are the root of my life. I wouldn't exchange my restlessness, your triumphs, our triumphs, our defeats, for anything. I will die knowing that we were one.

I have *definitively* broken with Breton, following a relatively calm discussion in the café. My decision was brought about by his frightful way of conversing when he has an audience. It's over, I will never participate in any activity with him again. I've had enough. Because of Breton, the whole thing all too often lacked a certain seriousness. I had long been determined not to put up with childishness and triviality and bad faith ever again. I want to be able to criticize without Breton relying for his answer on people who don't give a damn about anything, on a herd of sheep. Surrealism shouldn't have become a school, a literary chapel where enthusiasm and god knows what pathetic activism had to answer to authority.[1]

To put an end to it, I will not contribute to *Cahiers d'Art*—the issue on the object—unless Breton, because of my defection, should refuse to contribute without me. Because I don't want to leave Zervos with all the pictures he had done. I will lend my paintings for the London exhibition, because Penrose[2] had given me some money and I committed myself to him. *And that's all.* I don't know what Breton and the others will do afterward. I categorically refuse to answer any request for clarification. It will surely change my life.

PAUL ELUARD

I don't know how. *Between us,* it rather feels like riding the wind. It's not unpleasant. After 18 years,[3] it had all become a habit, an order. Leave the well-established life to others.

When you get back, Zervos will ask Dali for some good photos of his paintings and he'll write a lovely article for *Cahiers d'Art.* The Zervoses are very nice, but shy. In London, I'll lend the 4 Dalis I have, 2 old and 2 new, one of which, the Canaries one, doesn't belong to me. There will be 10 large paintings by Ernst, 10 very important ones by Miró, 8 very large Klees, etc. . . You'll have to tell me where I can borrow some: Noailles and who? And perhaps you might write to the lenders to ask them. Also, lend an important recent painting. This exhibition will be very big (200 important canvases!). Where is the large painting from the *Indépendants:* the *Lénine à la grande fesse?*[4] Etc. . . All paintings must be ready by 6 May. Also write to Caillet[5] immediately and tell him that he must do any photos I choose on your account. We need them *urgently* for the catalog and the English newspapers that are requesting them. Please do that one more thing for me. After that, I won't ask you for anything more to do with collective activity. Who took the picture of my portrait by Dali? I need it.

Other than that, Max Ernst and Man Ray are not far from completely sharing my feelings and my attitude.

I'll send you Tuesday—because we're in Montlignon until then—some issues of the Danish review *Concrétion,* in which Dali is well represented and in which you can read some of my new poems, in French.

Cécile loves you devotedly. So do I.

Ys. frvr.
Paul

217

Postcard: The Eiffel Tower
[Paris, May? 1936]

I'll call tomorrow.

Paul

The statue (on the back) is by M. Salvador Dali, official artist of the Popular Front.

218

Letterhead: Éditions "Cahiers d'Art," 14, rue du Dragon, Paris VIe
[Paris, 15 May 1936]

Friday

My beloved little Gala, today, extraordinarily, I feel very well physically, but I miss you unbearably. An unconquerable melancholy.

I wish I could lean on your shoulder, see you, be with you. You're lucky never to feel such yearning for the past. It's horrible.

And I am so calm, I feel so little need to mope, to shout. Sorry for telling you this. We couldn't have lived otherwise. I am imperfect, childishly complex, edgy, etc. . . But you must not forget me, ever, ever. I have such little attachment to life.

Enough, I felt like tearing this up and writing you only the following:

Monday, Cécile's birthday. She got a lot of presents and was very happy. Yesterday, too, she was at Man Ray's; he has a radio, and she heard me read some poems. She was shaken and moved. She's very, very sweet and loves you fiercely.

PAUL ELUARD

The paintings (150) have left for London. Keller is in America. We couldn't get any Dalis, except for the 4 that were at my place, the 2 paintings (*Le piano aux Lénines* and a very empty one with soft watches) that were at Colle's, and Marie-Laure's *Le Rêve*. Dali will be poorly represented. Max Ernst has 21 paintings, Miró 12 large ones, etc. . . And yet I was pretty insistent on you telling me where to find the large painting from the *Indépendants* (the *Lénine à la grande fesse*). Penrose is going to badger Edward James.[1] But does he have any that can be lent for this? *L'Homme invisible* would have been good. Anyhow, if you tell me where some large and beautiful ones can be had, I'll do the impossible to get them into the catalog on time. And all the other painters except Dali have large drawings? Make an effort, I beg of you.

I've been hearing some strange things about the surrealists' activities, from all over!

Come back soon!

Answer me at once. Because I shall probably leave afterward to rest up at Char's for 3 weeks. I love you, I kiss you all over.

Ys. frvr.
Paul

219

Letterhead: Central Hôtel, Le Mans
[around 20 May 1936]

Sunday

Here since yesterday with the manager of Adler manufacturing and a German driver in a fantastic car that does 155 and sometimes 198 [kilometers per hour] like a dream. It's fun.

Dali's article is on the way. Gala's magnificent object will be well reproduced. I hope you're coming back soon. Write to me. I hope to be better by your return, they'll soon be finished operating on my foot. I'll be moving like the engine of the Adler car.

Write me. Come back soon. I expect to have sold something by your return, and I also expect that Gala will be lucky. It's been a catastrophe for a while now, and I'm looking for work.

Yours forever.
Paul

Yvonne Zervos, with my best wishes

Regards. Nusch

Most fondly Man Ray

Best wishes Christian Zervos

Paul von Guillaume[1]

220

[Paris] 23 May [1936]

My darling little Gala,

Penrose will do as you wish, but he's disappointed. Nevertheless, to compensate him a little, please fix the date on which Dali will give his lecture in London. My own lecture will earn me £10, that is 750 francs. I'll give it on 24 June. Please, write him at once. He's really a very sweet boy, very generous, very nice.

The final operation has been done on my foot. I hope to be walking magnificently soon. In the meantime, I'm very tired. It's cold, I've been coughing. Eight days ago I was spitting blood all day. I think it's because they put an overly strong odorizer in the room to kill the mites. (!!!! hi! hi!)

When are you coming back? When you do, I hope to give you a big surprise. I was told about a surrealist manifesto by the Barcelonians. Try to get it for me. Apparently the art exhibit is very good.

Ys. frvr.
Paul

PAUL ELUARD

221

Postcard: Saint-Raphaël (Var). A section of the port and the sand plot.
Postmark: Saint-Raphaël, 17 July 1936
Addressee: Mme. Dali, 101*bis,* rue de la Tombe-Issoire, Paris 14e

Galotchka dorogaya,

the weather is fine, but I feel a little out of my element here. I hope you received my letter about Cécile in London[1]: *answer me:*
> Eluard-Grindel
> Hôtel des Algues
> Saint-Raphaël (Var)

Don't send anything registered in the name of Eugène Grindel. I kiss you very, very. [*sic*]

Ys. frvr.
Paul

My very best to Dali.

222

[Mougins, first days of September 1936]

Monday

My darling little Gala,

write me at 54, rue Legendre, as we'll be leaving here around the middle of the week. That makes over a month and a half of vacation and we've had enough. Your Fr 1,000 helped me a lot.

I'm sending you a poem and the second half of a poem dedicated to Picasso; the first is in Paris, you'll get it.[1] Tell me what you think of it. I want you to take full advantage of your vacation, to really regain your strength. I expect to see a lot of you when you get back. Send Dali my very best. You also didn't tell me how you found Cecile, her health, her haircut and her memories.

She seems to have taken all the high spirits with her from here. I love you. I'm thinking of you.
I kiss you all over.

Ys. frvr.
Paul

223

[Paris] Tuesday, 15 September [1936]

My beautiful little Gala, I'm very sad that you haven't had good weather. Try to take advantage of the cure even so. Rest a lot, go only for scheduled walks. Don't let events upset you. It's pointless. I myself was somewhat disheartened.

Since I've been back, I've been suffering from my nerves, my head, my skin. I have to see Mabille[1] this afternoon and I hope he'll be able to bring me some relief.

My book of poems comes out next month, illustrated by Picasso (cost: Fr 10). Title: *GRAND AIR*.[2]

Jacqueline left Breton, for good I think.[3] She found work in Algeria. Breton is alone with the child. Breton's parents have lost interest in him.

This morning's newspapers announce that Picasso has been named director of the Prado. Is it true? In that case, he'll have to return there. He's still in Mougins.[4]

Write me. Take good care of yourself. You must be strong. This is not the time to let yourself be beaten down. Everything will be looking up soon. I kiss you all over.

Ys. frvr.
Paul

Best to Dali and to Peter Watson.[5]

224

[Paris, late September 1936]

Saturday

My beautiful little Gala,

I'm impatiently awaiting you.

Dali should send me *at once* a drawing that can be line-blocked for the program of the production of *Ubu* in Paris.[1] The program will be printed very luxuriously. I'm contributing to it. *But it's urgent, very urgent.* He'll have to send it to me by return of post.

Furthermore, I'm leaving for a few days in Belgium, in the middle of next week. I think Dali is familiar with Ubu.

Cécile stayed with me these last two days. I had given her your new address in Cortina d'Ampezzo. I'm writing to her.

My next book: *Grand air,* comes out on 20 October. Tell me what you think of the title?

I can't wait to speak to you about a whole pile of things.

Friendly greetings to Dali and to Peter Watson.

The drawing, this very day, all right?

Yours forever.
Paul Eluard

225

[Paris, 17 December 1936]

Maya dorogaya,

I'm not too sure of your address. Man Ray will give you this letter. I hope, and I'm happy for you that you're beginning to get used to America.[1] I hope you'll have great success there and that it will shelter you from material want for a long time to come.

Nothing new here. Except that the poem herewith included came out this morning in *L'Humanité*. I had lent it to a boy I know and Aragon asked him for it.[2] It's the first time that one of my poems has had a 450,000 run. I can guess what Breton will think of it.[3] But, if I don't change my poetry, I don't see why I shouldn't rather contribute to *L'Humanité,* read by workers, than to N.R.F. or elsewhere, read exclusively by the middle classes. What do you think of the poem?

I'm counting on you to send anything that might be of interest: catalogs, newspapers, reviews, etc. . .

It's not difficult for you, and it keeps me entertained.

I'm also counting on you to write me, to tell me what you're doing, how you're feeling and especially whether you love me, that you're not forgetting me. Your portrait is in front of me. I often dream of you when I'm asleep, always when I'm awake.

I'm doing well, trying to work hard. Cécile's leaving on the 23d to do some winter sports. She's radiant.

I kiss you all over.

Ys. frvr.
Paul

And my very best to little Dali.

226

[Paris]

6 January 1937

My little Galotchka,

our letters crossed. I hope you got mine. Not being sure of the address, I had sent it to Man Ray.

I'm glad the Dali exhibition is doing well.[1] If it continues to, I hope that you'll be able to raise your prices considerably and that you should be freed from material worries for a long time to come.

PAUL ELUARD

I think we'll be able to leave for Le Cannet in 3 or 4 days, to spend a fortnight with Char. But don't let that stop you from writing me. Even if your answer is by return of post, I will have returned by the time it arrives. Write me.

I saw Barr's sumptuous catalog at Mme. Bûcher's.[2] I haven't received it. In any case, *try to bring one back for Cécile*. The reproductions of ancient objects will surely please her. The latter, our daughter, came back enraptured from Chamonix. The trip seems to have given her happy thoughts of independence. She's given her grandmother a shock, as it should be.

I have written over 30 poems in recent days. I've been taken by a great hunger for work. Think about laying aside any document that can put me in touch with the American scene.

I've been offered the directorship of a Spanish-English review. I will be payed but modestly (Fr 700 a month + my contribution). I can do with it as I please. I'm a little hesitant, fearful of giving up my freedom. I'd have a secretary for all the menial work. But it's a real shame you're not here to advise me. I have an appointment with Bergamin later. Maybe that will decide me?

Minotaure seems to be stagnating. Skira's trying to raise money from the Generalitad [sic] to do an issue on Spanish art. I don't think it'll work. *Write me*. I love you. You are forever ubiquitous to me, for the rest of my life. I kiss you all over.

Paul

227

Postcard: flowers
[Le Cannet] 14 January [19]37

My beautiful little Gala,

I've already written you, but you'll only get my letter with this one, since you're in Canada, where, I hope, you'll rest up from the exhaustions of NY. I'm very glad that you're coming back earlier than you had thought. For the moment, we're at Char's in Le Cannet, but we're going home around the 24th.

Pay close attention to my last letter. Tell James what I told you about Skira. I saw the latter on the day I left. He told me that there was more than enough time for me to submit Dali's text upon my return, which I will do. *Minotaure* does not seem very likely to come out.

Bring me back what I asked of you. If you have the time, find out from Levy[1] and at Barr's about the paintings I left with them (because funds are low).

I love you. I kiss you all over. Ys. frvr.

Paul

My very best to Dali.

228

[Paris] 14 February [19]37

My darling little Gala,

how glad this lovely trip you're on makes me. You won't regret it, but you'll have to remain calm and rest well afterward. I received your letter this morning, an adorable letter, a rare, precious pleasure.

I was in bed all week. Since I came back from Cannes I have been constantly in pain. I've only been out once at night, to a Poulenc concert featuring 9 of my poems.[1] Great success. I have heart pains, caused by my stomach. And my ear has been constantly bleeding and festering. I always have a headache. But a deeper and deeper loathing of doctors.

Despite everything, I'm working hard. I did 40 poems to illustrate Man Ray's drawings,[2] I'm finishing a 200-page book of prose (all my prosework) for the N.R.F.[3] and I promised a large book of poems by July for Éditions Kra.[4] If the Writers' Congress is held in Madrid as they say, I hope to be healthy enough to attend. I'm also participating in a congress on aesthetics to be held at the Exhibition in August, where I will read a paper on the following subject: "The Physics of Poetry: Picasso, Ernst, Dali."

Try to bring me back as many documents as possible and especially, for Cécile, books by Barr and Levy. Also the two Dali cards that I had given to Levy. Also, ask Barr *amiably* for a receipt for *Les 2 enfants menacés par un rossignol,*[5] which they forgot to include on the general receipt. Badger them about trying to sell one of my paintings: Chirico, Ernst, or another. Bring me back some photos.

As for *Minotaure,* its publication seems more and more unlikely. It seems that Skira is counting on James's return to work things out. That would be best. Or else that James should decide to found a new review, which I could run.

Breton is going to open a shop selling artwork, paintings, and books. He's being lent the funds.[6] I see him now and then. He's very involved in this Moscow Trials business.[7] Not me.

Cécile is sad that you don't write to her. We were very concerned about the floods. She's very sweet, she adores you. As do I.

Nothing will tear me from you, ever. You are still little Gala, be happy, gay, I'll be seeing you again.

Herewith 4 poems for Man Ray.

[unsigned]

PORTABLE WOMAN

Of a solemn effect in solitude

Earthly mocking the woman
When her heart is elsewhere

If what I love is given me
I am saved

If what I love withdraws
Obliterates itself
I am lost

I don't like my dreams but I tell them
And I do like others' when they are shown me

LETTERS TO GALA

ANGUISH AND ANXIETY

To purify rarefy sterilize destroy
To sow multiply nourish destroy

PARANOIA

In sight of the coast
Heard speak of certain fish
Neighbors of the earth

Let us leave the sea
Let us cling to the movement
Of the solid shores

The river descends like an egg
And we are the birds

STERILE EYES

She is like a bud
The space of flame
Artless she bears the scent
Of lovers intertwined.

229

[Paris, April 1937]

Friday

Galotchka, dorogaya,

   your sweet letter gave me great pleasure. Yesterday, I had Corti send you two English books. He didn't have much. Also the catalog with the Shakespeares in it.

PAUL ELUARD

I did indeed receive Dali's registered letter, two or three days after I wrote to you. The Narcissus-hand is surprising. I'll have it reproduced in my book. But Dali's commentary on his own poetry isn't of much use to me.[1] Anyhow, I'll work it out. A thousand thanks anyway. It was very sweet.

You don't say whether you received the N.R.F. and the page from *Marianne*. I hope so.

I am not very well: constant headaches, dizziness, etc. . . The ear is getting worse and worse. Once again I'm having quite a hard time working.

Cécile came home, well tanned, happy. She's met some young admirers of mine who are delighted to learn that she's my daughter (!!!)

I'm sending along my London lecture. You'll get a luxury edition (!!!)

I'm expecting Mme. Bûcher, who wants to see me about exhibiting Benquet. Perhaps I could sell some, which would be excellent.

Tell me everything you have to do in Paris, I'll do it. You know that I live for you, as always. You are a poor little darling. I want you to be happy. Rest well. Build up your health.

Send my regards to little Dali and to James.

I kiss you most attentively.

                Ys. frvr.
                Paul

                            Saturday morning

I reopen my letter. Last night, Mme. Bûcher came by. She took some Benquets, a Picasso etching and a tiny little Tanguy that I had bought (taken in exchange for) Fr 200. She'll give me Fr 1,000 on account against the future sales of these items.

I reopen my letter because I've just had a terrible dream. We were spending our vacation together. I was telling you that I had never been so happy. There were flowers in all the fields, the paths, the trees.

We get onto a mountain path. Near the path, a chess game is buried.[3]

There is a little path along the mountainside. You can get through. I scream at you, order you: "Get back, get back," because I've just seen that the earth is giving way, the path is crumbling.

You get through, behind you the path falls away into the abyss. Now I'm screaming: "Gala, why, why?" You get through, but suddenly you're sliding away with the path, you're yelling, the earth crushes you, I feel myself going mad. And suddenly I have an idea, I'm going to run all the way to the bottom. I'll reach you or be buried with you. I wake up, I have a hideous headache. I have a 100° temperature. And last night, I purposely didn't eat. I'll stay in bed and end up taking an aspirin, which I had quit doing.

230

[Paris, April 1937]

My beautiful little Galotchka,

I sent you 2 other English books yesterday, as well as some of Levis-Mano's[1] publications. They're always worth a few minutes' entertainment.

I'll go to Corti today to have him send you the book on Nietzsche. It's a shame you didn't receive the N.R.F. with my poems. I'm sending you the clipping. Please be good enough to keep it so I can have it back.

Nusch has been in bed for 4 days. She had a strong attack of fever with kidney pains. My ear is doing rather badly. But rest easy, I'm leading a very regulated life. I don't go out anymore. I go to bed at 9. I haven't been drinking for a long time. I try not to see anybody.

I'm glad you're getting a tan. Stay off your feet and rest a lot, in the open air.

And delay your return as long as possible.

PAUL ELUARD

I hope Dali is able to work well.
Au revoir, my precious Gala.

                Ys. frvr.
                Paul

I'm also sending along a poem that may interest you.

    The loop of your cool and melodious arms[2]
    A springtime affair in the heat
    Green in the white meadows
    Riddled with hope and with dew.

            ◆

    Let us not forget the nightingale
    Nor the chess game hidden in the mud
    Nor the bones of the dead
    Nor the dead leaves joined
    In the eternity of December

            ◆

    A look as wide as silence
    At that moment we are born
    Fortune of the eyes love is without bounds
    An ancient trust preserved
    Generous arms repeated arms
    Fed on dreams
    As if on earth there were but we two
    And the smile of our simple gestures.

            ◆

    We can allow ourselves
    To forget nothing
    Vows without rhyme all was sworn
    From the beginning

    We have nothing left to contrive

    And we lead everywhere.

                      April 1937.

231

[Paris] 1 May [1937]

Galotchka dorogaya,

I hope you've received *The Madness of Nietzsche*[1] by now. I especially hope that you'll waste no time coming home. It's still a little cold now and then, but that's nearly over. It's going to be lovely. I'm feeling well at the moment. I look very healthy. And I'm working.

Did I tell you how magnificent Dali's Narcissus is for my book? It will make an excellent reproduction.

Mr. James passed through Paris. I didn't have the pleasure of seeing him. Never mind. Everybody says he's going to lose his trial.[2] In any case, I don't think that *Minotaure* will rise again from its ashes. It's a real shame.

No news of Julien Levy.

If you write me that you're staying in Semmering[3] a little while longer, I'll send you a book or two. Have you read *The Eagle and the Serpent?*[4] It's the story of Pancho Villa, the Mexican dictator. Fascinating.

I am filled with incommensurable rage at the massacres in Guernica. But I don't know what to do.[5]

When you get back, you'll come to see me. For sure.

I'm thinking of you. We're having lunch with Breton at noon. His store isn't coming along. Breton's not cut out for this kind of business,

Neither is Jacqueline.

I love you. Ys. frvr.

Paul

PAUL ELUARD

232

Postcard: View of the cliffs—Northcottmouth—Bude
Postmark: Truro Cornwall [date illegible]
Addressee: M. and Mme. Salvador Dali, 101*bis* rue de la Tombe-Issoire, Paris XIV (France)
[July 1937]

                                          Wednesday

Dorogaya Galotchka,

this marvelous countryside is very healthful, but not too warm. I was very happy for Cécile's success on the written. If it goes well tomorrow, I swear to you that I shall be more cheerful on her account.

I'm thinking of you. I'm going to try to work. Behave yourself and send me the book fast and your address later.

Regards to little Darys. I kiss you.

                          Paul
                        Lee Miller[1]
                        Regards, Roland Penrose
                        kisses, Nusch
                        Eileen Agar[2]
                        Affect., Man Ray

233

Postcard: humorous
[Truro, Cornwall] Friday [16 July 1937]

We'll be in Paris at the end of next week.

I am steeped in joy by that blessed exam, which people will still be talking about at the end of the century.

We kiss you both[1] very deeply.

                                          Paul

234

[August 1937]

Tuesday

Maya Galotchka dorogaya,

I hope the letter adressed to Saint-Moritz was forwarded to you. I got that address by calling the Faucigny-Lucinges.[1]

You know, it's deplorable that you haven't sent me Dali's book.[2] Passing through Paris, I got a glimpse of it at Breton's. Well!

Speaking of Breton, he published a tract protesting the Jeu de Paume exhibition, an open letter to the ministers, signed (and for the defense) by an "Abstraction-creation" of the 14th order.[3] I've heard that I am regarded at the moment as the worst of pariahs. As I feel the same way about them, it makes no difference. We shall see.

Take care of yourself, rest as much as possible. I'm curious to see Dali's new paintings. I'm glad he likes Nice.

Send him my regards.

I kiss you all over.

Ys. frvr.
Paul

I'm leaving here around 3 September.

235

[Paris, late March 1938]

Here's my address for the next 2 months:
Shadyrock, La Garoupe, Antibes (Alpes-Maritimes).
I had you sent *Cours naturel,* while waiting for the luxury edition.
Little child, I'm glad to be going for a rest.
If you can come to see us, you're invited. It's at Mme. Cuttoli's,[1] a magnificent place.

PAUL ELUARD

I'm leaving. I love you, I kiss you.

Paul

236

[Antibes, early April 1938]

Dear little lovely, dorogaya, I sent you the book in Taormina. I hope it'll be forwarded to you.

No, Antibes is by the sea, but I think it wouldn't do you any harm for a few days.

In any case, I'll still be here at the time of the Ballets Russes in Monte Carlo.[1] And if you come, we'll see one another. Man [Ray] is with us.

I know that you are my best fan. I will know it for all eternity. And I appreciate it.

And I never forget you, my great little Galotchka.

I'll write you again soon.

Ys. frvr.
Paul

237

Postcard: The sandbanks of the Loire, seen from Tours.
[Late July/early August 1938]

Maya Galotchka dorogaya,
we're visiting Tours, looking for a house here.

I hope you received the *Ode to Dali* in good order, with a second copy.[1]

We get home Sunday night and leave again on Tuesday for Mougins (Alpes-Maritimes), Hôtel Vaste-Horizon.

On the off chance, I'll stop by your place for lunch on Monday, around 12:30. But if you have to go out, don't worry about it.

My very best to little Darys. Nusch sends you a kiss.
And so do I, a big one.

Paul

238

Postcard: Hôtel-Restaurant La Pergola, Mougins
Postmark: Cannes, 5 August 1938
Addressee: Mme. Dali, 88, rue de l'Université, Paris VIIe

Dorogaya Galotchka,
we're all settled in here. Come, but with warning, because there's a limited number of rooms and a crowd is expected.
The weather is charming.
We kiss you.

Paul

Received Fr 500 for Cécile.
Hôtel Vaste-Horizon
Mougins, Alpes-Maritimes, train station: Cannes.

239

Postmark: Cannes, 29 August 1938.
Sender: Eluard, 54, rue Legendre, Paris 17e
Addressee: Mme. Dali, Villa Pozzaccio de Marchi, Colonnato (Quinto), Florence (Italy)

Mougins, Monday August 29

Dorogaya Galotchka,

finally, your address, through Cécile's letters. We're returning to Paris tomorrow. Cécile stayed here three weeks, at the hotel, then went camping with Decaunes.[1] She's doing very well, very sweet. She left two days ago for the Pyrénées.

I've worked a lot here, notably on some bizarre little prose texts (you'll find one on the back). Some long poems too. I'll send you some from Paris.

Picasso did but a few paintings, though very beautiful (portraits of Dora,[2] of Nusch and of Mouginois).

I'll do my best to send Cécile the extra Fr 500 you promised her. Send me a check (Grindel), even a crossed one, it doesn't matter.

I've often dreamt of you here. You loved me deeply. How long life is!

Nusch gives you all her best.

I love you and kiss you.

Ys. frvr.

Paul

UNITED[3]

A cavern whose entrance is at the foot of a rock taller than me, and which itself serves as the base of a mountain taller than you. A few paces from the entrance there is a passageway, which leads to a chamber in which we unite, foot to foot, head to head.

240

Letterhead: Hôtel de la Licorne, Lyons-la-Forêt (Eure)
[September 1938]

My little girl,

It will soon be time for the mail. I was very glad to get your letter. I've been thinking of you so much.

I'm doing a little better. I'll write you again.

I love you forever.

Yours, Paul

241

[Paris, around 25 September 1938]

Sunday morning

Maya Galotchka dorogaya,

you can't know how happy I am that you're back in France. I was consumed with anxiety, knowing you were in Italy with this war coming.

Indeed, the day before yesterday we rented a house in Saint-Germain, where I'll go to live soon if we can stay out of war. And yesterday, that partial mobilization (a general mobilization would have been too brutal, but this one is almost as worrying). We were told once before, in 1914, that "mobilization is not war." Officers of all ages (up to 58) have been called up.[1] And great numbers of men.

Is Dali with you? When will you come home to Paris?

Anyhow, I rest easy, happy. Think how I would have suffered, had you been unable to return. Without news. You Russian, Dali Catalonian. And his painting! Everything would have seemed incredibly horrible and impossible to me.

I called Cécile in Montlignon this morning, with your address. Come home, sweet, beautiful, precious little girl.

Nusch sends both of you all her love. I kiss you a.o.

Ys. frvr.
Paul

242

[Paris] Monday, 3 October [19]38

Dorogaya Galotchka,

I'm glad you're thinking of coming home. I was frightfully worried.

I wrote you 8 days ago. You don't seem to have received the letter.

I'm leaving tomorrow for London, where I will stay 3 days. Then, next week, we're moving to Saint-Germain.

Come home soon. I'll have a lot to tell you.

I love you. I kiss you a.o.

       Ys. frvr.
       Paul

Our deepest regards to little Dali.
Nusch sends you a kiss.

243

[Le Pecq, late October 1938]

       Sunday

Galotchka dorogaya,

lovely, subtle, and clear, your letter gave me pleasure. Life here passes peacefully. I'm feeling better. I've started planting flowers and I really hope you'll come see the curtain rise on them.

Fraysse[1] came to see me. He doesn't spare his praises of you.

Cécile is weak. She's coming next week to spend 2 or 3 days here. She's sad. She's been humiliated, wounded by everything we told her about her choice.[2] At her age, one would rather hear speak of love than of the object of love. The reality is love. The object takes on its proportions, its qualities.

Write her a nice letter. At the moment she's just a poor little girl who's bored. And who loves you deeply.

Unfortunately, I haven't written anything since you left. As soon as I have some new poems I'll send them to you.

I kiss you. I love you, you are an adorable little marvel.

       Ys. frvr.
       Paul

All our regards to little Darys.

244

[Le Pecq, October 1938]

Tuesday

Dorogaya Galotchka,

More than 10 days ago, Mme. Cuttoli told me she'd pay for the painting within ten days or so. I don't dare dun her for it. I think it's a sure thing, because she's already had it framed in red morocco by Hugnet.[1] (Espinoza had repaired the tiny scratches.) I'll call Mme. Cuttoli in two days. If I get the money, I'll send it to you at once.

We have a dog, young but very intelligent and already quite big. Well trained, very gentle.

My mother telephoned me today that Cécile is very happy with your sweet letter. She's begun her classes: stenography and law. Neither Nusch nor I are feeling too well. There's too much rain. We never go to Paris. The country is a cure of silence. I think and think of you. I've been kissing you for 25 years.

Paul

245

Postcard: Saint-Germain-en-Laye, the castle and the chapel.
Sender: [Paul Eluard], "Gray House," Allée du Perruchet, Le Pecq (S. et O.)
Addressee: Mme. Dali, c/o Mme. Chanel,[1] Villa Pausa, Roquebrune Cap-Martin (Alpes-Maritimes)

[November 1938]

Dorogaya,

you can live with us. The train is like a subway ride. There's one every 10 minutes until 1 A.M. And it's heated.

I still don't know the date of the wedding. I'll wire it to you. Even so, it would be best for you to come a day in advance.

We're settled in now. We'll be getting a telephone.

My very best to little Darys.

I kiss you. Ys. frvr.

Paul

246

[Le Pecq, late November/early December 1938]

Monday

Dorogaya,

if you're not coming back immediately, I'll send you a few little books. Let me know by return of mail.

My long relationship with Breton and the surrealists is quite over.[1] For your entertainment, here is the latest from M. Breton. Seeing that, in past G.L.M. surveys on poetry,[2] I was often quoted, Breton ordered all his good-for-nothings to answer this time without quoting me.[3] It's shabby. I'm only well in with Ernst, Maurice Heine, Man Ray, Penrose, Mesens, Hugnet, Hayter, Pastoureau, Duchamp, Scutenaire, Nougé, Magritte, Chavée, Arp, Bellmer, Matta, Miró, Picasso, and little Darys.

In my response, I've quoted Breton, Péret; and also, by the way, our fair and worthy Darys.

Dali should respond.

It's not so bad anyway.

I haven't been to Paris in a month. I don't ever expect to be going there again.

The García Lorca booklet is coming out around Christmas. G.L.M. would like to find some subscribers for the Japanese vellum [edition]. Do you have any addresses?

Write me at length. I love you frvr.

Paul

Our kisses to little Darys.

INDISPENSABLE POETRY.[4]
We asked the following question: against any attempt to co-opt, stabilize, or define limits to Poetry, designate for us 20 poems, irrespective of country or era, in which you have recognized the INDISPENSABLE required of you not by the everlastingness of your times but by the mysterious passage of your life.
    respond to: G.L.M.
    6, rue Huyghens, Paris XIVe.

247

[Le Pecq] January 1939

Dorogaya Galotchka,

I received your letter yesterday. I was waiting for it before writing you. We, too, wish you both happiness. That is *most* important to us. And do not put that happiness at risk. And may Dali paint ever more beautiful paintings—and the kind of poetry I like, such as *Le Grand Masturbateur, L'Amour et la mémoire,* and *La métamorphose.*

I gave Cécile the Fr 500 you told me to give her. Mme. Cuttoli's leaving for America in 2 days. She telephoned this morning that she would stop by to see me today or tomorrow and pay me for the painting. I'll send you the money as soon as she does.

As I told you in my last letter, all is *over* between Breton (and those in his retinue) and me. Hugnet was expelled and is receiving threatening letters, mostly because he sees me. Max Ernst, so I've been told, has written a short humorous piece—in the form of a chapter of a novel—against Breton, Péret, Tanguy.[1] Still on my side are also Man Ray, Pastoureau, Penrose, Mesens (these last two not yet in Breton's bad books, thanks to the distance), Nougé, Magritte, and a few others, among whom you two above all. Picasso's wavering between the two.

PAUL ELUARD

I brought a book of prose of about 200 pages to the N.R.F. It will come out, they tell me, in early April. Title: *Donner à voir*.² What do you think? Little Darys will pronounce it: "Donner à boire."

The *Ode à Salvador Dali* is finished being printed. You'll have it, I think, by the end of the week.

M. Levis-Mano, 6, rue Huyghens—Paris XIVe—would be most grateful to you for sending him the addresses of potential subscribers to the Japanese vellum edition. If you get a minute, do so. The book, I think, will be extremely pretty.

I would have liked you to respond to the survey on your 20 favorite poems by signing Gala and Salvador Dali. I know what you like by Péret, Baudelaire, or me, but Pushkin or Rimbaud are harder. And Dali surely likes other things.

I quoted Dali in my previously published response. I'm sending you a few little booklets that will certainly amuse you. Arp, Chirico, Savinio, and Kafka are remarkable. I'll send you some poems soon. Answer me at once. We kiss you.

Ys. frvr., your happiness is essential.

Paul

248

[Le Pecq] 10 January [1939]

Dorogaya Galotchka,

two days before the letter in which I told you I had got the money, I had given Dora Maar quite a thick letter containing five or six booklets (Kafka, Chirico, Savinio, etc...) to mail for me. I'm starting to be fed up with letters that get lost. This one was very intimate, confidential even. Really! And my address was on the back. I'll see if it comes back. But what a bore. Write me at once if you receive it.

Understood, I'll keep the dollars for you (exactly 90 dollars).

Come to think of it, I'll keep 100 for you. And you'll give me Fr 300 back. I think that'll solve your problems. It solved mine.

Don't wear yourself out skiing. Don't break your legs. Be strong. I kiss you. Ys. frvr.

Paul

Nusch sends you both all her love.

249

[Le Pecq] 24 March [1939]

Galotchka dorogaya,

I was worried about the story published in *Paris-Soir* about how the irascible little Dali went through a plate-glass window and was arrested. I should very much have liked to hear the follow-up. Wasn't he injured? Won't they do anything to him? In any case, it can't have hurt his exhibition, quite the contrary.[1]

We're waiting for you. Life is slow in the country. And our nice dog has been very sick. He had the twitches, and meningitis was feared. Even now it's a lugubrious sight. But they'll save him, I hope.

Cécile is in Hyères (Mme. Decaunes, "Val-Rose," blvd. d'Orient, Hyères-les-Palmes, Var). I think she'll regain her strength there.

My guests have left, in very good spirits.

What else to tell you? That the 2 Magots are spreading frightful slander about Dali, who shall certainly be forced to react one day.[2] Otherwise, they'll cause him the worst sort of bother.

I'm not writing. I'm living a quite frightful idleness.

I don't forget you one instant. I dream...

Nusch sends you all her regards. We hope to see you again soon. I love you. I kiss you a.o.

Ys. frvr.
Paul

PAUL ELUARD

250

[Le Pecq] 4 May [1939]

Dorogaya Galotchka,

and yet I wrote you a little while ago. And I was expecting your return. But you're always away so long.

The country's doing fine. So are we. I spend all my days working in the garden. It's giving me a fine slouch, but also a healthy look, very tanned cheeks, forehead, and hands.

I've taken the first steps towards curing my ear, was at the hospital, they're going to x-ray me. Because the sun is making me bleed.

I'm hoping my two books will come out in the coming months: the thick one of prose, and a slim one of verse. Both at the N.R.F.[1] I made a long radio presentation on Rimbaud for America. You might have heard it 24 April. I don't like this type of necessity, and if it didn't pay I wouldn't do it anymore.

You really should send a card to Valentine (2, rue de Sontay, Paris XVIe). The poor thing is floundering in some atrocious difficulties and it would make her very happy.

Cécile often comes to see us. The people she meets at my place entertain her. Her grandmother is ill, she's growing old, but her personality is improving.

I received a letter this morning from an "emigrée princess," Natalie... (illegible), who traveled with you from Berlin to Riga twelve years ago, and kept an ineradicable memory of you. She's in Le Touquet and asks for news of you.

Despite their brevity, your letters always put me in a good mood, mollify me, and give me dreams. I trust you, you can love me, for you never leave my heart. A long life, you see, together.

Goodbye, see you soon, beautiful little Gala. Be calm and happy.

Paul

Nusch sends all her regards to you both. And tell Dali he is well loved. Perhaps he'll come to Le Pecq one day, the sweet "thug"! Have them remove the glass shards from his head.

251

[Le Pecq] Tuesday 6 [June] [1939]

Beautiful little Gala,

I didn't want to alarm you. I don't know who could have told you about this little illness? Nor how?

This is what happened: three weeks ago, I had been coughing for 3 days when, working in the garden on Ascension Day, I had a slight hemorrhage. I took to my bed straightaway. A little more blood came. Mabille arrived an hour later. As I was very weak and they were afraid of a relapse (and I've had a bad time of it in the country), after several shots I was brought to a clinic in Neuilly. I was very assiduously x-rayed with new equipment, which allowed them to see some very dilated and congested bronchi in my darkened lung. And a *very* tired heart. But neither there nor in the analysis, any Koch bacilli. *For certain:* no tuberculosis.

For a long time I had been too steady, as if empty. They're taking care of my heart and my blood circulation and I'm already feeling better. The weather's very fine in Le Pecq, but as I mustn't do any gardening or even stay in the sun, at least for this summer, it's no fun anymore. Life is bland, bland. I'll have to return to Paris over the winter, that's the wisest move, apparently. And perhaps go to the mountains for a bit. The money, all the money, will be gone. Too bad.

But anyhow, don't worry. This occurrence will have been beneficial: without it I shouldn't have taken care of myself. Suddenly, my ear cleared up too, I don't even think about it.

I hope you'll be coming back. My books come out this week, both of them at the N.R.F.

I love you. I kiss you.

Ys. frvr.
Paul

My very best to little Darys.

Thanks for the money. It's Bousquet. I've already received Fr 600, sweet.

252

[Le Pecq, September 1939]

Friday

My little Gala,

we're still in Le Pecq. I may have to leave on short notice.
Cécile is in Montlignon (Seine-et-Oise), 22, rue des Écoles, at her grandmother's. As I don't know my future address, send me a letter through Cécile, who will get it to me.
I think you're well off in Arcachon. Be calm and healthy and behave yourself there.
We kiss you both very deeply.

Paul
Cécile
Nusch

253

Postmark: Mignères,[1] Loiret, 28 September 1939
Addressee: Mme. Dali, 231, boulevard de la Plage (Villa Flamberge), Arcachon (Gironde)

27 Sept[ember] [19]39

Darling Galotchka,

your long letter and Dali's note raised my spirits. Though I'm doing my best in a service that isn't too unpleasant—since it prevents you from thinking 12 hours a day—I feel quite exhausted and depressed on certain mornings and evenings. Because I've been coughing and so has Nusch. (Did I tell you that our dog died?) I don't look unhealthy, I'm tan and already quite fit from walking. Perhaps I'll make it?

I had visits from Cécile and my mother, then from Man Ray, then from Valentine.

But it was your letter that really did me good. It is your affection that is most necessary to me. Don't worry about money. I've been paid and we're spending little. But Nusch won't be able to stay here alone in her room all day, and when it's cold I'll be sleeping at the post. They're going to build me an office and a bedroom at my workplace. The men working with me are all very nice. I'm afraid that if I asked to return to Paris, I would be compelled to remain in an office, which I hate (I fall asleep).

I'm becoming a funny sort of man, ready to forget everything except for a certain fierce hope—which keeps me alive.

Paulhan writes me. He'll publish some of my poems in the November or December issue of the N.R.F.[2]

Behave yourselves and be strong. If I didn't have you, my entire inner structure would crumble. And would my hope survive? I throw great bridges across life, but you are their foundation. Never leave me. Your happiness and confidence in life are indispensable to me. It is not wars that can keep us apart in reality, but that misery hidden within us and which we must kill. We love each other in order to live.

Write to me, little girl.

Kiss Dali for us. I kiss you awf.

> Ys. frvr.
> Paul

Lieutenant Grindel
Commissary Post
Mignères-Gondreville (Loiret).

PAUL ELUARD

254

Mignères [Loiret] [late 1939]

I'm doing fine. I have a lot of work. I'm worried about your future: write me soon.
I kiss you very, very hard, my little girl,

Paul

Lieutenant Grindel
Commissary Post
of Mignères-Gondreville (Loiret).

255

[Mignères] 18 May [1940]

Dear Gala, little one,

write me. I think you got my last letter, in which I told you about my quest for the second fly.[1]
Cécile has probably been evacuated along with the department where she works. She's had no news of her husband.[2]
I have a lot of work.
A line from you would console me.
Regards to Darys.
Nusch kisses you.
Me, you know.

Paul

256

[Mignères] 9 June 1940

Darling Gala,

the second fly has been sold, alas!
I'm worried about having had no news from you for a long while.
Write me.
I'm doing fine, so is Nusch.
We kiss you both, very tenderly,
Ys frvr.

Paul

257

Lieutenant Grindel
c/o M. Charles Bleys   20 June [19]40
Esplanade Octave Médale
Saint-Sulpice—Tarn[1]

Darling Gala,

I arrived in Saint-Sulpice, Tarn, two days ago, after quite a lively trip of 3 days and 3 nights on the road. Nusch had left 24 hours before me. There was just enough time to cross the Loire and beat the awful congestion.

Naturally, I have no news of Cécile, withdrawn 8 days ago to Pougues-les-Eaux, near Nevers, with her department. She's probably left there. If you have any news from her, write me and send me her address.

My mother must have stayed in Paris. I hope so.

You should stay in Arcachon. That would be wisest. Where would you go, anyway?

Why didn't you emigrate to America.

Write me soon. I think that, *under any circumstances,* we'll be staying here a while, until things calm down a bit. Life is going to be very difficult—perhaps impossible for me.

Kiss Dali for both of us.

I kiss you.

Ys. frvr.

Paul

We received the Fr 300. Thanks very much.

258

[*in fine*] Lieutenant Grindel   7 July [19]40
    c/o M. C. Bleys
        Esplanade Octave Médale
           Saint-Sulpice-la-Pointe
              (Tarn) France

Dear Gala,

I have no news of Cécile, who's at your place in Arcachon with your maid. She has money.

As for me, I'm here with Nusch, for how long I don't know. My mother must still be in Paris. I hope nothing's been destroyed in Montlignon, where I have all my things.

Where will we go if I'm demobilized, I don't know?

You can guess how eager I am to get news of you. Write me at once. Will you stay in Figueras?[1]

I am tired and sad. Write.

I kiss you with all my heart, and Dali too.

Paul

259

Lieutenant Grindel 27 July [1940]
c/o M. Bleys
Saint-Sulpice-la-Pointe
(Tarn) France

Darling Gala,

I have your letter of the 22d. I'm very happy for you. When you're in America, write me regularly, I beg you. But have you given any thought to your Paris apartment? What do you hope to do with everything that's in it, because it may be that, 1) you have no interest in keeping it; 2) you won't be able to keep it. Write me about this: if I can help you, I'll do so, either by paying for you, or moving it all out (with authorization), and putting it all in a storage room or elsewhere.

I've been demobilized and I'm hoping that we'll be able to leave for Paris any day now. For the time being, the cost of living is no higher than before. I'll have to find some tiny little lodgings in Paris (though the move from Montlignon will be difficult—there are no cars)—then some work. I saw Gallimard and Paulhan here: there's little chance of the N.R.F. or the other houses picking up again. Very tricky.

Cécile must have written you that Decaunes has been taken prisoner.

Despite everything I'm working. For myself alone, henceforth. Everything's very gloomy. But getting news from you quite often will be a great consolation to me. I love you. Gala, I'll never forget you, whatever happens. Nusch joins me in kissing you.

If you write me by return of mail, there's still time for me to receive your letter here.

[unsigned]

PAUL ELUARD

260

[Paris] Monday, 7 October 1940[1]

Darling Gala, I'll be living at 35, rue de la Chapelle, it's cheap and near my mother's, which will make life easier, hers as well as ours. Every day everything gets harder. Tomorrow I'm publishing a little book, *Le livre ouvert,* at *Cahiers d'Art.*[2] I'll try to send it to you.

If you see Man [Ray], the Barrs, Julien, give them our regards.

We hope that Dali is working and selling his paintings. You must be happy. We'll see each other again one day. We kiss Dali and you, as you can imagine.

Ys. frvr.
Paul

261

[Paris] 18 March 1945

Galotchka dorogaya,

Cécile and I were greatly overjoyed to get your address. Our separation from you had taken on the proportions of a catastrophe. And we would like to know when we will see our little Gala again. It's been too long, too long. I remind myself of an old dodderer now. I can't read without glasses. Everything has changed, except my heart. And the whole past is very distant, except you, for you have always been present within me. Little Gala . . .

I don't quite know what I can tell you about these five years. We had some unhappy times and some happy times. But our misfortune was not so great compared to that of so many others. And we suffered for others, and I assure you there was cause enough. And as my understanding of justice and gentleness hasn't changed, I suffered. Horror was almost always before our eyes. We hoped, despaired, raged, struggled as we could—and aged. I don't know how to laugh too well anymore. But how beautiful were the days of the Insurrection.

Since August of '40, we've been living on the rue de la Chapelle, no. 35 (XVIIIth *arrondissement*), right near by my mother's, which was a good thing, as we were able to take care of one another. Cécile has lodgings at 34, rue du Bac (VIIth). Her husband, Luc Decaunes, is still a prisoner. He has often been in disciplinary camps, for trying to escape. He must be in one at this very moment. He has been very unhappy. And I'm afraid his relationship with Cécile is in deep trouble. Your big girl is beautiful as anything. She's your daughter and I love her all the more for that. She still has her baby face. She's doing film reviews and little articles for the papers. She has talent and, since the liberation, she's been earning her own keep.

For a year, Nusch and I were obliged to go into hiding.[1]

We were lucky to escape the Gestapo.

We managed to save your apartment. But as it's going to be requisitioned any day now (so the concierge has been informed), we'd rather sublet it to people who will formally commit to giving it up if you return. Because that's the risk: as housing is short, occupants can't be made to leave. We'll put anything fragile or valuable in the drawing room, which we'll lock, as well as the study, which is still tidy. Your concierge has been faultless. But I've just found out that you have some things in a storage room here. I'm concerned, afraid they'll sell it to pay the rent. Send me the address quickly, I'll pay the arrears.

Since liberation, I've been earning pretty good change with my poems, more than I could ever have hoped to earn. According to our 1917 agreement, I owe you a fortune.[2] Perhaps you may have received a little book from me. Soon I'll send you an enlarged, complete reissue of it.[3] I'll soon be publishing *Le livre ouvert* (1937–1945): 400 pages.[4]

Published in Switzerland a very beautiful book on Picasso (140 reproductions).[5] Etc...

In any case, remind yourself that life is very difficult here. Many people are falling sick. I've been in bed for a fortnight, I'm feeling better but I can't get up because there's no fire. In January, all the frames were burnt. And it's not even easy to procure heating fuel on the black market. It was exceptionally cold this winter. The snow didn't melt for 3 weeks.

You must find a way to visit us, but not to stay for the winter. Life is *very* hard. And sad. But it would be less sad if you were here.

Kiss Dali very affectionately for us. As we kiss you.

Yours frvr. Paul

Little darling Gala, my father told you everything, we should find a way to tell you the rest in person. We miss you and I love you deeply.

I kiss you, and Dali too. Write us.

Cécile

262

Envelope: Paul Eluard, 35, rue de la Chapelle, Paris (France), airmail
Postmark: Paris, 2 November 1945
Addressee: Mme. Gala Dali, Hotel St. Regis, 55th Street and Fifth Ave, New York N.Y. (U.S.A.)

7 Nov[ember] [19]45

My darling little Gala, it really seems to me as if none of my long letters has reached you.

For a year I was very much taken up with a lot of more or less interesting, more or less practical things. I've begun to have a little peace recently. I systematically refuse whatever I'm asked to do.

You never told me whether you had received my little book: *Au rendez-vous allemand*. I sent it to you through at least five different people. I think we've received all of your parcels, and we thank you for them. But avoid the *Coffix:* a strange and undrinkable concoction. Some concentrated milk would be more useful. Some oil. And some real coffee: in beans. As for Aragon and Picasso, they have what they need. We're doing all right ourselves, for that matter.

Little Cécile is starting to age faster than us. She's going to be remarried. And again at the same altitude.[1] Anyhow, we shouldn't begrudge her this. She was quite alone for many long years. We're a family in which our youth is spent deprived of what we love. She loves you nostalgically.

Thanks to your help a few years ago, we pulled ourselves out of our financial hole. That is what allowed us to rebound somewhat. Nowadays, on this side, we're okay. My books are selling very well. I've got more requests than I can handle.

I'm writing you from my bed. As always on the threshold of winter, I'm coughing. But I'm taking advantage of it to work.

These days, we dream that you'll call us: Fr 600 for 3 minutes. Anyhow, if it's possible, ask for Paris: North 26–40.

My mother's getting very old. Nusch is going to have her gray hair dyed.

Me, I'm going very blond. I kiss you as always.

Paul

Nusch sends you all her regards and we kiss Dali.

263

Envelope: airmail
Postmark: Paris, 9 January 1946
Sender: 35, rue de la Chapelle (Marx-Dormoy), Paris XVIIIe
Addressee: Mme. Gala Dali, Hotel St. Regis, Fifth Avenue and 55th St., New York N.Y. (U.S.A.)

9 January [19]46

Maya Dorogaya Galotchka,

Cécile and I waited in vain for the phone call you had promised for Monday afternoon. We were in a fever over it. Try again as soon as it is possible. We also haven't gotten the photos that Robert de Saint Jean[1] was supposed to bring.

I've been in bed for about two months. Nothing more than the usual winter cough. Nusch is coughing too. Anyhow, our life is no picnic, but we're managing fairly well materially. For I am now very honorably paid for my "writings." I often think about my 1917 promise to share all my author's rights with you. I don't know how I can keep it. I've bought you a few very beautiful books, but that's far from representative of my debt to you. All of this to entertain you, little girl.

What is less funny is the slander spread by Breton and Co. I quash it where I can, but I'd especially like to be able to give the lie formally to the rumor that S[alvador] D[ali] painted the portrait of Franco's ambassador. There are a number of bastards whose traps I'd like to shut.

I think your tenants are leaving in late March. It's no joke, because others who may be less amenable will certainly be put in your apartment.

You should warn me if you're coming back. Because otherwise, I'll try to find someone who is a) neat, and b) who will sign a commitment to leave as soon as you arrive. The apartment problem here is acute: you can't have two, and you also can't have more rooms than are strictly necessary.

Did Cécile tell you that we paid your taxes[?] You're up-to-date. There's nothing to worry about from the landlord.

I'm still concerned about the books you must have left in Arcachon. If they're in a trunk, the marine climate might damage them and even just about destroy them.

Nusch wishes you both a happy New Year. So do I. And I kiss you as always. Please believe that I will always serve and defend you.

Ys. frvr.
Paul

264

Envelope letterhead: Cahiers d'Art 14, rue du Dragon, Paris VIe
Postmark: Paris, 4 March 1946
Addressee: Mme. Gala Dali, 1801 Angelo Drive, Beverly Hills, California (U.S.A.)
Sender: Paul Eluard, 35, rue Marx-Dormoy,[1] Paris 18e

Sunday, 3 March

Dorogaya Galotchka,

I was distressed last night (at midnight) by your phone call and your despair at being unable to hear anything. I could hear you just fine. The sound of your voice was a little distorted, but I recognized your accent and your clipped, innocent way of speaking. Sweet of you to ask if I was cold! Paris is snowbound. I had so many things to tell you, to repeat to you *viva voce*.

Don't fret over Parrot's book. Many others have been written about you, me, Dali, about our personal lives. I didn't read the text before its publication.[2] And let people say what they want: my poems will surely reestablish a little of the *truth*. I myself would not for a second consider reproaching Dali for his disclosure of his earliest relations with you.[3] The purity of our relationship, the great secret, is buried within me and what I or anyone else might say can never destroy it. Therefore smile, little girl, be happy.

Cécile is fine. She was here with her husband yesterday,[4] left as usual loaded down with presents, happy. Her husband's no genius, but he loves her deeply. He is naive and very sweet with her. She's remained very much the little girl, very innocent, very youthful. The same little Cécile.

We received a very lovely package from you today, shipped by the Victory Gift Parcel Co. of New York. It's great and we are very grateful to you for it, for life is once again *quite* difficult.

We came home two days ago from Biarritz, where I gave many classes and lectures at the American University. Nusch had a good rest. Stayed there ten days, very well treated, with countless honors and niceties.

As concerns your return, I think you have everything to lose by it. The political situation is not stable yet. And you can hardly count on many sales of your paintings. The market is bad at the moment. People are holding onto their money. Furthermore, you must realize that life is difficult, very difficult. You need a lot of money. And, above all, everything is tiring. I can't see you forever in the *métro*, and walking, and your apartment is difficult to heat. Mine is tiny, but Nusch never lets up for a minute. In my opinion, you should first make a visit, an investigative and setting-to-rights trip, if you really care to leave America, where Dali enjoys a popularity and benefits that you'll have a hard time recreating here.

The book I asked you for: the *Complete Poetic Works* of Victor Hugo in one bound volume. It costs 4 and a half dollars. But it's in Canada and I forget the name of the publisher. Anyway, it's of no importance.

I would love to have gotten that lout's *VVV*.[5] In general, you should be sure to send me anything to do with modern art and poetry: books in French or English, reviews, etc. . . I'm still a bibliophile. I never got the Dali catalogues that I saw at Marie-Laure's.[6] I only have *The Secret Life*.

My mother's going along very slowly, she's getting old and can barely support herself. We're helping her, because she can't adapt to the changes in the standard of living.

I'm going to send you my latest book, *Poésie ininterrompue*,[7] in which you'll find a 700-line poem.

Always believe that your peace and your happiness matter to me. Kiss Dali for us. Ys. frvr.

      Paul

I'm keeping anything that might interest you.

265

Envelope: airmail
Postmark: Paris, 28 March 1946
Addressee: Mme. Gala Dali, 1801 Angelo Drive, Beverly Hills, California (U.S.A.)
Sender: Paul Eluard, 35, rue Marx-Dormoy, Paris 18e

27 March [19]46

Dorogoya Galotchka,

I really wish you had answered the long letter I wrote you after the aborted phone call. I did receive yours and we saw the notary about your apartment. It will be sublet as if to Casanova, and you'll be guaranteed of being able to reoccupy it whenever you want.

We received your wonderful packages, so did Cécile.

We're leaving for Prague in 3 days (lectures). Nusch will come home 15 April, but I'll be going to Yugoslavia, Italy, and maybe Greece.

Cécile will be going to Switzerland with her husband sometime in April.

Write to me in late April. Try to have someone get me *Arcane 17* by M. Breton,[1] well wrapped (so it won't be damaged—I'm still a bibliophile).

Thanks for the photos. You are still just as youthful and just as beautiful.

Nusch sends her regards to both of you. My love to little bewhiskered Darys.

Ys. frvr.
Paul

PAUL ELUARD

266

Envelope: airmail
Postmark: Paris, 6 August 1946
Addressee: Mme. Gala Dali, Del Monte Lodge, Pebble Beach, California (U.S.A.)
Sender: Eluard, 35, rue Marx-Dormoy, Paris XVIIIe

6 August

Galotchka dorogaya,

perhaps some echoes have reached you about the long trip I took to Czechoslovakia, Italy, Greece, and Yugoslavia. A very difficult, very tiring 3-month trip, but one that did me much good. I was welcomed everywhere with enthusiasm. I had all sorts of affairs and that helped me to feel less old than I am. All of Italy by car. I went from Naples to Athens, then on a slow boat to Salonika. From Salonika to Belgrade by road and train. Came home via Trieste, Venice, Milan.

I've been overworked here since my return. Life is a little less difficult now, but we received your latest, very lovely packages with joy. The catalog and the photos of Dali, too. I like his latest paintings a lot: The Bread, your portraits especially. Galarina is the most brilliant of Stars. I would have liked to have the *Dali News*.[1] I'm going to try to find someone going to America who would be willing to bring you the new editions of my *Choix de poèmes*[2] and *Poésie ininterrompue,* which I don't think I managed to get to you. Needless to say, I would be very happy if you wrote me what you think of them, even in one sentence. For you know very well that you are still my best reader.

Don't worry about your apartment. Everything's arranged in your best interests. I think that if I hadn't chosen Hugnet, you wouldn't have gotten it back. Because the fighting is fierce and the laws ever more draconian.

My little Galotchkou, life has imposed an overly hard separation on us. Try to answer my letters, word for word. And I know that, deep down, you are still the same, my Gala from Clavadel, my eternal little girl.

Ys. frvr.
Paul

267

Envelope: airmail
Postmark: Montana-Vermala, 27 November 1946
Addressee: Mme. Gala Dali, [Del Monte Lodge Pebble Beach California—*address crossed out*] 5th Ave. and 55 St. New York N.Y. (U.S.A.)
Sender: Eluard, Mirabeau—Montana (Switzerland)

Montana, 25 Nov[ember] [19]46[1]

Maya dorogaya Galotchka, here I am once again in Switzerland, not for long (alas, since I'm having a good rest here), for 3 weeks in all. I stayed a week in Geneva, where I had myself examined from head to toe, for I was too exhausted and subject to too much discomfort. The results were not too bad: what is stifling me are my pleuresy adhesions constricting the base of my heart and the movements of my diaphragm. My liver is too big, there's a stone embedded in my gallbladder. Nothing else. But I'm alone here (Nusch stayed in Paris, fortunately, because my mother is very weak and ill, and I fear having to return home any day now—the news was better today), I speak to no one, I work.

For two years I had not been entirely alone one single day. It's made me a little neurasthenic. I'm afraid that you'll find me old when we see each other again. I really don't know how to laugh as before. But I can smile for you, my little Gala forever, even from afar, even in these mountains that we both know so well. Your last letter was very sweet, very helpful to me. From afar, after so long, I need a lot of coddling. I wonder when you're coming home, for I must see you again. It's awful . . .

After having smiled, here I go crumbling under this absence. But forgive me for it: because it's awful to count in years!

Cécile is expecting her little one in April. She's doing well. Write her often. Try to get her something for Christmas, it would make her very happy. She is sweet, beautiful, affectionate, intelligent (the articles she writes are among the best of their kind—she writes very well) and above all, in my eyes, what is sacred about her is that she adores you. Her husband, what can you expect—he's a good boy, not nearly so good as she is, but she must find it more comfortable to rule over inferiors. Nothing to be done about it. You can't hold it against her. It's her business (I hope you think as I do).

In any case, she lacks for nothing. She's earning a little money, and when I have any I give it to her regularly (especially during these months of pregnancy). She even uses it very skillfully to make little deals!

As for me, I am very soon to publish a lovely book illustrated by Chagall[2] and several others illustrated by young artists. Probably, also at Skira, *Cours naturel,* in a typographic milestone illustrated with color lithos by F. Léger.[3] I can see Dali foaming at the mouth from here.[4]

It takes a lot of money to live in France.

I hope you think as I do (I'm even sure of it), that we should avoid leaving any trace of our private life behind us. Thus, I am ripping up your letters . . .

M. Breton, whom I have not met (or glimpsed) since his return, has become petrified in a historic pose, very much the exile—forever and everywhere.[5] Take care not to be too indulgent to his memory, for he never misses a chance to slander Dali. It's not even painful to me anymore to see Breton supported by all the worst kind of reactionaries.

As for me, I am entirely at the disposal of my party, which demands nothing unpleasant from me. On the contrary. I fully approve its politics.[6]

What else to tell you? I have secretly set myself a great task: to rebuild my poetic life from scratch. But I tell you this in the greatest confidence: if you ever hear the name *Didier Desroches,* you'll know that it's me. I haven't told anyone besides Nusch. I'm sick of people buying my poems for the sake of their signature. I'll shortly be sending you what Desroches will have published, his first published poetry, like in Clavadel.[7] How beautiful and unchanged you were in that photo a few months ago, in that evening gown. Send me your photos often.

It's snowing. All is serene. Write me in Paris, where I'm returning next week. Make me a list of books by me that you've had since you left. I sent some to you through Hayter.[8] Do you have them?

Also send me books—catalogs—by Dali—and whatever strikes you as amusing, with pictures.

Give Dali a big kiss from me.

I kiss you with all my heart.

Ys. frvr.
Paul

268

[Paris] 10 March [1947]

My darling little Gala,[1]

it's been a long time since you've written to me. It must be a month since I wrote to you. I had told you that I received some packages from you: all in all, three large ones and a little one since (and my father the same). You're really a savior because there's often a complete lack of meat and I can't run around so much anymore looking for food. I'm really quite round now and starting to be fed up with swelling. The birth is coming up in 4 or 5 weeks now—it's soon and I'm a little nervous. But my health is normal. The doctor examines me every month and says it's going fine. The last time he told me that the baby's head is pointing down, as it should. Even so I get tired faster and stay at home more. I see my father fairly often and we talk about you together. He is affectionate and sweet with me and I think he's happy that I'm expecting, but he isn't getting over Nusch's death and I don't know what to do to help because of course he is independent despite everything. He gives me books, paintings, to cheer me up, he says, but what can I do to cheer him up.

Write me soon, so that I have more of your news before the birth. So long as nothing out of the ordinary happens!! I've been knitting and sewing since I can't run around much but I hope afterward to take up some activity besides motherhood.

If you want to send me some clothes for the baby, I've heard that in America they make a sort of suit for when the child goes out, that covers in one piece the feet, the hands, the legs and the body—with zippers, I think. I've put everything you've already sent me, almost all in blue, together with what I've made. I hope it's a boy but if it's a girl I'll take her anyway.

I'd also like some toothpaste. If you could send me some, and again thanks for the packages.

My grandmother still doesn't go out[2] but she's doing a little better. This makes almost 4 months that she's been sick. The winter is very hard and very long this year and everyone has the flu. I did too. And Dali's books? Have they come out and *will I get to see them?*

How much longer do you expect to stay in New York and what are your plans?

WRITE ME

I love you very, very dearly and think of you. I kiss you and Dali too. Regards from Gérard [Vulliamy].

Cécile

Send me articles on Dali if you have any.

I'm going to a clinic to give birth and I'll be staying there about ten days I think.

Galotchka dorogaya,[3] time passes as it may. I don't do much, I don't go out a lot, I have some nice friends helping me. And Cécile is a little mother just like you were. Still a good month to go!

Living is very difficult. I have a lot of courage. I talk about you every day, even to strangers. But I don't think I'll write anymore. I often dream of you, but I'm afraid of never seeing you again. It's been cold these past months. The earth is still frozen. But I've always had a little fire going.

Cécile is healthy, happy, she lacks for nothing.

Your packages were a big help to us. It's very convenient for me, as I am often alone at mealtimes.

I think of you, I love you, my little Gala. We have truly never been apart. I kiss you very gently. Ys. frvr.

Paul

269

Envelope: airmail
Postmark: illegible
Addressee: Mme. Gala Dali, Del Monte Lodge, Pebble Beach, California (U.S.A.)
Sender: Eluard, 35, rue Marx-Dormoy, Paris 18e

16 June 1947

Galotchka dorogaya,

I should have answered you sooner, but I've been through a very painful patch recently. The pain may have abated, but the emptiness within me and around me is now very great. Without the help of two young friends, a man and a woman,[1] I would certainly not be alive today. Death, the feeling of death, has taken too firm a hold within me. I hadn't thought about it before, nothing had prepared me for it, it was an all too crushing blow. I try to work and for some [time] I've been managing to a little, because they come to give me shots every day.

Neither Cécile nor I have ever seen *L'Énigme de Guillaume Tell.*[2] With M. Levitzki I made an inventory of everything in the apartment, but there are still two 2-meter-long crates and one of books in storage. We'll have them opened when M. Levitzki is back from Italy. And resealed, of course. I'll pay the storage bills, and, I think, have the crates insured, on their advice.

Thanks for all the packages. They have been very helpful to me, especially in my solitary situation. And without them, I really don't know how I could have eaten at home most of the time. The restaurants are very expensive.

Cécile's little daughter is very pretty and well behaved. I don't see her too often, nor my mother, for I've been feeling less and less familial. But anyway, I regularly give Cécile material assistance, as life is terribly expensive if one cares to eat a little.

Thanks for the *Macbeth,* which is very beautiful, and for the dedication drawing too. I was very moved by it. In a large book I'm doing for Switzerland, I'm reproducing in color Dali's painting from Cadaqués that's at your place, *L'âne pourri et les cailloux,* and my poem.[3]

I think of you, of your life, of mine, so threatened now. You'll soon be receiving a book with photos of Nusch. I've signed it with a new pseudonym: Didier Desroches.

I was invited to go to Russia, Poland, Hungary, and Brazil, but I don't have the strength.

I kiss you both. Ys. frvr.

Paul

270

Envelope: airmail
Postmark: Paris, rue de la Chapelle, 13 October 1947
Addressee: Mme. Gala Dali, Pebble Beach, Del Monte Lodge (California) U.S.A.
Sender: Eluard, 35, rue Marx-Dormoy, Paris 18e

13 Oct[ober] 1947

Dorogaya Galotchka,

life goes on for me in curious fashion. I hope to tell you about it some day. I go through long phases of patience and, periodically, fits of despair, rage, drawn-out anger.

I hope you received the book signed by Didier Desroches with the portraits of Nusch. I had entrusted it to Caresse.[1] I should like to have received Dali's *Don Quixote.*

I'm grateful for all your packages. I don't know how I'd get by without them.

I dream of being detached from everything. But there's little chance, alas, of that happening.

I'll never go to America. No strength for it. But perhaps I'll see you again here.

My Gala, forgive my tone. The blow I received was too great. My life is empty.

I kiss you all over. Ys. frvr.

Paul

271

Envelope: airmail
Postmark: Paris, 8 November 1947
Addressee: Mme. Gala Dali, [Del Monte Lodge, Pebble Beach, California—*address crossed out*] Hotel St. Regis 5th Ave. and 55th Street. New York, N.Y. U.S.A.
Sender: Eluard, 35, rue Marx-Dormoy, Paris 18e

8 Nov[ember] [19]47

Dorogaya Galotchka,

it's been quite a while since you wrote to Cécile and me. We're bored and anxious.

Our granddaughter is gorgeous. She's 6 months and 3 teeth old. Even so, she laughs a lot and seems very intelligent.

I'm sending you a bill that's hard for me to pay. For this year, the tax on your apartment comes to Fr 16,000. Hugnet will be paying it. Money is getting entirely out of hand here. Everything is getting more and more expensive. I'm working hard, which allows me to help Cécile regularly. But I can't expect to be buying any more books or paintings.

I wanted to come see you, but I can't get used to the idea of leaving my apartment and also Nusch's grave, all that I have left of her.

Kiss Dali.

You should write to me.

Paul

familial. But anyway, I regularly give Cécile material assistance, as life is terribly expensive if one cares to eat a little.

Thanks for the *Macbeth,* which is very beautiful, and for the dedication drawing too. I was very moved by it. In a large book I'm doing for Switzerland, I'm reproducing in color Dali's painting from Cadaqués that's at your place, *L'âne pourri et les cailloux,* and my poem.[3]

I think of you, of your life, of mine, so threatened now. You'll soon be receiving a book with photos of Nusch. I've signed it with a new pseudonym: Didier Desroches.

I was invited to go to Russia, Poland, Hungary, and Brazil, but I don't have the strength.

I kiss you both. Ys. frvr.

Paul

270

Envelope: airmail
Postmark: Paris, rue de la Chapelle, 13 October 1947
Addressee: Mme. Gala Dali, Pebble Beach, Del Monte Lodge (California) U.S.A.
Sender: Eluard, 35, rue Marx-Dormoy, Paris 18e

13 Oct[ober] 1947

Dorogaya Galotchka,

life goes on for me in curious fashion. I hope to tell you about it some day. I go through long phases of patience and, periodically, fits of despair, rage, drawn-out anger.

I hope you received the book signed by Didier Desroches with the portraits of Nusch. I had entrusted it to Caresse.[1] I should like to have received Dali's *Don Quixote.*

I'm grateful for all your packages. I don't know how I'd get by without them.

I dream of being detached from everything. But there's little chance, alas, of that happening.

I'll never go to America. No strength for it. But perhaps I'll see you again here.

My Gala, forgive my tone. The blow I received was too great. My life is empty.

I kiss you all over. Ys. frvr.

Paul

271

Envelope: airmail
Postmark: Paris, 8 November 1947
Addressee: Mme. Gala Dali, [Del Monte Lodge, Pebble Beach, California—*address crossed out*] Hotel St. Regis 5th Ave. and 55th Street. New York, N.Y. U.S.A.
Sender: Eluard, 35, rue Marx-Dormoy, Paris 18e

8 Nov[ember] [19]47

Dorogaya Galotchka,

it's been quite a while since you wrote to Cécile and me. We're bored and anxious.

Our granddaughter is gorgeous. She's 6 months and 3 teeth old. Even so, she laughs a lot and seems very intelligent.

I'm sending you a bill that's hard for me to pay. For this year, the tax on your apartment comes to Fr 16,000. Hugnet will be paying it. Money is getting entirely out of hand here. Everything is getting more and more expensive. I'm working hard, which allows me to help Cécile regularly. But I can't expect to be buying any more books or paintings.

I wanted to come see you, but I can't get used to the idea of leaving my apartment and also Nusch's grave, all that I have left of her.

Kiss Dali.
You should write to me.

Paul

PAUL ELUARD

272

Envelope: airmail. Please forward
Postmark: Paris, 21 February 1948
Addressee: Mme. Gala Dali, The St. Regis, Fifth Avenue and 55th Street, New York (U.S.A.).
Sender: Paul Eluard, 35, rue Marx-Dormoy, Paris 18e

21 February, [19]48

Little darling Galotchka, I dreamt of you two last night. We were in the country.

You should—and I know you don't write easily—but you should write often and nicely to Cécile, who's being a little neurasthenic, and suffering the consequences of childbirth (stomach and kidney pains, weight loss). This winter, life has again become very difficult. The 1,000-franc note has tended to become the standard unit of currency. Her husband's earning nothing anymore, nobody's buying. Me, I've been giving her Fr 10,000 a month for a while, but that's not nearly enough. Her daughter is costing her. Everything is very difficult. Nobody pays me anymore, and I've been living more and more alone. And now it's snowing and very cold. I only have a miserable little wood stove to heat my four rooms, and it's a problem preparing my meals. Your packages were very helpful to us. But they're not coming anymore. Please understand me. I don't like to worry you, but Cécile especially is in distress. She's very proud, never asks for anything (her grandmother has no more money), but she is morally and materially unhappy. The child keeps her at home. She can barely work anymore. And she's got the idea that you don't love her anymore and that she won't see you again. Although she is fairly hardened, she cries every time she speaks of you.

Once again, my little Gala forever, don't torment yourself over it. You can smooth it out by writing her nicely once in a while and by sending her packages that prove you're thinking of her. She reads English well, and a book like Dali's *Don Quixote*, which I saw in London, would make her happy. Me too, by the way hi! hi! . . .

LETTERS TO GALA

I've been invited to spend a month in Algeria, but I don't think I can leave my home again, Nusch's absence.

Little Galotchka, how I'd like to see you again.

Ys. frvr.
Paul

Give little Dali a big kiss for me. I saw some photos of some very beautiful paintings.

Poems
for
Gala

All the poems published in this volume were found in Gala's home in Cadaqués, along with the letters from Eluard.

Wherever it was possible, the poems were placed alongside the letters with which they were originally sent. The poems that figure in this appendix were those for which this task proved impossible.

These poems offer a threefold interest:

First, the fact that Eluard chose to send them to Gala, a privileged recipient, indicates that these are either poems written specifically for her, or poems to which Eluard attached particular importance—those that required Gala's advice, "the only being whose compliments move [him]," and occasionally that of Dali, "the most authoritative of all."

Secondly, other than a few rare unpublished verses—and Eluard's unpublished verses are extremely rare—they offer us a certain number of variants apparently unknown to the editors of the *Complete Works* in the Bibliothèque de la Pléiade edition. These variants are revealed to be particularly interesting in the case of the anthology *À toute épreuve* (written at the time of Eluard's separation from Gala), for which the Pléiade edition indicates no variants, the poems published here undoubtedly constituting the earliest drafts.

Finally, for some of the poems, certain evidence allows us to suggest specific dates for their composition (see the poems from *La rose publique*).

It will be noted that at least three manuscript poems are absent—*Salvador Dali, Man Ray* and *To Pablo Picasso*—which Eluard claims to have sent to Gala, in letters 140, 181, and 222 respectively. The French editors are unable to account for the missing manuscripts.

[SONG FOR GALA]

My dear, my beloved beauty, there would be a fine song to sing

I do not love, I will not love women
I hate them
I have never loved but Gala

LETTERS TO GALA

If I deny other women it is to affirm this
That I have found no other woman than Gala
To give me a little taste for living
And a great taste for suicide

The little, the tiniest share of happiness she gave me
Was so very pure
That it had to be pulled from a vast dark mine where
nothing else was ever found
From a vast mine of evil like a great threatening fist
closed about a diamond a tiny nothing that can yet blind
he who dares to open the frightful hand
I hate all women I hate antidotes clouds more fair
than hummingbirds, all ceilings, all prisons
I hate love, I love Gala

                    Paul

From *Mourir de ne pas mourir* (1924)

WITHOUT MALICE

Tears to the eyes, misery to the miserable,
Prosaic miseries and colorless tears.
He asks for nothing, he is not unaware,
Sad is he in prison and sad if he is free

The weather is sad, the night is black enough
To keep the blind indoors. The strong
Are sitting, the weak hold power
And the king stands by the sitting queen.

Smiles and sighs of insults rot
In the mouths of mutes and the eyes of cowards.
Take nothing: this one burns, that one blazes!
Your hands are made for your pockets and your brows.

A shadow
All the world's misfortune

PAUL ELUARD

And my love upon it
Like a naked beast.

From *Au défaut du silence* (1925) and *Mourir de ne pas mourir* (1924)

Make up on the she-devil
Makes her pale
She lived to forget.

Spinning in place in the fog
And her face that all surrounds

Get her to laugh, the zealot,
Was she made of stone?
She will crumble.

From *Capitale de la douleur*
(N.R.F. 1926)

♦ ♦

The curve of your eyes is wrapped around my heart,
Dancing in circles of gentle ways
And if I can't say what it is that I've lived
It's just that your eyes have not always seen me.

You really must try not to forget me,
I really must try to be outside the world
I'm afraid of existing through this poem alone
Or even yet through this changing sky.

♦ ♦

The curve of your eyes is wrapped around my heart,
Dancing in circles of gentle ways,
Firm nocturnal cradle, the halo of time
And if I can't say all it is that I've lived
It's just that your eyes have not always seen me.

LETTERS TO GALA

Leaves of day and foam of dew,
Reeds of wind and scented smiles,
Wings that wash the world with light,
Boats with freight of sky and sea,
Hunters of sound and wells of color,

Clutch of pearls, bouquet of dawns
Embalming under straw, embalming under snow.

From *A toute Epreuve*
(October 15, 1930)

COMMENTARY

The scales
From one
day to
another
   or else
the memory
   of just
death
  un-
   to
birth.

The bliss
one day or
another,
of memory
unto just death,
just toward birth.

White trees black trees
Tonight revived the day
And randomness but birth
To forget its aging
Or rediscover nature.

White trees black trees
The youngest of them, nature
Cannot find at random
Its place of birth or aging.

PAUL ELUARD

IN THE LIGHT OF WHIPS

I

These lovely white apotheosis walls,
Are of great usefulness to me
But in earnest, he who does not pay the piper
Juggles with your trousseau, lavender queen.

Is he free? With imperious finger his throat points out
Hallways where the rustlings of his ankles glide.
From dawn to dusk, his hue outmodes his tattooed skin
And the shelter of his eyes bears cloudless doors.

Oh, regicide! your corset belongs to the minions
And to minions of all kinds. Your simple flesh therein evolves
Oh new mediator, there in your ermine you lick yourself all over
Through the cracks in your smile takes flight a howling beast

That joys only in the heights.

                              Paul Eluard

II

Blighting metal, daytime metal, nesting star,
Point of dread, fruit in rags, predatory love,
Knife at rest, useless stain, flooded lamp,
Love's desires, fruits of spite, whorish mirrors.

Of course, greetings to my face!
Where great desires more clearly catch the light than landscapes
Of course, greetings to your spears,
To your cries, to your leaps, to your belly gone to hide!

I have lost, I have won, see what I am mounted on.

♦ ♦

    The violence of the wayward winds
    Ships with grizzled faces
    A permanent home
    And arms for self-defense

An unfrequented beach
A gunshot just the one
Astoundment of the father
Who has been long since dead.

♦ ♦

You should not see reality as I am

Specter of your nudity
Specter child of your simplicity
Puerile tamer carnal sleep
Of imaginary freedoms

Feather of clear water fragile rain
Veil of cool caresses
but the hand caressing me
Is opened by my laugh
By my throat is restrained
And repressed

    Treasures of love
If I speak of your mouth
It's your mouth you should display
It is born it grows it flowers and it dies
It sleeps
Beneath the heavens of your eyes
Where your stars admire and adore
Each other

White trees black trees
Are younger still than nature
To find this randomness of birth one needs
To age

Incredible the conspiracy of angles
  soft as wings

Veil of cool glances

♦ ♦

Feather of clear water fragile rain
Veil of cool caresses

PAUL ELUARD

Of glances and of words
Love that veils that which I love.

Profane men and bodies
Incredible conspiracy
Of angles soft as wings

But the hand caressing me
Is opened by my laugh
By my throat is restrained
And repressed.

Incredible conspiracy
Of discoveries and surprises

♦ ♦

By their intelligence and tact
An abnormal existence

By this strange taste for risk
A mysterious path

In this dangerous game
Bitterness dies at their feet.

♦ ♦

Simplicity itself to write
The hand is here for now.
My eyes have shut behind me
The light is burnt the night beheaded
Heavier than the winds, the birds
Have lost their perch.
In feeble sufferings in folds of laughter
I seek my fellow man no more
Life has declined my images are deaf
All the world's denials have had their final say
They no longer meet but ignore one another
Alone I am alone all alone I have never changed.

♦ ♦

This prison uncrowned
In the open air
This window in flames

LETTERS TO GALA

Where the lightning bares its breasts
A night all green
No one smiles in this solitude
Here the fire sleeps on its feet
Through me.
But this gloom is pointless
I can smile
Doltish face whose desires death cares not to wither
Perfectly free face
That will forever keeps its look and its smile.

If I live today
If I am not alone
If someone comes to the window
And if I am that window
If someone comes
His new eyes do not see me
Do not know my thoughts
Refuse to be my cohorts

And divide so as to love.

♦ ♦

He who sleeps can he have rest
He doesn't see the night nor the invisible
He has some heavy blankets
And pillows of blood over pillows of mire.

His head is in the garret and his hands are closed
About the tools of weariness
He sleeps to test his strength
The shame of being blind in so great a silence.

On the shores thrown back by the sea
He doesn't see the night with heavy storming eyes
Quiet he doesn't see the silent stances
Of the wind that makes man enter his statues.

Sleeping in goodwill
All the way through death.

♦ ♦

PAUL ELUARD

Villages of lassitude
Where the girls bare their arms
Like fountains
Youth grows within them
And laughs on pointed toes

Villages of lassitude
Where every being is the same.

One woman every night
Travels in deep secret.

◆ ◆

The mountain the sea and the bathing beauty
In the houses of the poor
Upon the wilted sky that takes the place of shade
A thousand somber lamps and more do hide.

Here is where the insects come
Sputtering shadows from the fire
A much-rusted flame
Splashes one's sleep
Its bed of flesh and its virtues.

The mass of light roles toward other cares
A field of reflections joins laughter to tears
And closes its eyes and all is fulfilled

To drain the cup of sight

From *La vie immédiate*
(15 June 1932)

◆ ◆

By reason for a panicked man
When the tree melts
When the seasons' sheaves collapse
When the stripped-down glacier
Displays the depths of its heart
Reason head held high

LETTERS TO GALA

Pathetic mast of fortune
Ant-headed lantern
Reason its yoke of indifference

Show me the exuberant prey
The man who burns his bonds.

◆ ◆

All the trees all their limbs all their leaves
Grass at the foot of the rocks and huddled houses
Far off the sea that your eye bathes
These images day after day
Vices and virtues so imperfect
The transparency of strollers on the streets of chance
And strolling girls exhaled by your stubborn pursuit
Your dogged obsessions with leaden heart and virgin lips
Vices and virtues so imperfect
The resemblance of permissive looks to the eyes that you have conquered

The confusion of bodies of lassitudes of fervors
The mimicking of words of attitudes of thoughts
Vices and virtues so imperfect
Love is the man who remains incomplete.

◆ ◆

In procession the convent must be put to flame.

◆

The black-tongued drawing room licks its master[2]
Embalming him his semblance of eternity

◆

Gold filings a treasure a platinum
Flask in the depths of a hideous vale
Whose dwellers have all lost their hands
Leads the gamers to leave themselves.

◆

A red-headed woman with large breasts crosses the Berezina.

◆

Far above the hats
A regiment of eagles galloping on by

PAUL ELUARD

It's a regiment of footwear
All the collections of thwarted fetishists
On their way to hell.

♦

Cataclysms of well-got gold
And ill-got coin.

♦

There was the sawlike door
There was the strength of walls
Boredom without cause
The accommodating floor
Turned to the die's winning forsworn face
There were the windows broken
On which the wind's tragic flesh was rent
There were the protean colors
The swampland borders

Common or garden time
In a forsaken room a room at risk
An empty room.

THE PROBLEM OF SERENITY

To yesterday's sunshine and breeze
That joins your lips
That coolest caress
To roam your modesty's winsome seas
In shade to make of them
The jasmine mirrors
The problem of serenity.

♦ ♦

And so
The natural stream
Is dying by the villas

The boss might talk to his silent son
It's not every day he laughs

LETTERS TO GALA

The whole thing valid for twenty minutes
And for four people
Kills your bent for laughter

The son is taken for a drunk.

EVERY RIGHT

Pretend
The flowering shade of flowers hung in springtime
The shortest day of the year and the eskimo night
The agony of the autumn visionaries
The scent of roses and the nettle's learned sting
Hanging out transparent sheets
In the clearing of your eyes
Display the fire's ravages its inspired works
And the Eden of its ash
The abstract phenomenon's fight against the hands of the clock
The wounds of truth the sermons that do not bend
Show yourself.

You can go out in a crystal gown
Your beauty perseveres
Your eyes shed tears caresses smiles
Your eyes have no secrets
No limits.

♦ ♦

Why are they made to run
They are not made to run
Arriving early
Leaving late

How backward the road
When a slowness is involved

Proofs to the contrary
And uselessness

♦ ♦

PAUL ELUARD

Fatal sun of the host of the living
Your heart is not preserved.

♦ ♦

Ancient actor playing water-plays
Worn out miseries quite transparent
The sweet red iron of dawn
Returns the blind their sight
I attend the raising of walls
The struggle between weakness and exhaustion
The speechless winter.
Images gone by are faithful in their way
They imagine fever and delirium
An entire maze in which my complex hand is lost
A long time ago I fell prey
To hallucinations of virtue
I saw myself hung from morality's tree
I beat the drum of goodness
I caressed my mother.

I have slept all night
I have lost the quiet
Here are voices that know only what they cannot say
And here am I talking
Deafened yet I still hear what I say

In listening to myself I learn.

From *La rose publique*
(December 1934)

THE SKY OFTEN SEES ITSELF AT NIGHT

Mondal is a Parisian
He is of the ancient race of bastards
He is poor frail alone
We see him scratch out a living
He does not attack his foes
His linen flees him

LETTERS TO GALA

His home is cracking
His heart weakening
His eyes have lost their spark
Too late for an idea
Neither sleep nor summer are any solace to him now
He doesn't think of dying
In the stormy plain
Not good not evil
The roots of moaning
Rot away
The green tapestries are folded
Piled up and leveled
Like books
Funereal violets ring the bone
And inertia like pallid lips
The locks of blocked-up ditches
And the hands that beg are seized
By the sweet trembling of the vase
Beneath the mahogany wind
The nerves
Beneath the swollen veins of the endless rain
The fatted earth
Beneath the muted sun
The heart

Magnificent the heavy trappings
Of the usual awful weather
Sure of his road despite mankind

Such misery
Such defiance

And yet there's laughter in the air
Applauding the promises of young blood
Without memories
Promises of cool sunshine
At the window
Of all the brows that mingle with the day

Inexplicably

PAUL ELUARD

Since Mondal son of everything and little
Is alone has nothing and wants nothing

Not even to engage his foes.

Paul Eluard

SHIVERING WITH THIRST, STARVING IN THE COLD

A sublime blue heat
Beats against the panes

Feathers mapping out the beauty to her limbs
The scented one the adult rose the poppy and the torch's virgin bloom

To compose the coated skin of naked women

Floodgates glisten in the door
One must pass despite the siren tower that's taken up the fight
Pass the hillsides the great vegetal beds
Sprinkled with sunshine

And go on
The storm in summer months is like a fingerless hand
Like a cat in a bag
An ostrich smoke announces the riotous summer
Glazed with poisons

Thirsts vary go through graded fogs
Up to the inn to the tide
Of burning stones saddled onto rabid drinkers.

HER GREED HAS NO EQUAL BUT ME

Prodigal world in motion
Cinched in pleasure like a fire
Better than a shadow you make your way through shade
Your mind in tune

LETTERS TO GALA

My heart beats throughout your body
In your favorite retreats
On the white grass of night
Beneath the drowned trees

We spend our lives
Turning back the hours
We invent our time

And suddenly as always
Some sunshine and some birds
Blow across your glances
Alight on your eyelids
Take care not to move
The garlands of your limbs
Are for less subtle feasts
Not one apparent move
We are thought to be still
So unrevealed are we

Give your righteous weight to the dawn
The sinew of the scales on the horizon
A cratered crown of pure air and of wind
Upon your wild hair
A thousand puffs of froth between the sun's lips
Or your blood's beating wing

Lend your strength your warmth
Heavy brutal bitter summer
From your palms and from your mouth
Lend your clear exhaustion

Lend your gentleness your trust
In the expanse of your eyes
There is sometimes a lovely castle
Like a butterfly open to all winds
Sometimes an awful shanty
A final caress
Fated to divide us
Sometimes wine sometimes a river

PAUL ELUARD

Shut in like a hive of bees
Come here docile come forget
So that all may start anew.

**THE FALSE, THE NEGATIVE
LEAD LIFE TO SELF-HATRED**

I

Do not say on a path of stone
Of thick houses smashed by culture
Say not I'm ashamed an unbreathable eagle
Would take you by the throat by the lamp of harvesting tongues
Fear like a faded flower on the current
The prow of nerves against the wind
Monarch don't get on your knees
Mighty continent
As vile as horse and bourgeois combined
Do not take the form of a machine for dealing death
Beware of the menacing topographies of new deliria
Of hands guided by the leafy and tenacious scents
Of the ear that leaves the parlor
Of caresses imposed by the frozen pity of dreams
Were you to run headlong into me
You'd merge once more with pinhead infinity.

II

The most familiar cogs will break
In the gloved hands of prisons
The glowing motion fades the shadows pass
Along the pathway taken at full speed
When the tropics would float on the sea of stars
When the bird-paved sky would sing in the suburbs
Comes to founder here
Our sights were set for raspberries and pearls

For breasts aware of miracles
For the savage roses of the storm

Instead we learn the alphabet of fools.

III

To return one's head to its destiny
The delirium of glowing valves gone wild
Of opposed reflections on upright and wan beds
The scissors of twin flames
Here is the awful fervor of speech not said to be heard
The gesture looking for the void
Hunting for the hanged fishing for the drowned
The great raging frosts the desert's glue
The fight to the death with appearances.

IV

The twilight that dying chameleon
That madman clinging on to me
It should be wrapped in cotton
Leave it just one eye and what else
My room has done its hair for the night
It's on the threshold of its nightwear
Like the rain before the carnival
My room is breaking from my universe
And I no longer know what isn't there

In a lovely witch's home there was a tray of milk
In a hideaway with impenetrable toys
I spoke of the desert's glue and the desert is a bee
Miserable little wormwood shrubs growing in the drought
In the skin of lazy silence
The way one speaks of one's misfortune
With words that only harm the innocent

I also know that clouds with heavy and low throat
Bend the virgin forests over tides of foam

PAUL ELUARD

That the ocean moves like a falling hoop
The stars are on the bridge
The wedded beaches now fly on just one wing

I know there was in the home of a girl better than the first white loaf
Audacity enough to be open to the truth

Truth with its endless procession
Of childish proofs.

◆ ◆

**SHE HAD HERSELF BUILT A PALACE
THAT RESEMBLED A RIVER IN A FOREST,
FOR ALL THE ORDERED APPEARANCES OF LIGHT
WERE BURIED AWAY IN MIRRORS.
AND THE DIAPHANOUS TREASURE OF HER VIRTUE
RESTED DEEP BENEATH THE GOLD AND EMERALDS,
LIKE A SCARAB.**

A copse of clouds on a solar roundabout
A straw-laden ship on a torrent of quartz
A little shade surpassing me
A woman smaller than myself
But weighing as much on pygmy scales
As the brain of a lark on the contrary wind
As the tender-eyed spring on the rising tide

One day further the horizon revives
And shows the rising day the day that would never end
The roof collapses to let the landscape in
Ragged walls akin to archaic dances
The sullen end to a duel to the death where candles and retreats
  begin
Laying to earth the way vermin are killed

Roaring laughter a palette forms
Color burns the stages
Runs from dazzlings to blindings
Shows the azure glaciers the trails of blood

LETTERS TO GALA

The crying wind rolls over its own ears in passing
The bursting sky quivers in the green arena
In a lake abuzz with insects
The valley's glass is full of sweet and limpid flame
Like a duvet
Seek out the earth
Seek out the roads the wells the subterranean veins
The bones of those who are not my peers
And whom no one loves any more
I cannot detect the roots
The light that sustains me

Seek out the night
As temperate as in a bed
Passionate the fairest of adoring girls
Prostrates herself before her lover's sleeping statues
She doesn't think that she's asleep
Life plays the shade the entire earth
Night and day the weather is improving
The fairest of lovers
Offers her outstretched hands
By which she comes from afar
From the end of the world of her dreams
Rushing along stairways of shivers and of moonlight
Through suffocations of jungle
Immobile storms
Hemlock borders
Bitter nights
Livid and forsaken waters
Through mental rusts
Walls of sleeplessness
Trembling little girl with ardent temples
Where the fingertips of kisses lean against the upper heart
Against a stump of fondness
Against the ship of birds
Infinite fidelity
It's about her head that the morrow's certain hours spin
On her brow caresses bring all mysteries to light

PAUL ELUARD

It's from her hair
From the curly gown of the fairest of her dreams
That memories will take to flight
Toward the future that bare window
A little shade surpassing me
An enchanted shade.

◆

A rooster at the gates of dawn
A rooster tolling the bell
Shatters nightly time on shingles of promptitude
A volley of birdsong
Between two unequal clarities
Not so soon shall we raise our head
Toward extinguished stars
Toward the gathering light
Lower it rather on a mouth more ravenous than an eel
On a mouth that hides beneath eyelids
And that soon will hide behind the eyes
Carrier of new dreams
Sweetest of the ploughs
Useless indispensable
She knows where each thing goes
She is fraught with silence
Broken bonds rebellious oaths
Another mouth as litter
The mate of feverish herbs
The enemy of traps
Pure and wild cut for every fit
A mouth oblivious of speech
A mouth illumined by the night's illusions

The first step on that candid road
Drab as a child
Myriad orchids without end
Glowing burning living bridge
Image echo reflection of an endless birth

To gain an extra second
Never more to doubt one will endure.

LETTERS TO GALA

From *Cours naturel*
(10 March 1938)

TO ONE WHO IS GUILTY

Eye you enemy of thorns your sadness is complete
Learn to hide the fact that torture
Pushes back the limits of your desert
Leave the mirthful hangmen to their good works

By great waves of heat in the summer of your thirst
May the dreary sun restrain the mills
Courage equals idle banter
May the spice of good advice rot upon its feet

The old mud is dry they cannot seize those slaves
Between their fettered fingers but your dust
You sustain the fire you refute the squalid hope
Tomorrow only vies don't think of it keep still.

Paul Eluard

Notes

LETTER I

1. San Cristobal, Solomon Islands.

2. On 24 March 1924, Eluard abruptly left France for the Pacific Islands. The causes for his journey, which he himself later called "stupid," are unknown, but increasing pressures from his father to involve himself in the family business, and tension at home due to his wife Gala's liaison with Max Ernst (see note 4), may have played a part. Eluard was gone for seven months, and little is known of his trip other than its itinerary: "The Antilles, Panama, Oceania—stopping in Tahiti, the Cook Islands, New Zealand, Australia—the Celebes [. . .] Java, Sumatra, Indochina and Ceylon." (Louis Parrot, *Paul Eluard,* Poètes d'aujourd'hui, 1972, p. 26).

3. Elena Dmitrievna Diakonova, whom Eluard called Gala.

4. In 1923, Eluard had moved into the villa at Eaubonne, near the Montmorency forest, with Gala, Cécile, and Max Ernst, who had been living with them since September 1922. Ernst covered the walls, ceilings, and doors in frescoes, which were rediscovered undamaged in 1968 by Cécile Eluard, and transferred to canvas.

5. Karl Nierendorf: founder, in 1917, of the publishing house Kairos Verlag, the review "Der Strom," and the "Société des Arts," which exhibited the works of Dada painters.

6. Roland Tual (1902–1956): Participant in surrealist activities between 1925 and 1927, and manager of the surrealist art gallery. Neither a painter nor a writer, he was primarily a great promoter of talent.

NOTES

LETTER 3

1. "Maya daragaya [dorogaya]": "my dear," "my darling," in Russian. Eluard will sometimes use the masculine form, "moy [my] dorogoy," in addressing Gala.
2. The fight between Ernst and Eluard was certainly caused by Marie-Berthe's jealousy over Ernst's affair with Gala.
3. Marie-Berthe Aurenche: Max Ernst's second wife, whom he married in 1927.
4. Clearly, a slip of the pen on Eluard's part, when he means to say "couldn't hold a candle to *you.*" It should be noted that this is not the only instance in which Eluard confused Gala with himself.
5. 3, rue Ordener, the home of Eluard's parents. M. Grindel was to die that year, 1927, and Mme. Grindel was to retain the apartment until her death in 1955.

LETTER 4

1. One of Eluard's aunts.
2. *Yves Tanguy et objets d'Amérique* at the Surrealist Gallery in May–June 1927.
3. Philippe Soupault had recently been expelled from the surrealist group.

LETTER 5

1. Théodore Fraenkel (1896–1964): Childhood friend of André Breton, he was a participant in many Dada demonstrations. In 1921, Eluard dedicated *Rendez-vous* to Fraenkel.
2. Painting by Giorgio de Chirico.
3. Alphonse Kann (1868–1948): Businessman and wealthy art collector connected to the Dada and surrealist movements.
4. The missing word at the end of this sentence may be an intentional omission.

NOTES

LETTER 6

1. Probably Max Berger, director of the Vavin-Raspail Gallery.
2. Mme. Grindel's chauffeur.

LETTER 7

1. The letter and telegram have not been found.
2. Marcel Noll: Connected with the surrealists from 1923 to 1929, he was briefly the manager of the surrealist gallery.

LETTER 8

1. Swiss sanatorium where Eluard stayed almost continuously in 1928–1929.
2. René Nelli (1906–1982): Essayist and bilingual poet, he was a key figure in the Occitanian (Languedoc) renaissance.
3. Eluard exchanged paintings for sculpture and other art objects with Nelli.
4. Joë Bousquet (1897–1950): French writer, co-founder with René Nelli of the review *Chantiers* in 1928, he was involved with the surrealists from 1924 onward. Wounded in combat in 1916, he remained bedridden until his death.

LETTER 10

1. From Marseille; see letter 11.
2. Notary clerk in charge of the building society founded by Eluard's father and of which Eluard was a shareholder. When he died in 1927, Eluard's father left a considerable inheritance to his wife and son. Eluard was thus one of the few surrealists who did not have to struggle for subsistence.
3. Eugénie Lavidière, one of Eluard's aunts.

NOTES

LETTER 11

1. The building society.
2. The country home which Mme. Grindel owned, not far from her son's house in Eaubonne.
3. Nickname ("Gappy") given by René Crevel to Cécile Grindel, Gala and Eluard's daughter, then age six.

LETTER 12

1. Charles Ratton, expert in African and Oceanian artwork.
2. Janine Bouissounouse (1905–1978): A friend of Eluard's, she took charge of the publication of his *L'amour la poésie* in 1928.

LETTER 13

1. One of the doctors caring for Eluard.
2. Art dealer, owner of a gallery on the rue de Seine, who mounted exhibitions of Max Ernst, Miro, and others.
3. Gala's dog.

LETTER 14

1. One of Eluard's shoulders was stooped, due to his pulmonary ailments.
2. Three poems of *Comme une image*, the second part of *L'amour la poésie*, were first published in the "Cahiers du Sud" (April 1928, No. 100) under the title *Décalques*.

LETTER 15

1. "I love you" in Russian.
2. Alexander Blok (1880–1921): Russian poet, supporter of the October Revolution; he was Gorki's collaborator in the paper "Chronicle."

NOTES

3. Eluard's reconciliation with Max Ernst was not completed until October 1928, with his dedication in *Défense de savoir:*

   > my dear Max
   > nothing, ever
   > will destroy our friendship
   >
   > Arosa, 15 Oct. 1928

4. The word here has been written illegibly on purpose.

LETTER 16

1. Finnish epic written by Elias Lönnrot in 1835.

2. Walter Bondy (1880–1940): Painter of Czech origin, he settled in Paris in 1906 and was a member of Dôme, a group of Central European artists.

3. First poem of *Comme une image.*

4. For Lucerne, to meet Gala.

LETTER 17

1. Paul Guillaume, art dealer.

LETTER 18

1. Issue No. 4 (April 1928) of *Chantiers* contains three poems by Eluard: *Je te l'ai dit, Porte comprise,* and *Vous êtes chez moi,* all from *L'amour la poésie.*

LETTER 20

1. Ninth poem of *Comme une image.*

NOTES

LETTER 21

1. "Why aren't you here, dear *Frau* Gala. The most beautiful weather on the most beautiful trip." The signature is illegible.

LETTER 23

1. No book of Eluard's was published without a title. The reference here must be to *L'amour la poésie,* published in April 1929.

LETTER 25

1. Of the real-estate concern of which Eluard was a shareholder.
2. Gala read cards. Eluard, like most of the surrealists, was interested in the occult and also occasionally had his fortune told with cards.
3. 1928 film directed by W.S. van Dyke and Robert Flaherty.
4. A friend of Eluard's from Germany.

LETTER 27

1. "Kniga" is Russian for "book." The reference is probably to a Berlin bookstore specializing in Russian-language literature.
2. Georges Salles, collector of primitive art, was curator at the Louvre in the 1930s.
3. Thea (Élisabeth Dorothea) Sternheim, better known under her pseudonym Mops or Mopsa, was a painter and set designer, and a friend of René Crevel.

LETTER 28

1. A young Berliner, Alice Apfel (whom Eluard called "the Apple," cf. Letters 34 and 39) lived a worldly existence with the adventurer Rudolf van Ripper—certainly the "young man" referred to later.
2. George Grosz (1893–1959): German painter and caricaturist, an early adherent of Huelsenbeck and Haussmann's dadaism.

NOTES

3. Wife and collaborator of Herwarth Walden (see Letter 7), she laid the foundation before World War I for the famous Walden public collection.

LETTER 30

1. Collection of caricatures (1915–1922) published in 1923.
2. *L'amour la poésie,* Gallimard, March 1929.

LETTER 34

1. Clavadel, where Eluard met Gala in 1912; Versailles, where Eluard and Gala lived for some time after World War I; Bray-et-Lu, where Cécile was born in 1918.
2. See note 1, Letter 28.
3. Town in the Tyrol, where Gala and Paul Eluard spent their vacation with Max Ernst in 1922. Imst was a favorite point of congregation for the surrealists.

LETTER 39

1. See note 1, Letter 28.
2. "Flows" ["*coulances*"]: euphemism invented by Gala.
3. This allusion to the "red woman" is untraceable, but probably refers to a woman working in the Moulin Rouge.
4. *Êtes-vous fous,* by René Crevel, Nouvelle Revue Française, Paris, 1929.

LETTER 43

1. Belgian illustrated monthly review, directed by P.G. Van Hecke. The June 1929 issue was dedicated to "Surrealism in 1929."

NOTES

LETTER 44

1. London dealer of African and Oceanian artworks.
2. Pierre Loeb, art dealer who's gallery on the rue des Beaux-Arts held the first surrealist exhibition in 1925.
3. André Gaillard (1894–1929): French poet, one of the founding fathers of *Cahiers du Sud*. Gaillard's accidental death in a fall from a cliff was to occur later that year.

LETTER 47

1. Jacques Baron: French poet, one of the earliest surrealists; he was expelled by Breton at the 11 March 1929 meeting.

LETTER 48

1. Medical treatment using platinum needles heated to white-hot.

LETTER 49

1. Keller, an art dealer, was director of the Georges-Petit gallery in Paris.

LETTER 50

1. This drawing has not been found.
2. Thirteenth poem of *L'univers solitude,* the first part of *À toute épreuve,* N.R.F., 1930.

LETTER 52

1. The Hôtel Regina in Marseille.
2. The reference is certainly to André Gaillard, but what occurred between him, Eluard, and Gala is unknown.
3. The editors were unable to identify "B." Perhaps he is the "Beer (from Arosa)" whom Eluard describes in Letter 159?

NOTES

4. Eluard may have meant an "ulu" (an Alaskan carving).
5. Adolphe Basler, *Henri Rousseau: sa vie, son oeuvre*, Librairie de France, Paris, 1927.
6. This telegram has not been found.

LETTER 53

1. The apartment on rue Becquerel, into which Eluard would not move until October. Eluard had, at first, planned to live there with Gala, but lived there practically alone until Gala and Dali took it over as their pied-à-terre in the spring of 1930.

LETTER 54

1. Camille Goemans (1900–1960): A participant in various surrealist activities, he opened the first gallery devoted entirely to surrealist painters in Paris, where, among others, Salvador Dali was given his first one-man exhibition. Goemans distanced himself from the surrealists around 1930.
2. The "Spaniards" were Salvador Dali and Luis Buñuel, whose film *Un chien andalou* was first screened at Studio 28 in October 1929.

LETTER 57

1. See note 4, Letter 1.

LETTER 59

1. Serge Moreux: decorator, architect, musicologist, and composer.

LETTER 60

1. The mirror of this dressing table was etched (in Eluard's handwriting) with the line: "*D'une seule caresse je te fais briller de tout ton éclat,*" from the seventeenth poem of the first part of *L'amour la poésie*.

NOTES

LETTER 62

1. Eluard was introduced to Salvador Dali in March 1929 in Paris, while Gala was in Switzerland. Accepting an invitation to Spain, Eluard, Gala, and Cécile went to Cadaqués in August. As soon as he met her, Dali, who was still a virgin, recognized in Gala his Gradiva, his "Galotchka rediviva." He decided to seduce her by scenting himself with goat's dung, sticking a geranium behind his ear, and flaying his armpits, spreading the blood around "out of coquetry." Gala, somewhat concerned about his supposed coprophagous tendencies discerned in certain elements of his *Jeu lugubre*, but believing him to be a "half-mad genius," decided to have the matter out. When, during a long walk on the beach, Dali assured her that he was not a coprophagist, they determined never to leave each other again. In September, when the guests—including Eluard, but not Cécile—returned to Paris, Gala remained behind with Dali. (From *La vie secrète de Salvador Dali*, Gallimard, 1979).

LETTER 63

1. A "12" or a "15" designates a painting of average size.

LETTER 65

1. Eluard, like Breton and Gala, collected Belle Époque postcards.

LETTER 67

1. The Vicomte de Noailles, a patron of the arts who owned a villa in Hyères, purchased a great many surrealist paintings.
2. Savinio (Andrea de Chirico) (1891–1952): Italian musician, writer, and painter, brother of Giorgio de Chirico. His poetical texts are a sort of lyric commentary on his common pursuit with his brother, notably in *Les chants de la mi-mort* ("Soirées de Paris," 1914).

LETTER 69

1. Yvonne Bernard, Camille Goemans' lover.

NOTES

2. Silent partner in the Goemans Gallery.

LETTER 70

1. *Un Cadavre* (Imprimerie spéciale du Cadavre, Paris, 1930), a title borrowed from the 1924 surrealist pamphlet against Anatole France, was a protest signed by many surrealists, including Jacques Baron, Raymond Queneau, Jacques Prévert, and Georges Bataille, against Breton's exclusion of others. On the front page, Breton is shown with his eyes closed, a crown of thorns around his head.
2. Poe, who like Baudelaire had been enshrined in the early surrealist pantheon, is attacked in Breton's *Second Manifesto* (Kra, Paris, 1930).
3. A letter signed by the surrealists Georges Sadoul and Jean Caupenne was sent to M. Keller, a senior cadet at the Saint-Cyr military school, threatening to give him a public spanking if he did not resign immediately. General Goureaud, the military governor of Paris, demanded public apologies, which Caupenne tendered, but Sadoul refused to give (he later gave in, in 1932). Sadoul was condemned to three months' imprisonment and a 100-franc fine, which he avoided by fleeing to the Soviet Union with Louis Aragon and Elsa Triolet to attend the Kharkov congress. This is the beginning of the "Aragon Affair."
4. Thirion had fled to Switzerland after unfounded rumors had circulated concerning his imminent arrest as a communist agitator.
5. Suzanne Muzard, a member of the surrealist group from 1927 to 1932, had become Breton's lover after Nadja's disappearance.
6. Probably one of Eluard's doctors.
7. This poem is previously unpublished.

LETTER 71

1. Gala was suffering from pleurisy.
2. Only one of Eluard's lungs was functioning as a result of his illness.
3. Eluard, René Char, and Alice Apfel.

NOTES

LETTER 72

1. The house at Eaubonne.
2. Dali made only two frontispieces for Breton's books, the *Second Manifesto* and *Le revolver à cheveux blancs* (1932). Neither of these can be the book in question, and the drawing must not have been used.

LETTER 73

1. See note 2, Letter 44.
2. *Ralentir travaux,* Éditions surréalistes, Paris, 1930.
3. *La peinture au défi,* Galérie Goemans, 1930. This is his first work devoted to collage.
4. See note 2, Letter 72.
5. *Le tombeau des secrets,* Larguier, Nîmes, 1930.
6. Nickname given to Marc Chadourne. *Vasco* is the title of his first popular novel, published in 1927.

LETTER 76

1. Poem without title in *L'univers solitude* (8).

LETTER 78

1. Expelled from the surrealist movement by Breton in 1930, at the time of the *Second Manifesto,* Robert Desnos was then writing a *Third Manifesto of Surrealism* in which he violently attacked Breton and Eluard.
2. Vladimir Mayakovski (1894–1930): Russian poet, adherent of futurism in 1912, political propagandist during the revolution. His suicide on 14 April, it is said, was caused by the Soviet authorities' refusal to allow him to travel abroad to join the woman he loved, who was not a communist.

NOTES

3. Elsa Triolet, whom the surrealists called Ella, was Mayakovski's sister-in-law.

LETTER 79

1. The apartment on rue Becquerel was finally ready to live in in October 1929. Gala left for her "honeymoon travels" with Dali on 18 November, rarely to return to Paris thereafter.
2. Eluard met Gala in 1912 when they were both 17.
3. Pierre Loeb.
4. 20 drawings by Max Ernst. Gala's is the only copy on Japanese vellum.
5. A monthly pre-surrealist review directed by Breton et al., running sporadically from 1919 to 1924.
6. Crevel was operated on for tuberculosis in Switzerland, in October 1929.
7. Singer who from 1925 to 1930 was the friend of Robert Desnos, who felt an unreciprocated passion for her.

LETTER 82

1. The envelope bears the letterhead of the café "Le Berry-Paris."
2. Dealer of African and Oceanian art.
3. *L'Âge d'or,* written by Buñuel and Dali, directed by Buñuel, financed by the Vicomte de Noailles.
4. *Le surréalisme au service de la révolution (Le surréalisme a.s.d.l.r.)* No. 1, Librairie Corti, July 1930. The front cover, when exposed to strong light, glows in the dark. The luxury edition on Dutch paper was limited to 15 copies, but all copies were "luminescent."

LETTER 83

1. Pierre Colle was a gallery owner in Paris.
2. *Le surréalisme a.s.d.l.r.* No. 2, pp. 24–25: "Vie de l'assassin Foch." Following the publication of this violent and satirical poem against

NOTES

Maréchal Foch, who had recently died, the literary critic of "La liberté" demanded that its author be shot.

3. Maria Benz, known as Nusch (Eluard sometimes writes Nush), whom Eluard had met in May 1930 and would marry in 1934.

LETTER 84

1. Albert Valentin was expelled from the surrealist group in 1931 for having collaborated with René Clair on the film *À nous la liberté*.
2. Coastal resort near Barcelona.
3. On the front cover of *Le surréalisme a.s.d.l.r.* The births of Breton and Aragon occurred during the conjunction of Uranus and Saturn from 1896 to 1898. Although Eluard was born in 1895, the symbolism was meant to include all three of them.

LETTER 86

1. Jacques Rigaut (1889–1929): Dadaist and contributor to *Littérature*. Suicide was a "vocation" for Rigaut—his second attempt was successful.
2. By Simon Schabacher, pseudonym Henri Duvernois (1875–1937).
3. Probably Mack Sennett's 1926 film, *Alice Be Good*.
4. Francis Picabia (1879–1953). French painter, Picabia was in the forefront of the Cubist, Orphist, and Dadaist movements.

LETTER 87

1. This drawing has not been found.

LETTER 90

1. César Moro, Peruvian poet and painter, and a participant in surrealist activities.
2. First part of *L'Immaculée Conception*, which appeared first in *Le surréalisme a.s.d.l.r.* No. 2., and was then published by Corti in November 1930.

NOTES

LETTER 91

1. Eluard and Gala were not divorced until January 1932.
2. Painting by de Chirico from 1914.

LETTER 94

1. Jean-Auguste-Gustave Binet, pseudonym Binet-Valmer (1875–1940): French novelist, inspirer of the cult of the Unknown Soldier. *Prosper Bourguillard, impuissant, Président du Conseil* was published in the monthly review *Les Oeuvres libres* No. 55, January 1926.
2. Perhaps a reference to Brice Parain, an ex-manager of *Détective* magazine. On Henri Barbusse, see note 2, Letter 170.
3. *L'Âge d'or* was shown at Studio 28 from October to December 1930. On December 3, representatives of the "League of Patriots" and the "Anti-Jewish League" ransacked the hall and slashed the surrealist paintings hanging in the lobby. The film was banned by the police.

LETTER 95

1. By turning the card over, one can make out a woman's genitals.

LETTER 96

1. See note 2, Letter 90.

LETTER 97

1. The auctioneer.
2. Valentine Gross-Hugo (1887–1968). A painter and musician, she married the painter Jean Hugo in 1919, and designed many sets for the theater and ballet. She became acquainted with the surrealists in 1930, and illustrated several of Eluard's books.
3. *La Femme visible,* by Salvador Dali, Editions surréalistes, December 1930.

NOTES

LETTER 98

1. *L'Âge d'or* had been commissioned by Noailles. After the *scandale* of its first showing at Studio 28, Noailles tried unsuccessfully to destroy the film.
2. At the 2d International Conference of Revolutionary Writers in Kharkov, Aragon (along with Sadoul and Triolet) signed a text denouncing the *Second Manifesto* ("to the extent that it opposes dialectical materialism"), Freudianism, and Trotskyism. Summoned by Breton to explain themselves, Aragon and Sadoul agreed to write a manifesto implicitly renouncing the positions they had taken in Kharkov and reaffirming solidarity with the surrealists. For the moment, the affair seemed to be resolved.

LETTER 99

1. See note 3, Letter 70.
2. Sadoul was originally from the city of Nancy.
3. René Gaffé, a wealthy collector of surrealist books and manuscripts, and author of a 1945 book on Eluard.

LETTER 100

1. Eluard certainly means "another letter *for* you."
2. A cousin of Eluard's.

LETTER 101

1. In 1931, Paul Eluard was denied a passport for two years. He was never able to determine the reasons for this denial, nor were his or his friends' protests to the Ministry of Foreign Affairs effective in reversing it.

LETTER 105

1. This "calligraphy," which in the next letter has become "galligraphy," most likely refers to the manuscript of a poem by Dali dedicated to

NOTES

Gala—perhaps a fragment of *L'amour et la mémoire* which was to be published in December 1931.

2. *Par une nuit nouvelle*, a poem from *La vie immédiate*.

LETTER 106

1. "That galligraphy" certainly refers here not to a Dali text (see note 1, Letter 105), but to Gala herself.

LETTER 111

1. Eluard, Nusch, Breton, Valentine Hugo, and Sadoul.
2. *Critique de la poésie*. *La vie immédiate* was published in June 1932. This poem was published for the first time in *Le surréalisme a.s.d.l.r.* No. 4, December 1931.
3. Gala suffered from fibroma for which she was operated on at the end of the year.
4. See note 2.

LETTER 115

1. Eluard had visited Gala at Vernet-les-Bains.

LETTER 116

1. See note 3, Letter 119.
2. Jacques Viot, member of the surrealist group.
3. Editions surréalistes, Librairie José Corti, Paris, July 1931.
4. Editions surréalistes, Paris, October 1931.
5. These poems were not found with the letter.
6. Pierre Unik (1909–1945): Welcomed at a very tender age among the surrealists, he published his first work, *Vive la mariée*, in *Le Révolution surrealiste* No. 6, 1926. He joined the communist party in 1927, along

NOTES

with Breton, Aragon, Péret, and Eluard, and would eventually break with the surrealists over the "Aragon Affair."

LETTER 117

1. The card shows an angel from the front and the back, with the captions "before" and "after."
2. Gala, Dali, and René Crevel.

LETTER 118

1. See note 3, Letter 119.
2. This document (a newspaper clipping?) has not been found.
3. Breton was at that time very discouraged by the highly personal, non-ideological tone of issues No. 1 and 2 of *Le surréalisme a.s.d.l.r.*, and was even considering abandoning plans for No. 3.
4. Eluard annotated at least one of his albums of postcards in this manner.

LETTER 119

1. Wife of Jorge de Piedrablanca de Guana, Marquis de Cuevas (1885–1961), a Spanish patron of the arts and friend of Crevel and Dali. She intervened several times on Eluard's behalf to try to obtain his passport.
2. The surrealists had recently come out in support of the Spanish revolutionaries who were at that time fighting the "Bourgeois Republic."
3. Dali's questionnaire, on "the vampire of Dusseldorf and the humanitarian emotions," was in fact very poorly received and remained unpublished.

LETTER 120

1. The Anti-colonialist Exhibition was organized in the Soviet pavilion by the communists in September 1931, in response to the Colonial Exhibition held that spring and denounced by the surrealists.

NOTES

LETTER 121

1. *Les vases communicants.*

LETTER 122

1. The reference may be to Dali's *Rêverie,* published in *Le surréalisme a.s.d.l.r.* (No. 4, December 1931). This text, condemned as pornographic by the French communist party, would be at the heart of the "Aragon Affair" in early 1932.
2. First poem (untitled) of *La vie immédiate.*

LETTER 123

1. The reference to an "altered sentence" is unverifiable.
2. These poems have not been found among the letters.

LETTER 124

1. The A.E.A.R. (Association des Écrivains et Artistes révolutionnaires), founded by Paul Vaillant-Couturier, brought together communists and supporters of Henri Barbusse.
2. Aragon was indicted in January 1932 for inciting military disobedience and murder in his poem *Front Rouge.* The surrealists immediately circulated a petition in Aragon's defense, a petition that brought them the censure of right and left. The surrealists were denounced in particular by the communist paper "L'Humanité" for rising only in defense of their own while remaining passive in the face of repression of the workers. Breton responded to these charges in his pamphlet *Misère de la poésie.*
3. Maurice Heine (1884–1940): Critic and essayist, he was a great champion of the works of the Marquis de Sade. He was a contributor to surrealist publications from 1930 on.

NOTES

LETTER 126

1. Aragon, Unik, Sadoul, and Maxime Alexandre, at that time the only surrealist members of the communist party, were summoned to a party meeting upon the publication of Dali's *Rêverie* (see note 1, Letter 122). They categorically refused the party's request to renounce surrealism.

LETTER 127

1. Clément Vaulet, pseudonym Vautel (1876–1954): a writer for "Le Journal."

LETTER 128

1. Picasso eventually signed the petition in support of Aragon.
2. The A.E.A.R. had in fact already been formed.
3. *Nadrealism danas i ovde*" ["*Surrealism Today and Here*"], Belgrade, June 1932.

LETTER 129

1. This article has not been found. The reference can only be to the anti-Aragon tract, *Paillasse,* which had not yet been published. Paillasse is a farcical character, a clown.
2. Poem published under the title *Le temps d'un éclair* in *La vie immédiate.*

LETTER 130

1. *Misère de la poésie* (see note 2, Letter 124).
2. Pierre Unik, like Maxime Alexandre and Georges Sadoul, chose to follow Aragon, thus cutting himself off definitively from surrealism, which the communist party characterized as a "movement of bourgeois degeneracy."

NOTES

LETTER 131

1. Books by Raymond Roussel.

LETTER 133

1. The manifesto was called *Paillasse! Fin de "l'Affaire Aragon"* (March 1932) and was signed by all the important surrealists.
2. This is how Aragon had described the Soviet Union in his 1924 contribution to *Un Cadavre*, "Avez-vous déjà giflé un mort."

LETTER 134

1. In March 1932, Breton and Valentine Hugo were staying with Dali in Cadaqués. This "note" has not been found.

LETTER 135

1. Mme. Grindel owned the house in Montlignon, and Eluard was hoping to persuade her to buy his in Eaubonne. The deal did not come off.
2. See note 4, Letter 137.
3. These poems have not been found.

LETTER 136

1. Upon becoming a communist, Buñuel may indeed have attempted to "repudiate" *L'Âge d'or* by expurgating certain scenes in order to bring the film into conciliation with Marxist ideology.
2. In 1930, Dali painted several versions of *Dormeuse-cheval-lion invisibles*. One version was hung at Studio 28 at the premiere of *L'Âge d'or*.
3. Of *Le surréalisme a.s.d.l.r.*, published simultaneously with No. 6 in May 1933.
4. This text appears to have remained unpublished.

NOTES

5. *La petite anthologie poétique du surréalisme,* edited by Breton and Eluard, was not published until 1934.

LETTER 137

1. An inquiry done by Marco Ristitch, a Yugoslavian surrealist, and published in *Nadrealism danas i ovde* No. 6, June 1932. The questions focused on the nature of desire, both secret and public.
2. Eluard did in fact include his response with this letter.
3. Mme. Grindel's business manager.
4. Eluard's poem, *Salvador Dali* (later published in *La vie immédiate*), was in fact published for the first time as the preface to the catalog of Dali's exhibition at the Pierre-Colle gallery in May/June 1932.

LETTER 138

1. A photograph showing Eluard and Gala dressed as "Pierrots" in Clavadel, 1913.

LETTER 141

1. *Yves Tanguy,* poem in *La vie immédiate.*
2. In 1932, Miró designed the sets for George Bizet's opera *Jeux d'enfants.* In 1926, the surrealists had indeed "heckled" Diaghilev's ballet *Romeo and Juliet,* whose sets were designed by Ernst and Miró.

LETTER 142

1. The surrealists, like everyone else, were feeling the effects of the Depression by 1932, and Eluard had moved into Breton's house on the rue Fontaine. His modest loft was a great contrast to the middle-class comforts of the rue Becquerel (see Thirion, *Révolutionnaires sans Révolution,* Laffont, 1972).

NOTES

LETTER 131

1. Books by Raymond Roussel.

LETTER 133

1. The manifesto was called *Paillasse! Fin de "l'Affaire Aragon"* (March 1932) and was signed by all the important surrealists.
2. This is how Aragon had described the Soviet Union in his 1924 contribution to *Un Cadavre*, "Avez-vous déjà giflé un mort."

LETTER 134

1. In March 1932, Breton and Valentine Hugo were staying with Dali in Cadaqués. This "note" has not been found.

LETTER 135

1. Mme. Grindel owned the house in Montlignon, and Eluard was hoping to persuade her to buy his in Eaubonne. The deal did not come off.
2. See note 4, Letter 137.
3. These poems have not been found.

LETTER 136

1. Upon becoming a communist, Buñuel may indeed have attempted to "repudiate" *L'Âge d'or* by expurgating certain scenes in order to bring the film into conciliation with Marxist ideology.
2. In 1930, Dali painted several versions of *Dormeuse-cheval-lion invisibles*. One version was hung at Studio 28 at the premiere of *L'Âge d'or*.
3. Of *Le surréalisme a.s.d.l.r.*, published simultaneously with No. 6 in May 1933.
4. This text appears to have remained unpublished.

NOTES

5. *La petite anthologie poétique du surréalisme,* edited by Breton and Eluard, was not published until 1934.

LETTER 137

1. An inquiry done by Marco Ristitch, a Yugoslavian surrealist, and published in *Nadrealism danas i ovde* No. 6, June 1932. The questions focused on the nature of desire, both secret and public.
2. Eluard did in fact include his response with this letter.
3. Mme. Grindel's business manager.
4. Eluard's poem, *Salvador Dali* (later published in *La vie immédiate*), was in fact published for the first time as the preface to the catalog of Dali's exhibition at the Pierre-Colle gallery in May/June 1932.

LETTER 138

1. A photograph showing Eluard and Gala dressed as "Pierrots" in Clavadel, 1913.

LETTER 141

1. *Yves Tanguy,* poem in *La vie immédiate.*
2. In 1932, Miró designed the sets for George Bizet's opera *Jeux d'enfants.* In 1926, the surrealists had indeed "heckled" Diaghilev's ballet *Romeo and Juliet,* whose sets were designed by Ernst and Miró.

LETTER 142

1. The surrealists, like everyone else, were feeling the effects of the Depression by 1932, and Eluard had moved into Breton's house on the rue Fontaine. His modest loft was a great contrast to the middle-class comforts of the rue Becquerel (see Thirion, *Révolutionnaires sans Révolution,* Laffont, 1972).

NOTES

LETTER 143

1. *La vie immédiate,* which was published by Éditions des Cahiers Libres in June 1932, simultaneously with Breton's *Le revolver à cheveux blancs* and Tzara's *Où boivent les loups.*

LETTER 145

1. René Laporte (1905–1954): Poet and publisher, he was head of the Éditions des Cahiers Libres, where he edited and promoted the surrealists' writings.
2. *Comme deux gouttes d'eau,* José Corti pub., Paris, 1933.
3. *Comme deux gouttes d'eau* was published without illustrations.
4. The manuscript contains many variants to the published version.
5. *Babaouo, un film surréaliste* by Dali was brought out by Cahiers Libres in mid-July 1932.
6. *This Quarter—Surrealist number* Vol. V, No. 1 (September 1932), containing Eluard's article *Poetry's evidence.*
7. Corti had actually published many books prior to this, most notably *L'Immaculée Conception* (1930). It seems, however, that Corti was widely regarded as a vanity publisher, whereas Laporte was editor of a large and prestigious house.

LETTER 146

1. Like Eluard, Valentine Hugo lived in a studio on the rue Fontaine. "That one room" must refer to Eluard's studio, which he did not give up until April 1933.

LETTER 147

1. Dullita is the name of the heroine in *Rêverie,* Matilde being her mother, while Ellena, also a character in *Rêverie,* surely represents Gala—Hélène.

NOTES

LETTER 148

1. Dali and Gala left 7, rue Becquerel, and moved into 7, rue Gauguet, in July 1932.

LETTER 153

1. Eluard's nickname for René Crevel.

LETTER 154

1. Jules Gonon, publisher, binder, and a friend of Eluard's, published Eluard's first book, *Le devoir et l'inquiétude* (1917).

LETTER 155

1. Printed text, glued to the head of the letter.

LETTER 157

1. Crevel, suffering from tuberculosis, joined Eluard at the sanatorium.
2. Probably *L'objectivité poétique* (see note 2, Letter 165).
3. The Marquise Cuevas de Vera (see note 1, Letter 119).

LETTER 159

1. See note 2, Letter 52.
2. *The System of Doctor Tarr and Professor Fether* (1845).
3. In 1933, Skira published *Les Chants de Maldoror* with 52 engravings by Salvador Dali.

LETTER 160

1. The reference is to *La lumière éteinte* . . . , a poem from *La rose publique* (1934).

NOTES

2. Eluard at first wrote "if Dali were to die (or to go mad)," then crossed out the second alternative.

3. Dali and Gala were married on 30 January 1934.

4. Dali had been estranged from his father since 1929, when his father learned that the caption beneath one of his son's paintings at an exhibition read: "Sometimes, just for the pleasure of it, I spit on my mother's portrait." This, as well as Dali's affair with Gala, were the cause of an estrangement that would last until Dali's return to Europe in 1948.

5. Issues Nos. 5 and 6 of *Le surréalisme a.s.d.l.r.* were published concurrently in May 1933, after an eighteen month hiatus.

LETTER 161

1. Eluard later modified the end of the title (see Letter 163).

2. Boris Kochno, choreographer of the Ballets Russes, and a friend of Dali.

LETTER 163

1. First published in *Le surréalisme a.s.d.l.r.*, this poem was then included in *La rose publique*, with significant differences to the manuscript version presented here.

LETTER 164

1. Jaroslav Hašek (1883–1923): Czech novelist and journalist, author of the classic *The Good Soldier Schweik,* a cycle of novels that remained unfinished at the author's death.

2. Albert Skira, publisher.

3. *Minotaure,* the first issue of which appeared in June 1933. Tériade ran it, while Breton, Eluard, Duchamp, Heine, and Mabille formed the editorial review board.

4. In issue No. 7 of *La Critique Sociale* (January 1933), Bataille says of Eluard's poetry that it is "avidly consumed by a certain type of enlightened *amateur* of modern literature, but has nothing to do with poetry."

NOTES

LETTER 165

1. *Les pieds dans le plat,* Éditions du Sagittaire, Paris, 1933.
2. First published in *Le surréalisme a.s.d.l.r.* No. 5, May 1933, this poem was then included in *La rose publique.*

LETTER 166

1. Final section of "Poetic Objectivity . . ." (see Letter 165).

LETTER 167

1. "My sweet," "my pretty" in Russian.
2. Eluard's nickname for Salvador Dali.

LETTER 168

1. "*Boeuf*" is French for "ox" or "beef."

LETTER 169

1. Dali's survey questions went as follows:
   Surrealist experimentation.
   1) What are the two *objects* or *things* (natural or artificial) that currently seem to you to be the most "poetic," that is, which constitute the rarest and most exceptional psychic images, phantasms, and collisions?
   2) What objective reasons can you give to justify your choice?
   3) What subjective reasons?
   4) What irrational reasons?
   same questions for objects or things in memory
   same questions for objects or things in dream.
2. No such tract, written in collaboration with Yves Tanguy, seems to exist; the nocturnal context leads to the supposition that Eluard is referring to a dream.

NOTES

LETTER 170

1. To the rue Legendre, where Eluard and Nusch lived until the fall of 1938.
2. Eluard was writing on the back of an announcement for a conference to be held by the A.E.A.R. on March 21: "FASCISM AGAINST CULTURE." The speakers included Eluard, André Gide, René Crevel, André Malraux, and Charles Vildrac, among others, but Eluard's "very bad company" refers specifically to the honorary chairs, Romain Rolland and Henri Barbusse. Barbusse, editor for "Le Feu," a socialist weekly, and Rolland, a prolific writer, apostle of Gandhi and heroic idealism, were, according to the surrealists, "the most dangerous propagators of a humanitarian mysticism more pernicious on the whole than any abstract theology." (Thirion, op. cit.)
3. After the Reichstag fire, Hitler, the new chancellor, accused the communists of arson. Blacklisted by the Nazis, Bertolt Brecht (d. 1956) and Ludwig Renn, both communists, were not killed but forced to emigrate.
4. *Spektrum*.
5. This poem has not been found.

LETTER 171

1. Alfred Kurella, a Comintern delegate, whose job in France, among others, was to "silence the surrealist cackle by whatever means necessary." (Thirion, op. cit.)
2. In fact, the surrealists did not quit the A.E.A.R. until June 1933, when Breton was expelled.

LETTER 172

1. Eluard had contracted to pay Laporte Fr 6,000 (Fr 3,000 of which as a loan) toward the publication of issues 5 & 6 of *Le surréalisme a.s.d.l.r.* To raise the Fr 5,000 he was short, Eluard arranged a swap of either paintings or manuscripts with the Vicomte de Noailles.

NOTES

2. Achim d'Arnim, *Contes bizarre,* introduction by André Breton, illustrations by Valentine Hugo, Cahiers Libres, 1933.
3. Emilio Terry, architect, was an underwriter of "Zodiaque," a circle of art collectors committed to ensuring Dali the regular purchase of his work.

LETTER 173

1. "Interprétation paranoïaque-critique de l'image obsédante 'l'Angélus de Millet,' " *Minotaure* No. 1, 1933.

LETTER 174

1. Mme. Grindel's chauffeur.

LETTER 177

1. *Man Ray,* final poem of *La rose publique,* first published in *Man Ray— Photographs 1920–1934,* James Thralle Soby, Hartford, Connecticut.
2. Survey published in *Minotaure* No. 3–4, December 1933.

LETTER 178

1. Ovid's *Metamorphoses,* illustrated by Picasso (1931) and Mallarmé's *Les poésies,* illustrated by Matisse (1932).

LETTER 179

1. Édouard Mesens (1903–1971): Poet, one of the founders of the Belgian surrealist group.
2. Paul Nougé (1895–1970): Early founder of the Belgian communist party after World War I, a regular contributor to many surrealist publications.

NOTES

LETTER 180

1. Eluard's optimism was justified. After this double issue (Nos. 3–4), the surrealists effectively controlled *Minotaure*.
2. Eluard's hostility toward Tériade, an art critic and contributor to *Cahiers d'Art*, stems from Tériade's 1929 bad review of the first Dali exhibition.
3. Six anonymous "involuntary sculptures" were reproduced in the issue: "Rolled-up bus ticket . . . ," "rolled-up bus number . . . ," "piece of soap exhibiting spontaneous art nouveau forms . . . ," "ornamental and art nouveau bread . . . ," "morphological randomness of toothpaste . . . ," "elementary curling found in a mental defective."
4. Man Ray, at Duchamp's request, provided photographs of art nouveau architecture in Barcelona for *Minotaure*.
5. Duchamp did not contribute to No. 3–4. An avid chess player, he had already written myriad articles on the subject.
6. Joseph-Vicente Foix, an early proponent and promoter of surrealism in Spain.

LETTER 181

1. "Le phénomène de l'extase," *Minotaure* No. 3–4, p. 77, is a photomontage of faces "in ecstasy."

LETTER 182

1. As Dali did not respond to the survey, and the involuntary sculptures remained anonymous, his name appears only four times.

LETTER 184

1. From 1926 to 1929, then from 1935 to 1936, Vriamont was a publisher of songs, such as those by Paul Magritte, the sheet music of which appeared with illustrations by his brother, René Magritte.
2. No book by Dali was published by Donoël during that period.

NOTES

3. The reference must be to Dali's *The Enigma of William Tell*. This enormous painting, measuring over three meters by two, was very poorly received by the surrealists because of its supposedly "gratuitously indecent" portrayal of Lenin, and in fact a surrealist "commando" made a thwarted attempt to slash it.

LETTER 185

1. During the rapid consolidation of Nazi power, Dali compared Hitler to Maldoror. As early as 1933, he felt that Hitler had to be judged "from the surrealist point of view," convinced that the surrealists were the only ones capable of "saying pretty things on the subject" (from a letter from S. Dali to A. Breton, 29 July 1933). Forty years later, associating Hitler and Lenin, he would reiterate that his sexual delirium was incited by Hitler's "plump edibility": ". . . Lenin and Hitler excited me to the highest degree. Hitler more than Lenin, for that matter. His plump back, especially when I saw him in his shoulder- and swordbelts that squeezed his flesh, elicited in me a delicious gustatory shiver of buccal origin that brought me to a Wagnerian frenzy. I often dreamed of Hitler as a woman" (Dali, *Comment on devient Dali*, Laffont, 1973).

2. Eluard is certainly refering here to the many Dali paintings inspired by Millet's *Angélus*.

LETTER 189

1. The meeting of 5 February. Order of the day: "Dali having been guilty on several occasions of counter-revolutionary activities tending to glorify Hitlerite fascism, we the undersigned propose [. . .] to expel him from surrealism as a fascist element and to fight against him by every means available." At this meeting, Dali's clownish behavior contrasted markedly to the solemn tone of the convocation. Feigning the flu, he discoursed with a thermometer in his mouth, interrupting himself to take his temperature. He lost his socks and knelt before Breton as if before the Holy Altar, read a startling tract demonstrating the surrealist character of his admiration for Hitler. Breton interrupted him brutally: "How much longer are you going to bother us with your Hitler?" To which Dali responded with an invocation of the theory of surrealist "ireponsibility" developed by Breton himself and illus-

NOTES

trated in a most unique fashion by Dali: " 'Therefore, André Breton,' I concluded, 'if I dream tonight of making love with you, tomorrow morning I will paint our favorite love-making positions with the most luxurious attention to detail.' Breton was transfixed; with his pipe clenched between his teeth he sputtered furiously: 'I wouldn't advise it, old chap.' " (S. Dali, op. cit). Dali was not expelled by the surrealists.

2. Eluard did in fact refuse to vote for Dali's expulsion.
3. Gala and Dali were married the week earlier.
4. Fascist riots had rocked Paris on 6 February, the day before.

LETTER 190

1. These documents have not been found.

LETTER 192

1. This poem has not been found.

LETTER 193

1. *Une personnalité toute nouvelle,* pp. 11–15, *Documents 34.* The first poem of *La rose publique.*

LETTER 195

1. No surrealist group exhibition was in fact held in Paris in June 1934.

LETTER 196

1. Jean-Louis-Ernest Meissonier (1815–1891): French genre painter whom Dali considered a genius.
2. Jeanne Bûcher indeed published the *Petite anthologie poétique du surréalisme* in June 1934.
3. No poem was found with this letter.

NOTES

LETTER 197

1. *La rose publique,* published by Gallimard in December 1934.

LETTER 198

1. This article has not been found.

LETTER 201

1. To 3, rue Ordener, where Eluard's mother would live until the end of her days. When they weren't in Paris, Mme. Grindel and her granddaughter lived in Montlignon.
2. See note 1, Letter 197.
3. In fact, lacking money, Eluard did not go, and Breton went to the Canaries with Benjamin Péret. The Spanish painter who organized their trip must have been Oscar Domínquez, who brought the Paris surrealists into contact with those from Teneriffe.

LETTER 202

1. Eluard married Nusch on Tuesday, 21 August 1934.

LETTER 203

1. Book by Jensen, interpreted by Freud. Dali makes several references to it in his *Vie secrète*.

LETTER 204

1. The beginning of the letter is in Nusch's hand. She gives Gala news of Eluard's health.
2. Eluard's anger with Skira seems to derive from the fact that, in *Minotaure* No. 7, a de Chirico painting (possibly *Melanchonia*) belonging to Mme. Grindel was reproduced without her permission and after Eluard had specifically declined the offer of Fr 500. Despite his assertion here, Eluard continued to contribute to *Minotaure* until 1938.

NOTES

3. Zwemmer: the Zwemmer Gallery in London, the sole *Minotaure* correspondent from England.
4. Painting by Dali, called *Day break* in the 1936 London exhibition catalog.
5. René Crevel who, having fallen ill once again, was staying in Davos with Eluard at the time.
6. René Crevel, *Dali ou l'antiobscurantisme*, Ed. surréalistes, Paris, 1931.

LETTER 205

1. See note 1, Letter 213.

LETTER 206

1. Vitezslav Nezval (1900–1958): Co-founder of "poetism" and of the first Prague surrealist group (1934). Prolific poet, novelist, dramatist, and translator.
2. Karel Teige (1900–1951): A theoretician of Czech literature and plastic arts, with Nezval she founded "poetism" and Czech surrealism. Also founded the artists' and writers' group "Devetsil," dedicated to "proletarian literature."
3. Jindrich Styrsky (1899–1942): Painter, photographer, occasional poet and essayist, Styrsky was the co-inventor, with Toyen, of "artificialism," an offshoot of "poetism."
4. Maria Germinova Toyen (1902–1980): Czech surrealist painter, Toyen was a strong contributor to all activities of "Devetsil," as well as Styrsky's lover.
5. Vincenc Makovsky (1900–1966): A sculptor, member of the Czech surrealist group.

LETTER 207

1. The Canaries were the site of the first international surrealist exhibition, at the Ateneo de Santa Cruz in Teneriffe in May 1935.
2. M.A. Cassanyes, Spanish art critic; Jaume Miratvilles, Spanish writer, author of *El ritme de la revolución*.
3. *Minotaure* No. 7, June 1935.

NOTES

LETTER 210

1. A mummified hand, a sort of good-luck charm that Gala had given to Eluard.
2. Alfred A. Barr, who, in late 1936, organized the enormous exhibition at the New York Museum of Modern Art, *Fantastic Art, Dada and Surrealism*.
3. *Sur*, an Argentinian monthly.
4. Pierre Matisse, a New York gallery owner and the son of Henri Matisse.
5. *Facile*, published in October 1935 with 12 photographs of Nusch by Man Ray.
6. Christian Zervos, director of the review *Cahiers d'Art*. As a publisher, Zervos produced the famous Picasso *Catalogue raisonné*.
7. *Du temps que les surréalistes avaient raison*, Ed. surréalistes, August 1935. Following the violent incidents between the communists and the surrealists at the *Congress of Writers in Defense of Culture* (incidents which may have contributed to René Crevel's then recent suicide), this pamphlet formalizes the rift between the two groups.

LETTER 211

1. Anne-Marie Hirtz ("Lise") Deharme, woman of letters and a friend of Eluard.

LETTER 212

1. This is almost certainly a reference to Benquet, a blacksmith and naif painter from the Landes region.
2. In issue no. 5–6 of *Cahiers d'Art* appeared for the first time Eluard's poems *La nuit est à une dimension, René Magritte,* and *Max Ernst*.

LETTER 213

1. *Nuits partagées,* with two drawings by Dali, Editions G.L.M., Paris, July 1935. These poems had been published in *La vie immédiate* in 1932.

NOTES

2. These poems, which were not found with the letters, were not published in *Sur* until April 1936. They are *Où la femme est secrète, l'homme est inutile, Un soir courbé,* and *Chasse.*

LETTER 214

1. On Picasso, at the time of a large Picasso exhibition in Spain. Ramon Gomez de la Serna: Spanish writer.

LETTER 215

1. *La barre d'appui,* with three engravings by Picasso, was published in June 1936.

LETTER 216

1. Eluard's definitive break with Breton did not occur until 1938. But the gap between them can be seen to be growing in these letters from 1934, as evinced by the disagreement over Eluard's title for his book *La rose publique* and the "Dali trial." (See note 1, Letter 189.)
2. Roland Penrose (1900–1984): painter, photographer and poet, the inaugurator and organizer of surrealism in England.
3. Eluard had met Breton in 1918.
4. *L'Énigme de Guillaume Tell* (see note 3, Letter 184).
5. Caillet, a photographer who took many pictures of surrealist artworks, especially for Eluard.

LETTER 218

1. Edward James, the poet, did indeed loan *Paranoiac Head* for the exhibition (#62 in the catalog).

LETTER 219

1. Paul von Guillaume, probably one of the drivers. The last signature is illegible.

NOTES

LETTER 220

1. The exhibition of surrealist objects held by Charles Ratton, expert on African art, in May 1936.

LETTER 221

1. This letter has not been found.

LETTER 222

1. The manuscript of this poem has not been found (the bottom of the page is cut away).

LETTER 223

1. Pierre Mabille (1904–1952): Doctor and essayist, contributor to and co-director of *Minotaure* from 1937 to 1938.
2. The definitive title would be *Les yeux fertiles*, illustrated by Picasso, G.L.M., October 1936. *Grand Air* is the title of one section of the anthology, of one of its poems, and of one of Picasso's illustrations.
3. Jacqueline Lamba, the muse of *L'amour fou*, married Breton in August 1934, a week before Eluard and Nusch's marriage. They remained together until 1943.
4. Picasso was indeed named director of the Prado, but never even considered accepting the nomination.
5. British art lover and promoter of Dali in England.

LETTER 224

1. *Ubu enchaîné*, by Alfred Jarry, produced by Sylvain Itkine in September 1937, sets designed by Max Ernst.

NOTES

LETTER 225

1. Dali and Gala had arrived in New York on 7 December 1936. They remained there for four months.
2. The reference is to *Novembre 1936*, published in *L'Humanité* on 17 December. A critical note appearing with the poem proclaims Eluard as "one of the greatest poets of his generation." The poem was not found with the letter.
3. Since August 1935, the surrealists had been in open battle with the communists, and therefore with *L'Humanité* (see note 7, Letter 210).

LETTER 226

1. *Fantastic Art, Dada and Surrealism,* Museum of Modern Art, New York, Dec. 1936–Jan. 1937.
2. Jeanne Bûcher, who published several of Eluard's books, also owned a gallery on the boulevard Montparnasse in Paris.

LETTER 227

1. The Julien Levy Gallery in New York, where Dali had his first New York exhibition. Julien Levy also published the first surrealist anthology in the United States: *Surrealism,* Black Son Press, NY, 1936.

LETTER 228

1. Francis Poulenc, *Tel jour telle nuit,* nine melodies on poems by Paul Eluard. The poems used were:
Bonne journée (À Pablo Picasso);
Une ruine coquille vide (je croyais le repos);
Le front comme un drapeau perdu (Être);
Une roulotte couverte en tuiles (Rideau);
À toutes brides (Intimes II);
Une herbe pauvre (Balances III);
Je n'ai envie que de t'aimer (Intimes V);

NOTES

Figures de force (Intimes IV);
Nous avons fait la nuit (Facile).

2. *Les mains libres,* drawings by Man Ray illustrated with poems by Paul Eluard, Éditions Jeanne Bûcher, Paris, November 1937.
3. *Donner à voir,* which was not published until 1939.
4. *Cours naturel,* Éditions du Sagittaire (Kra), March 1938.
5. Painting by Max Ernst that Eluard owned and which was used in the *Fantastic Art, Dada, Surrealism* exhibition.
6. The Gradiva Gallery.
7. In January 1937, Breton spoke before the Trotskyist International Workers' Party, denouncing the second Moscow Trials.
8. Published in *Oeuvres Complètes* by the Bibliothèque de la Pléiade.

LETTER 229

1. An example of Dali's commentary on his own poetry can be found in a letter to Eluard written in April 1937:

   Dali believes that poetry is "the most lyrical expression of thought," from which it follows that the *musical* expression of thought corresponds to the actual verses, when man is truly inspired, begins to sing like a nightingale and immediately creates opera, *Rhyme,* therefore, corresponds to actual poetic technique, especially as *constraints* of this type are favorable to the blossoming of interesting automatisms, as (. . .) for Vermeer, constrained by technique and freer than anyone. Surrealist automatism is indispensable, it is a kind of diarrhea, a torrential colic (. . .)

2. *L'évidence poétique,* lecture read in London on 24 June 1936, and published in *Cahiers d'Art,* No. 6–7, 1936.
3. See the second stanza of the poem adjoining Letter 230:

   "Let us not forget the nightingale
   Nor the chess game hidden in the mud . . ."

LETTER 230

1. Guy Levis Mano, Parisian publisher (Éditions G.L.M.).

NOTES

LETTER 225

1. Dali and Gala had arrived in New York on 7 December 1936. They remained there for four months.
2. The reference is to *Novembre 1936*, published in *L'Humanité* on 17 December. A critical note appearing with the poem proclaims Eluard as "one of the greatest poets of his generation." The poem was not found with the letter.
3. Since August 1935, the surrealists had been in open battle with the communists, and therefore with *L'Humanité* (see note 7, Letter 210).

LETTER 226

1. *Fantastic Art, Dada and Surrealism,* Museum of Modern Art, New York, Dec. 1936–Jan. 1937.
2. Jeanne Bûcher, who published several of Eluard's books, also owned a gallery on the boulevard Montparnasse in Paris.

LETTER 227

1. The Julien Levy Gallery in New York, where Dali had his first New York exhibition. Julien Levy also published the first surrealist anthology in the United States: *Surrealism,* Black Son Press, NY, 1936.

LETTER 228

1. Francis Poulenc, *Tel jour telle nuit,* nine melodies on poems by Paul Eluard. The poems used were:
Bonne journée (À Pablo Picasso);
Une ruine coquille vide (je croyais le repos);
Le front comme un drapeau perdu (Être);
Une roulotte couverte en tuiles (Rideau);
À toutes brides (Intimes II);
Une herbe pauvre (Balances III);
Je n'ai envie que de t'aimer (Intimes V);

NOTES

Figures de force (Intimes IV);
Nous avons fait la nuit (Facile).

2. *Les mains libres,* drawings by Man Ray illustrated with poems by Paul Eluard, Éditions Jeanne Bûcher, Paris, November 1937.
3. *Donner à voir,* which was not published until 1939.
4. *Cours naturel,* Éditions du Sagittaire (Kra), March 1938.
5. Painting by Max Ernst that Eluard owned and which was used in the *Fantastic Art, Dada, Surrealism* exhibition.
6. The Gradiva Gallery.
7. In January 1937, Breton spoke before the Trotskyist International Workers' Party, denouncing the second Moscow Trials.
8. Published in *Oeuvres Complètes* by the Bibliothèque de la Pléiade.

LETTER 229

1. An example of Dali's commentary on his own poetry can be found in a letter to Eluard written in April 1937:

   Dali believes that poetry is "the most lyrical expression of thought," from which it follows that the *musical* expression of thought corresponds to the actual verses, when man is truly inspired, begins to sing like a nightingale and immediately creates opera, Rhyme, therefore, corresponds to actual poetic technique, especially as *constraints* of this type are favorable to the blossoming of interesting automatisms, as (. . .) for Vermeer, constrained by technique and freer than anyone. Surrealist automatism is indispensable, it is a kind of diarrhea, a torrential colic (. . .)

2. *L'évidence poétique,* lecture read in London on 24 June 1936, and published in *Cahiers d'Art,* No. 6–7, 1936.
3. See the second stanza of the poem adjoining Letter 230:

   "Let us not forget the nightingale
   Nor the chess game hidden in the mud . . ."

LETTER 230

1. Guy Levis Mano, Parisian publisher (Éditions G.L.M.).

NOTES

2. Undated poem published in *Cours naturel* (March 1938) under the title *Toute la vie*.

LETTER 231

1. Erich Friedrich Podach, *Nietzsches Zusammenbruch*, N. Kampmann, Heidelberg, 1930.
2. The reference must be to a lawsuit by Edward James against Skira concerning *Minotaure*, but both the causes and the outcome of this suit are unknown.
3. In the Austrian Alps.
4. *El Aquila y la serpiente* (1928), by Martin Luis Guzman, Mexican novelist and revolutionary.
5. Guernica was bombed and utterly destroyed by the German airforce on 26 April 1937, with 1,654 dead and 889 wounded, almost all civilians. After the massacre, Eluard wrote *La victoire de Guernica*, a poem first published in *Cahiers d'Art* No. 1–3, 1937, then in anthology in *Cours naturel* in 1938.

LETTER 232

1. Man Ray's assistant, married to Roland Penrose in 1947.
2. Painter, a member of the English surrealists since 1936.

LETTER 233

1. Gala and Cécile.

LETTER 234

1. Prince Faucigny-Lucinge, member of Zodiaque and a friend of Dali.
2. *La Métamorphose de Narcisse*, Éditions surréalistes, June 1937.
3. Dali had eight paintings at the exhibition *Origines et developpement de l'art international indépendant* held at the Jeu de Paume from July to October 1937. A tract endorsed by 50 signatures—with Breton's on

NOTES

top—protested the "unjust" exclusion of certain "universally known" artists and the overrepresentation of "certain others," who are not named, though the allusion is certainly to Dali.

LETTER 235

1. The wife of an Algerian senator, the friend of Eluard, Picasso, etc., Marie Cuttoli had taken over the Kahnweiller Gallery to exhibit tapestries she owned by Braque, Léger, Miró, and Picasso.

LETTER 236

1. Dali was working on the set of a Ballet Russe production, *Bacchanale,* costumes by Coco Chanel, choreography by Leonid Massine. Because of the war, the production was delayed a year and finally opened at the New York Metropolitan Opera House in November 1939.

LETTER 237

1. *Ode to Salvador Dali* by Federico García Lorca, published in *La Revista de Occidente,* April 1926.

LETTER 239

1. Luc Decaunes (1913–   ): French poet, the first husband of Cécile Eluard, to whom he was married in November 1938.
2. Dora Maar, photographer and member of the surrealists since 1934. Introduced by Eluard to Picasso in 1936, she became his lover and is the subject of many of his portraits.
3. *Unis,* nineteenth poem in the first part of *Donner à voir.*

LETTER 241

1. Eluard, at the age of 43, held the rank of lieutenant in the Reserves.

NOTES

LETTER 243

1. Jean Fraysse, writer, co-director with Roger Lannes of the review *Les Feux de Paris*.
2. The reference must be to Cécile's projected marriage to Luc Decaunes.

LETTER 244

1. Georges Hugnet (1906–1975): Poet, creator of "book-objects," he was a member of the surrealists from 1933 to 1939.

LETTER 245

1. See note 1, Letter 236.

LETTER 246

1. For the specific occasion of the break between Breton and Eluard, we have only Breton's explanation in his *Entretiens*, published in 1952, the year of Eluard's death. While in Mexico, Breton learned of attacks published against him in the review *Commune*, directed by Romain Rolland and Louis Aragon, which published shortly thereafter, in May 1938, an Eluard poem on the Spanish Civil War, *Les vainqueurs d'hier périront*. Breton protested by letter to Eluard, who declined to answer. On his return, he found that Eluard was ready to defend his decision to publish in *Commune*, on the grounds that it implied no solidarity on his part with the review's publishers and that his poetry was strong enough to be judged on its own merits, regardless of the vehicle. Breton, at that point, informed Eluard that any further meeting between them was pointless. Without questioning Breton's account, we can assume that this disagreement was merely a pretext for a definitive end to their relationship that had been brewing for at least four years (see note 1, Letter 216, and note 3, Letter 225). Finally, we can also note that, in his letters to Gala, Eluard had ceased to mention Breton's name eighteen months earlier (since Letter 234), though he had mentioned it often prior to that.
2. *Les Cahiers G.L.M.*, a monthly review.

NOTES

3. Max Ernst, in *Écritures* (N.R.F., 1970) and in *Propos et présence* (P. Gonthier, Seghers) has corroborated this assertion. "... [Breton] had asked all the members of his group to undertake to boycott Paul Eluard's poetry by every possible means." Hans Bellmer, "the chief's emissary," came to inform him that "each member of the surrealist group had to commit himself to sabotaging Eluard's poetry by every means available to him. Any refusal would entail expulsion..."

4. Press clipping stapled to the letter.

LETTER 247

1. *L'Homme qui a perdu son squelette* [*The man who lost his skeleton*], a novel by Hans Arp, Léonora Carrington, Marcel Duchamp, Paul Eluard, Max Ernst, Georges Hugnet, Henri Pastoureau, Gisèle Prassinos, etc. Published in *Plastique* No. 3 and No. 4, imprimerie Jourde, Paris 1939.

2. *Donner à voir*, Gallimard, Paris, June 1939.

LETTER 249

1. Dali had been asked to dress a window for Bonwit Teller on Fifth Avenue, on the theme of the "Narcissus complex." His display featured a bathtub filled with water and floating narcissi, mirrors, and a headless mannequin dressed in a green negligee. The display attracted a large crowd, and the store manager replaced the offending mannequin with more conventional ones. Seeing this, Dali demanded that his name be removed from the display, and when this request was refused, he entered the window, demolished the mannequins, and went to overturn the tub. But the tub slipped and smashed through the window, showering Dali with glass. He was taken into police custody and ordered to pay the cost of the broken window.

2. The surrealists, who held meetings at the café Les Deux Magots.

LETTER 250

1. The "thick one," *Donner à voir*, would be published in June 1939, and the slim one, *Chanson complète*, in May.

NOTES

LETTER 253

1. On 3 September 1939, Eluard was mobilized with the rank of lieutenant into the Commissariat at the commissary in Mignères-Gondreville in the Loiret region.

2. *Pour vivre ici*, first published in *Nouvelle Revue Française* No. 314, November 1939, then in anthology in *Le livre ouvert* in 1940. Jean Paulhan, the *éminence grise* of French letters, had introduced Eluard and André Breton in 1919.

LETTER 255

1. Gala collected flies.

2. Luc Decaunes remained a prisoner of the Germans throughout the war.

LETTER 257

1. After the rout, the Commissariat fell back to Saint-Sulpice in the Tarn region.

LETTER 258

1. As the Germans advanced, Gala and Dali left Bordeaux, which was under bombardment, and managed to reach Spain two days before the Germans took the Hendaye bridge. Gala went to Lisbon to arrange their passage to America, and Dali visited his father in Figueras.

LETTER 260

1. The beginning of the letter is in Cécile's hand, and is not reproduced here.

2. *Le livre ouvert (1938–1940)*, Cahiers d'Art, Paris, 1940.

NOTES

LETTER 261

1. In late 1942, Eluard and Nusch left their apartment on the rue de la Chapelle and went to live incognito on the rue de Tournon. In November 1943, they took refuge in Saint-Alban-sur-Limagnole, in the Lozère region, in the psychiatric hospital of Doctor Bonnafé, who sheltered members of the resistance, where they remained until February 1944.
2. On Eluard's authorship rights, see Letter 263. 1917 is the year Eluard and Gala were married.
3. *Au rendez-vous allemand,* December 1944.
4. *Le livre ouvert* (I–II) (1938–1944) was not be published until 1947.
5. *À Pablo Picasso,* Éditions des Trois Collines, Geneva-Paris, December 1944.

LETTER 262

1. Both of Cécile's weddings took place in the mountains.

LETTER 263

1. One of the twelve original members of Zodiaque.

LETTER 264

1. Formerly rue de la Chapelle.
2. Louis Parrot, *Paul Eluard,* Seghers, Paris, 1944. The book contains nothing of a nature that should have alarmed Gala.
3. In S. Dali, *The Secret Life of Salvador Dali,* published in 1942 (see note 1, Letter 62).
4. After the war, Cécile Grindel was remarried to the painter Gérard Vulliamy, who, in 1946, illustrated Eluard's *Souvenirs de la maison des fous,* written while in hiding in Bonnafé's hospital.

NOTES

5. *VVV,* a surrealist review founded by André Breton in America during the war, and directed by Breton, Marcel Duchamp, and Max Ernst. "That lout" may refer either to Breton or to Ernst.
6. Marie-Laure de Noailles (see note 1, Letter 67).
7. *Poésie ininterrompue* (I), Gallimard, Paris, January 1946.

LETTER 265

1. André Breton, *Arcane 17*, Brentano's, New York, 1945.

LETTER 266

1. *Dali News, Monarch of the Dailies,* first issue published in New York in 1945 in conjunction with the Dali exhibition at the Bignou Gallery.
2. First published in 1941, *Choix de poèmes* was reissued by Gallimard in a new, enlarged edition in July 1946.

LETTER 267

1. Three days after writing this letter, Eluard, while resting in Montana, learned by telephone of Nusch's sudden death of a cerebral hemorrhage.
2. *Le dur désir de durer,* with 25 original drawings and a frontispiece by Marc Chagall, Arnold-Bordas pub., Paris, November 1946.
3. This project was never brought to completion.
4. Dali considered Chagall "today's most inept painter." (Dali, *Entretiens avec A. Bosquet,* P. Befond, 1966.)
5. Breton returned from the United States in the spring of 1946.
6. In the spring of 1942, Eluard requested reinstatement into the communist party, then illegal.
7. It was in Clavadel that Eluard wrote his first poems.
8. Stanley William Hayter, engraver, who worked on the illustrations of *Solidarité* in 1938, and was the sole illustrator of *Facile proie,* which also appeared in 1938.

NOTES

LETTER 268

1. The first half of the letter was written by Cécile Grindel.
2. Up to her death in 1955, Mme. Grindel refused to step outside her home.
3. Eluard's handwriting, usually so neat, trembles here.

LETTER 269

1. Jacqueline and Alain Trutat, to whom Eluard dedicated *Le temps déborde*.
2. See note 3, Letter 184.
3. *Voir,* poems, paintings, drawings, Éditions des Trois Collines, Geneva, April 1948. *L'âne pourri* (1928), a Dali painting, was reproduced here with the poem *Salvador Dali,* from *La vie immédiate*.

LETTER 270

1. Caresse Crosby, a wealthy American and a friend of Dali, with whom Dali and Gala had left for the United States. It was at Caresse Crosby's home that Dali wrote his "secret life."

Index

Agar, Eileen, 231
Alexandre, Maxime, 125, 126, 136, 312
Andre, M., 197, 198
Apfel, Dr., 167
Apfel, Alice (the Apple), 30, 32, 35, 37, 39–40, 42, 43, 53, 54, 74, 75, 98, 298, 303
Apollinaire, Guillaume, 170, 206
Apple, the, see Apfel, Alice
Aragon, Louis, 39, 73, 77, 78, 94, 98, 103, 113, 119, 120, 121, 122, 123, 125, 126, 127, 130, 131, 135, 158, 190, 222, 253, 303, 306, 308, 310, 311, 312, 313, 333
Armani, M. Jules, 65
Arnim, Achim d', 170, 174, 320
Arp, Hans, 239, 241, 334
Ascher Gallery, 84
Aurenche, Marie-Berthe, 4, 6, 43, 294

Barbusse, Henri, 94, 307, 311, 319
Baron, Jacques, 47, 300, 303

Barr, Alfred A., 208, 210, 223, 224, 225, 251, 326
Basler, Adolphe, 53
Bataille, Georges, 69, 157, 167, 168, 170, 171, 172, 303, 317
Baudelaire, Charles, 172, 174, 241, 303
Beer, see Gaillard, André
Bellier, Maître, 101, 105
Bellmer, Hans, 239, 334
Benquet, A., 227, 326
Benz, Maria, see Grindel, Nusch
Bergamin, José, 223
Berger, Max, 8, 30, 295
Benard, Yvonne, 69, 70, 76, 302
Beaudin, Andre, 178
Binet, Jean-Auguste-Gustave (pseudonym Binet Valmer), 94, 307
Bizet, George, 314
Blake, William, 52
Blok, Alexander, 17
Blum, Léon, 42, 149
Bondy, Walter, 18, 297
Bonnafé, Dr., 336
Bores, 178

INDEX

Bouissounouse, Janine, 13, 14, 17, 20–21, 25, 28, 31, 32, 33, 36, 42, 296
Bousquet, Joë, 10, 20–21, 39, 43, 245, 295
Brancusi, Constantin, 179
Braque, Georges, 183, 194, 332
Brassai, 178, 179, 181, 183
Brecht, Bertolt, 167, 319
Breton, André, 6, 7, 12, 39, 41, 42, 55, 64, 65, 69–80 *passim,* 91, 98, 99, 100, 101, 102, 112, 115, 116, 117, 119, 120–39 *passim,* 144, 156, 157, 158, 165–80 *passim,* 182, 185, 187, 190, 194, 196, 199, 200, 204, 205, 206, 207, 209, 214–15, 220, 222, 225, 230, 232, 239, 240, 255, 258, 261, 294, 300, 303, 304, 305, 306, 308, 310, 313, 314, 315, 317, 319, 320, 322–23, 324, 327, 330, 331–32, 333, 334, 335, 337
Bûcher, Jeanne, 195, 223, 227, 323, 329, 330
Buñuel, Luis, 64, 84–85, 119, 120, 125, 126, 127, 130, 136, 301, 305, 313
Burne-Jones, Edward, 207

Caillet, Andre, 215, 327
Carré, Louis, 102
Carrington, Léonara, 334

Cassanyes, M. A., 207, 325
Caupenne, Jean, 70, 303
Chadourne, Marc (Vasco), 73, 304
Chagall, Marc, 261, 337
Chanel, Coco, 332
Char, René, 65, 66, 67, 70, 71, 73, 76, 78, 80, 81, 83, 86–97 *passim,* 100, 105, 107, 112, 113, 123–29 *passim,* 132, 137, 188, 199, 217, 223, 224, 303
Chavée, Achille, 239
Chirico, Andrea de, *see* Savinio
Chirico, Giorgio de, 19, 52, 90, 167, 194, 196, 208, 210, 225, 241, 294, 302, 324
Clair, René, 306
Clemenceau, Georges, 86
Cohen (architect), 80
Colle, Pierre, 85, 174, 217, 305
Corti, José, 115, 138, 139, 147, 148, 150, 151, 226, 228, 306, 315
Crastre, Victor, 88
Crécre, *see* Crevel, René
Crevel, René (Crécre), 12, 13, 14, 16, 18, 20, 24, 37, 41, 42, 43, 55, 58, 61, 80, 85, 107, 113, 114, 115, 116, 127, 130, 132, 141, 144, 146, 148, 150, 151, 153, 157, 158, 159, 163, 167, 168, 169, 170, 172, 174, 200, 203, 296,

INDEX

Crével, René, (*continued*) 298, 305, 310, 316, 319, 326
Cros, Charles, 170
Crosby, Caresse, 265, 338
Cuevas, Marquis de (Jorge de Piedrablanca de Guana), 310
Cuevas, Marquise (Tota), 115, 147, 158, 163, 170, 205, 212, 310, 316
Cuttoli, Marie, 232, 238, 240, 332

Dali, Salvador, 63, 64, 66, 70–268 *passim*, 301–24 *passim*, 326, 329, 331, 332, 334, 336, 337, 338; father of, 151, 317, 335
Decaunes, Luc, 235, 250, 252, 332, 335
Deharme, Anne-Marie Hirtz (Lise), 209, 211, 326
Delamour (business manager), 132, 314
Demikeli, Dr., 37
Derain, André, 194
Desnos, Robert, 78, 305
Diaghilev, Sergei, 314
Dietrich, Marlene, 175
Dranem, Armand Menard, 12
Domínquez, Oscar, 324
Duchamp, Marcel, 86, 180, 182, 239, 317, 321, 334, 337
Duvernois, Henri (pseudonym), 88, 306

Ernst, Mame, *see* Aurenche, Marie-Berthe
Ernst, Max, 4–5, 7, 8, 17, 25, 38, 39, 41, 42, 43, 47, 119, 127, 132, 180, 196, 208, 215, 217, 225, 239, 240, 294, 297, 299, 305, 314, 328, 330, 334, 337
Espinoza, 238

Faucigny-Lucinge, Prince, 232, 331
Flaherty, Robert, 28
Flechtheim, Albert, 30, 39
Flemming, Max, 9
Foch, Maréchal, 86, 305–306
Foix, Joseph-Vincente, 180, 207, 321
Fort, Paul, 122
Fortugé, 12, 41
Fourrier (lawyer), 151
Fraenkel, Théodore, 7, 12, 294
France, Anatole, 303
Franco, Francisco, 255
Fraysse, Jean, 237, 333
Freud, Sigmund, 75, 324
Froiss-Wittmann, Jean, 86, 88, 178

Gabriel (chauffeur), 8, 172
Gaffe, René, 99, 102, 176, 308
Gaillard, André (Beer), 44–50 *passim*, 52, 149, 199, 250, 300, 324, 337
Gandhi, 319
Georges, Yvonne, 80

INDEX

Giacometti, Alberto, 119, 127, 136, 179, 183, 204
Gide, André, 88, 123, 168, 319
Giraudoux, Jean, 22
Gobineau, Joseph Arthur, 189
Goemans, Camille, 55, 62, 63, 69, 70, 80, 89, 301, 302
Goethe, Johann Wolfgang von, 52, 58
Gomez de la Serna, Ramon, 212, 327
Gonon, Jules, 144, 316
Goureaud, General Henri-Eugene, 70, 303
Grellety-Bosviel, Dr., 165, 170, 171, 173
Grindel, Cécile (daughter), 6, 12, 14, 23, 26, 54, 55, 57, 59–64 *passim*, 78, 80, 81, 83, 84, 91, 93, 100, 110, 119, 125, 139, 142, 153, 164, 170, 172, 175, 176, 177, 181, 182, 183, 190, 192–93, 195, 196, 197, 199, 203, 208, 210, 212–27 *passim*, 231, 234–67 *passim*, 296, 302, 331, 336; daughter of, 264, 266, 267
Grindel, M. (father), 17, 294, 295
Grindel, Mlle. (mother), 11, 13, 15, 17, 25, 26, 31, 32, 39, 52, 54, 59, 63, 78, 81, 83, 85, 89, 91, 106, 119, 120, 121, 124, 126, 127, 129, 132, 134, 172, 173, 175, 176, 177, 192, 197, 202, 238, 243, 246, 248, 251, 252, 254, 257, 260, 263, 264, 267, 294, 295, 313, 324, 338
Grindel, Nusch (second wife), 86, 92, 105, 106, 112–13, 124, 126, 129, 139, 144, 145, 147, 150, 158, 163, 173–74, 175, 177, 186, 198, 200, 201, 202, 204, 208, 228, 231, 234–67 *passim*, 306, 309, 319, 324, 326, 336, 337
Gross-Hugo, Valentine, *see* Hugo, Valentine
Grosz, George, 30, 31, 32, 33, 298
Guenot, Dr., 14, 296
Guillaume, Paul, 19, 218, 297, 327
Gurlitt, 3

Hannesse, 25, 28
Hašek, Jaroslav, 317
Haussmann (dadaist), 298
Hayter, Stanley William, 239, 262, 337
Heine, Maurice, 85–86, 119, 170, 239, 311, 317
Herriot, Édouard, 149
Hitler, Adolf, 185, 189, 319, 322
Huelsenbeck (dadaist), 298
Hugnet, Georges, 238, 239, 240, 259, 266, 333, 334
Hugo, Jean, 307

INDEX

Hugo, Valentine, 97, 102, 112, 131, 133, 134, 139, 144, 192, 243, 246, 307, 309, 313, 315, 320
Hugo, Victor, 257
Huysman, Joris-Karl, 175

Itkine, Sylvain, 328

James, Edward, 217, 224, 225, 227, 230, 331
Janet, Pierre, 70
Jarry, Alfred, 170, 328
Jouk (dog), 15, 16, 190, 246

Kafka, Franz, 241
Kann, Alphonse, 7, 294
Keaton, Buster, 88
Keller, Georges E., 48, 57, 63, 64, 65, 66, 72, 80, 85, 88, 102, 217, 303
Kisch, Erwin, 167
Klee, Paul, 9, 32, 199, 215
Kochno, Boris, 152, 157, 317
Kra Éditions, 77
Kurella, Alfred, 168, 319

Lacan, Jacques, 183
Lagrange, 84
Lamba, Jacqueline, 220, 328
Laporte, René, 138, 139, 141, 145, 146, 150, 157, 170, 172, 315, 319
Laurens, Henri, 179
Lautréamont, Isidore Ducasse, 131, 170, 178, 183
Lavidière, Eugenie (Nini), 11, 12, 245

Léger, F., 261, 332
Leiris, Michel, 179
Lenin, Vladimir Ilyich, 171, 185, 322
Levis-Mano, Guy, 228, 241, 330
Levitzki, M., 264
Levy, Julien, 224, 225, 230, 329
Lise, see Deharme, Anne-Marie Hirtz
Loeb, Pierre, 44, 73, 80, 81, 300, 305
Lönnrot, Elias, 297
Lorca, Federico García, 239, 332

Maar, Dora, 235, 241, 332
Mabille, Pierre, 220, 244, 317, 328
Magritte, René, 176, 239, 240
Maillol, Aristide, 179
Makovsky, Vincenc, 205, 325
Maldoror, 182, 322
Mallarmé, Stéphane, 184, 320
Malraux, André, 168, 319
Mann, Klaus, 43
Mann, Thomas, 43
Manoukine, Dr., 37, 53
Marx, Karl, 69
Massine, Leonid, 332
Masson, André, 25, 157, 178
Matisse, Henri, 172, 174, 184, 194, 320
Matisse, Pierre, 208, 209, 210
Matta, Roberto, 239
Mayakovski, Vladimir, 78, 80, 304

INDEX

Meissonier, Jean-Louis-
  Ernest, 195, 323
Mesens, Edouard, 176, 184,
  197, 198, 239, 240, 320
Miller, Lee, 231
Millet, Jean François, 210, 322
Miratvilles, Jaume, 207, 325
Miró, Juan, 136, 183, 199,
  215, 217, 239, 314, 332
Mops, *see* Sternheim, Thea
  Elisabeth Dorothea
Moreux, Serge, 60, 61, 301
Moro, César, 91, 306
Mouginois, 235
Murray, Hubert, 10
Muzard, Suzanne, 70, 71, 76,
  78, 303

Napoleon, 87, 88
Nelli, René, 10, 14, 20,
  295
Nesens, 193
Nezval, Vitezslav, 205, 206,
  325
Nierendorf, Karl, 3, 7, 18, 20,
  30, 293
Nietzsche, Friedrich, 228
Noll, Marcel, 9, 80, 295
Noailles, Vicomte de (Marie-
  Laure), 67, 97–98, 128,
  134, 170, 215, 257, 302,
  308, 319, 337
Nougé, Paul, 176, 193, 239,
  240, 320
Nouveau, Germain, 170
Nunez de Arenas, Manuel,
  212
Nusch, *see* Grindel, Nusch

Ocampo, Mme., 208
Odette, 69, 84, 86, 97
Oger, 11
Oldman, O. W., 44
Ovid, 176, 320

Parain, Brice, 94, 307
Parrot, Louis, 256, 336
Pastoureau, Henri, 239, 240,
  334
Paulhan, Jean, 246, 250, 335
Penrose, Roland, 214, 217,
  218, 231, 239, 240, 327,
  331
Petitjean, 213
Péret, Benjamin, 43, 59, 86,
  127, 128, 178, 180, 199,
  207, 239, 240, 241, 310,
  324
Philippon, Dr., 16, 106,
  129
Piaget, Jean, 178, 183
Picabia, Francis, 88, 306
Picasso, Pablo, 4, 7, 78, 80,
  81, 102, 122, 168, 170,
  176, 183, 194, 196, 199,
  201, 213, 219, 220, 225,
  227, 235, 239, 240, 252,
  253, 312, 320, 327, 328,
  332
Podach, Erich Friedrich, 331
Poe, Edgar Allan, 69, 149,
  303
Portier (auctioneer), 97, 104,
  105
Poulenc, Francis, 224, 329
Prassinos, Gisèle, 334
Prévert, Jacques, 303

INDEX

Prévost, Marcel, 145
Pushkin, Aleksandr Sergeyevich, 24

Queneau, Raymond, 303

Ramlot, 208, 209
Ratton, Charles, 13, 14, 25, 29, 43, 63, 80, 101, 102, 296, 328
Ray, Man, 175, 179, 181, 183, 195, 199, 211, 215, 216, 221, 222, 224, 225, 231, 233, 239, 240, 246, 251, 321, 326, 330, 331
Real, Dr., 20
Renéville, 121
Renn, Ludwig, 167, 319
Reverdy, Pierre, 122, 179, 183
Rigaut, Jacques, 88, 90, 306
Rimbaud, Arthur, 5, 170, 178, 183, 241, 243
Ristitch, Marco, 133, 314
Rolland, Romain, 319, 333
Romains, Jules, 122
Rott, 69, 70, 84
Rousseau, Henri, 16, 53, 191, 197, 202
Roussel, Raymond, 179, 183, 313
Roux, 178

Sade, Marquis de (D. A. F.), 171, 311
Sadoul, Georges, 70, 98–99, 112, 125, 126, 136, 303, 308, 309, 312
Saint Jean, Robert de, 254

Salahum, Vve., 6
Salles, Georges, 29, 298
Savinio (Andrea de Chirico), 67, 302
Savinio, Alberto, 241
Schabacher, Simon, see Duvernois, Henri
Scutenaire, Louis, 239
Sennett, Mack, 88, 306
Serner, Dr., 46
Sgard, 14, 26
Skira, Albert, 157, 167–80 passim, 182, 202, 204, 223, 224, 225, 261, 316, 317, 324, 331
Soupault, Philippe, 6, 294
Stephan, E., 10
Sternheim, Thea Élisabeth Dorothea (Mops), 29, 30, 31, 32, 33, 35, 37, 39, 43, 298
Styrsky, Jindrich, 205, 325

Tanguy, Yves, 109, 119, 127, 135, 166, 172, 194, 196, 227, 240, 318
Tchang, Raymond, 190, 193, 194
Teige, Karel, 205, 325
Tériade, E., 178, 182, 183, 196, 321
Terry, Emilio, 170, 320
Thiorion, André, 70, 117, 127, 303
Thorner, Dr., 20
Touraine, Dr., 70
Tota, see Cuevas, Marquise

INDEX

Toyen, Maria Germinova, 205, 325
Triolet, Elsa, 78, 80, 303, 305
Trutat, Alain, 264, 338
Trutat, Jacqueline, 264, 338
Tual, Roland, 3, 6, 7, 8, 77, 293
Tzara, Tristan, 127, 132, 136, 137, 171, 172, 178, 185, 186, 188

Unik, Pierre, 114, 125, 126, 128, 130, 136, 309–10, 312

Vaillant-Couturier, Paul, 311
Valentin, Albert, 85, 86
van Dyke, W. S., 298
Van Hecke, P. G., 299
Van Leer (art dealer), 14, 296
van Ripper, Rudolf, 298
Vasco, *see* Chadourne, Marc
Vautel, Clément (pseudonym Voutel), 121, 312
Verlaine, Paul, 5
Vermeer, Jan, 330
Vildrac, Charles, 319
Villa, Pancho, 230
Viot, Jacques, 113, 309
Vriamont, 184, 321
Vulliamy, Gérard, 256, 258, 261, 263, 267, 336

Walden, Herwarth, 9, 299
Walden, Nell, 30, 33, 299
Watson, Peter, 220, 221

Zervos, Christian, 209, 214, 215, 218, 326
Zervos, Yvonne, 218
Zwemmer Gallery, 202, 325